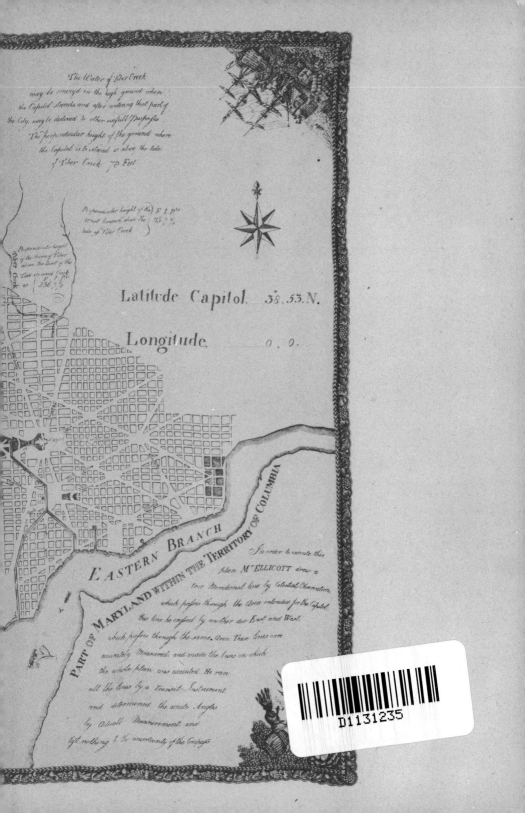

SOCIETY IN AMERICA SERIES

WASHINGTON CAVALCADE

By CHARLES HURD
Author of
The White House and *The Veterans' Program*

Historically accurate, entertainingly written, full of colorful, dramatic stories of Washington life — political, diplomatic and social — here is a delightful presentation of Washington Society from its beginnings to the present day.

No city in the country has changed its social character as much as has Washington, D. C. Yet, in a very real sense, it has, since its foundings, mirrored the events which have shaped the United States, and the faces of those who have played their several parts in the American pageant. From the aristocratic river culture of its first period, Washington suffered all the growing pains peculiar to adolescence. In the War of 1812 it endured the ignominy of capture and destruction by the British. With the inauguration of Andrew Jackson a new and democratic phase began, to be in turn followed by mellow days of careless elegance.

Washington remained provincial in character until the outcome of the Civil War was decided. Lincoln, in making this a nation in the true sense of the word, inadvertently transformed Washington into a National Capital. Through the gaudy years that followed, through the gay nineties and through the early years of the new century no one visiting Washington could mistake it for any other American city. Slowly, through a succession of administrations, a certain outward graciousness emerged which could not be disturbed by the raucous politicians.

Then came another transformation. This time it was Woodrow Wilson. Washington moved one more step and became the Capital of the world, something it has remained ever since. Throughout World War II the citizens of Washington were the citizens of

(Continued on flap II)

WASHINGTON
CAVALCADE

the World Capital that guided the destinies of all the nations. And, as its destiny became manifest, Washington outgrew its earlier confines, becoming a city of great physical beauty and possessing all the bustle, elegance and charm of other world capitals.

But even today, Washington has retained two of its early characteristics: Society is divided into three groups just as it was in the days of Jackson and Buchanan. And despite its cosmopolitanism and sophistication it is still a combination of an international capital and an American crossroads.

Here is Washington Society in all its colorful detail — a brilliant tapestry of men and women who have influenced and have been influenced by the life of our nation's capital.

About the author . . .

As a staff member of the N. Y. *Times* Washington Bureau, and as a member by marriage of an old Washington family, Charles Hurd has had a unique opportunity to observe Washington Society in exactly the right proportions.

He spent his boyhood in Oklahoma, attended Washington University in St. Louis, Missouri, and Northwestern University in Evanston, Illinois. Even in those days, he found newspaper work fascinating. Beginning his newspaper career on the St. Louis *Post-Dispatch,* he then spent five years with the Associated Press in Chicago and New York. In 1926 he became an associate editor on *Liberty* Magazine, went with the N. Y. *Times* in 1929. Later that year he was assigned to the *Times* Washington Bureau, where he has remained ever since, with the exception of short periods with the *Times* London Bureau and *Newsweek*.

PUBLISHER'S NOTE

Another volume in the Society in America Series,
independent volumes by distinguished writers
devoted to the important cities and sections of
this country. The aim of these volumes is to por-
tray the individual characteristics, to underscore
the idiosyncrasies, and to trace the growth of sec-
tional societies with special emphasis on local
traditions and on the personalities who embodied
them.

Malcolm S. Huey

X mas 1947

D. P. Madison.

Washington Cavalcade

CHARLES HURD

ϒ

New York 1948 E P Dutton & Co Inc

Jacket, binding and title page designed by
NATHANIEL FARMER

This Book is for

E.B.H.

(*a veritable Washingtonian*)

CONTENTS

vii

Frontispiece portrait of Dolly Madison drawn by J. Herring after J. Wood.

The map in the endpapers is reproduced from a large silk handkerchief hand blocked prior to 1814 and now in the Library of Congress. It was adapted from L'Enfant's drawing of the District of Columbia by commission of George Washington in 1792.

WASHINGTON
CAVALCADE

Chapter One

THE RIVER CULTURE

GENERAL GEORGE WASHINGTON and Thomas Jefferson, mulling
their port and planning their city, would have resented bitterly
the later accusations that they sold the country a swamp for a
Capital. But then, perhaps, long exposure to the mists of the rivers had given them a certain immunity to malaria. Certainly,
the Virginians, although no whit hardier than the Northerners,
had survived numerous plagues in Philadelphia and other more
northerly cities.

But as for that "swamp," it is true that a lot of brackish water
stood among richly scented magnolias where some of the more
important Washington buildings now rise. A boathouse once
was built on the southern edge of the White House grounds, at
the edge of the Potomac, now pushed a mile or more away from
its doors.

But Georgetown was not a "swamp" and most certainly not
the larger and more important city of Alexandria. Here were
proud little cities built up in the century before 1800. There
were forests around them, true, but it was hard to drive more
than five miles in any direction without finding really splendid
plantations. Life was little different, except for warmer sum-
mers, from that on country estates in England in the Georgian
period, and England also had its forests. The women's clothes
were as luxurious, the food as good and more varied, and a gentleman wore the same quality satin in his breeches.

Alexandria was the port for upper Virginia and Georgetown

11

for southern Maryland. Alexandria had more traffic and an edge in the fact that it was a county seat for Fairfax County. Georgetown resented that distinction; even tried to have the Montgomery County Court House moved down from Rockville to its boundaries.

But these were little things. And Georgetown won the final round when the Northern members of Congress, always with a suspicious eye on Virginian pretensions, exacted a pledge that no Federal building should be erected south of the Potomac. As a result, Alexandria passes out of our picture almost immediately, because it is today, what it was then, only a suburb of Washington.

While Georgetown grew, and finally became absorbed into Washington, the population of Alexandria changed very little from 1800 until 1940, when the Washington housing shortage gave it a building boom. Its port declined. Today an investor can buy waterfront property in this old port for about the same price that George Washington, a very canny husbander of money, paid for lots in the same location.

It was Georgetown that supplied much housing for new officials, that sent its ladies to pay the calls that plagued the wives of Presidents from the start, and that gradually melted into the life of the Capital.

From Washington to Baltimore there was little worth mentioning. The region supported a river civilization and people clung to the rivers—in this case, the Potomac. Annapolis, the Capital of Maryland, was the center of a little world on the Severn River. Baltimore nestled on the tip of Chesapeake Bay. None realized the value of river development better than the shrewd, kerchiefed and almost royal Martha Custis Washington, who put her wealth at the disposal of her second husband, George Washington, and was "Lady" of the southern bank of the Potomac for half a century, with "connections" in the other communities.

Politics and society were synonymous, and there was nothing

new then, or today, in the fact that Jefferson worked his deal
over punch and Madeira. Life was a gambling affair—a gamble
on weather, crops and politics. The chips were held by a very
few people. Neither were the piles small.

Within a day's ride of Washington, at the time it was laid out,
were feudal estates rivaling those of the wealthier Britons.
These were absolutely complete, compact living communities
in which few imports were required beyond salt, sugar, tea, coffee and such luxuries as the clothes worn by the master's family.
There was a tight solidarity of interests. Almost every family
was related in some degree to the others. One factor of strength
that enabled the Virginia gentlemen to dominate the Congress
and hold the Presidency from 1800 through 1824 was this
family inter-connection.

Lord Fairfax and his immediate family held social ascendancy
and lived in palatial state at Belvoir, situated on the Potomac
near Alexandria on the road that ended at Mount Vernon.
Another nest of Fairfaxes held forth at Ravensworth, south of
Alexandria. John Parke Custis, son of Martha Washington, was
established in near-by Abingdon. Still another Fairfax, Bryan,
occupied Mount Eagle. George Mason was the seigneur of Gun-
ston Hall.

Across the Potomac River from Alexandria, in Maryland,
Thomas Addison had built a manor house on the banks of the
Potomac, on a grant which he named Oxon Hill in memory of
Oxford University, where he had gone for his education. And
Thomas Addison also owned, for a while in partnership with
James Stoddert, a 3000-acre tract between Rock Creek and the
Potomac. When his daughter Nancy married William Murdock
she inherited the Rock Creek property and built there another
mansion.

This house was the home of Murdock in 1765 when, as a delegate from Maryland to the "Stamp Act Congress" in New York,
he and Robert Livingston and Samuel Johnson signed the fa-

mous address to the king protesting the Stamp Act. The Murdocks called their estate Friendship and occupied it for 50 years.

Georgetown lived for the river and on the river, very small in space and most compact. There were the wharves on the water front west of Rock Creek, spread haphazardly over a distance of a quarter mile. Behind the wharves were warehouses where Negro slaves trundled hogsheads of tobacco that had more consistent, solid worth than any money then in circulation. Tobacco was the currency of the day. Parson Alexander Williamson was a wealthy man, since he could measure his income at 90 hogsheads of tobacco a year. It is hardly likely that Washington had as much income—certainly not Jefferson, or Madison.

On the bluffs above the river were some of the better town houses, and Georgetown rambled thence north for a dozen blocks. Its cluttered and usually small buildings flanked off to left and right, through devious little streets and alleys, from what was Main Street and is now Thirty-third Street in Washington. Up this hilly street straining teams of horses and oxen pulled the goods generally brought from England, the spices that had come from India and the stuffs and furniture, also of English craftsmanship, that came in trade for tobacco. The workmen stopped for a refreshing pint halfway up the hill at the Yellow and White Tavern.

Two of the better-known Georgetown gentlemen-merchants in the latter days before Washington was formally established were Major Benjamin Stoddert and General Uriah Forest. They were gallant soldiers, good livers and, like most of their compatriots, bankrupts of the Revolution. They mended their fortunes quickly in the postwar boom by founding a joint business.

Major Stoddert soon built a fashionable house at Prospect and Frederick Streets. It served him well as a social center when he became Secretary of the Navy. General Forest, satisfying a taste for horses and sport, built and occupied a modest home at Rosedale, just north of Georgetown. Stoddert held on to his

money, but General Forest could not resist a taste for speculation. He went broke. Mrs. Forest was enabled to live in her
home only because Philip Barton Key, the noted and wealthy
lawyer, brother-in-law of General Forest, bought the estate at a
bankruptcy sale for her benefit.

This was a neighborly thing for Key to do, because he had
also an estate carved out of Rosedale, known as Woodley. Woodley is still there, in recent years the luxurious and beautifully
preserved home of Henry L. Stimson, elder statesman who was
successively Secretary of War under President Taft, Secretary of
State under President Hoover and Secretary of War under President Franklin D. Roosevelt.

A little farther north, or an hour's ride on horseback, was
the estate named Hayes, where Parson Williamson, secure in his
fixed tobacco income, rode to hounds, took his three bottles of
an evening, raced horses and played whist for double-eagle
points and five on the rubber. This estate was probably the most
pretentious of a number founded on patent from the Lord Pro-
prietary of Maryland and Avalon.

Near Parson Williamson lived Charles Jones, Esq., who built
his house in 1750 and called it Clean Drinking Manor, because
of the purity of a spring on the property. But "Uncle Charlie's"
personal drinking preference went more toward Madeira or
rum than water, and his house was famous for the parties given
in it.

A notable guest at Clean Drinking, although he then was not
rated as very much, was George Washington, who stopped to
rest for several days on his way home to Alexandria from Ft.
Duquesne in 1755. Much later, in 1814, when the British made
Washington uninhabitable for the government for a little
while, Thomas Munroe, then Postmaster General, fled to Clean
Drinking and ran the postal service between the north and south
from this house.

Swinging around toward the east, near Bladensburg, itself
a busy little port on the Eastern Branch, a visitor found the

this incipient stage, I should deem that the most unfortunate of all consequence, to avert which all partial and temporary evils should be yielded. I proposed to him, however, to dine with me the next day, and I would invite another friend or two; bring them into conference together, and I thought it impossible that reasonable men, consulting together coolly, could fail by some mutual sacrifices of opinion, to form a compromise which was to save the Union.

"The discussion took place. I could take no part in it but an exhortatory one, because I was a stranger in the circumstances that should govern it. But it was finally agreed that, whatever importance had been attached to the rejection of this proposition, the preservation of the Union and of concord among the States was more important and that therefore it would be better that the vote of rejection should be rescinded, to effect which some members should change their votes. But it was observed that this bill would be peculiarly bitter to the Southern States, and that some concomitant measure should be adopted to sweeten it a little to them.

"There had been propositions to fix the seat of government either at Philadelphia, at Germantown, or on the Potomac, and it was thought that by giving it to Philadelphia for ten years more, and to Georgetown permanently afterwards, this might, as an anodyne, calm in some degree the ferment which might be excited by the other measure also.

"So two of the Potomac members agreed to change their votes and Hamilton undertook to carry the other point. It doing this, the influence he had established over the eastern members, with the agency of Robert Morris with those of the Middle States, effected his side of the engagement, and so the assumption was passed, and twenty millions of stock divided among favored States and thrown in as a pabulum to the stock-jobbing herd."

Chapter Two

GROPING DAYS

MOVING TO WASHINGTON in 1800 meant either hunting for a boarding house where almost none existed or setting up housekeeping under real pioneer conditions. Mrs. Samuel Harrison Smith, whose husband moved down from Philadelphia in 1801 at Jefferson's suggestion to found the *National Intelligencer,* was genuinely grateful when Mrs. Bell, one of the first callers at Sidney, their farm, brought a basket of sweet potatoes and cabbages.

The Madisons (a Secretary of State must have some influence) found a house to lease in Georgetown, where Dolly started the famous charm career that carried through eight Administrations. She immediately began to act as the widower Jefferson's hostess. Colonel John Tayloe came up briefly from Mt. Airy, his country estate, to live at the Octagon House, two squares southwest of the Palace, and give social life a lift, but he soon fled. He never liked the city; probably resented having let George Washington talk him into building a town house there instead of in Philadelphia. George Washington wanted to spur real-estate development.

Thomas Law, who had married Martha Washington's granddaughter and built a house on the south slope of Capitol Hill, turned that home over to the innkeeper Conrad. Jefferson as Vice-President became the "star boarder," and the only paying guest to have two private rooms. Law went on to become the town character. He sometimes forgot his own name in the ec-

19

centricity of introspection. A little later his wife divorced him, but not before they had inaugurated the Washington Dancing Assembly.

Captain Thomas Tingey, former British naval officer who had joined the Colonies in the Revolution, moved to Washington to begin angling for a job he got in 1804—Commander of the Washington Navy Yard. Old Captain Tingey finally died in 1829, still Commander of the Yard, and so confused in his feeling of ownership that he tried to dispose of the official residence in his will.

Dr. Frederick May had set up practice as the first physician in Washington in 1795, and survived to do very well.

William Greenleaf and Robert Morris, the latter the financier of the Revolution, had undertaken large real-estate developments, which ended eventually in bankruptcy, but a land boom was underway in this oddly hybrid city. Yet everything was unfinished. Much would remain so for a couple of generations.

There was much money changing hands, even though Congress could not afford a chaplain and only six rooms in the Palace were habitable on June 4, 1800, when potbellied John Adams and his disillusioned Abigail arrived to open the city formally as the seat of government, and visit for a few days.

On the fourth day after Mrs. John Adams returned to the White House in November for her brief "permanent" residence, she jounced in her carriage to Georgetown to return fifteen calls. Such was the social pace. That phase has never stopped.

The residents from the first were not going to let Philadelphia or New York outshine them in maintaining the amenities. A century or more would pass before harassed hostesses would decide that good taste could be served equally well by sending around a messenger with the first cards.

One may assume that sex had its place in life in Washington, as it always does. But not for the record. Otherwise, Washington began in minute form to express what was general in the United States. It took its politics in flowery phrases and dissimulation.

It always was "correct," on the surface. And it trotted itself to death on social non-essentials.

Washington talked and drank, and worshipped protocol. Mrs. Anthony Merry, wife of one of the first British Ministers to the new Capital, raised the devil when Jefferson did not seat her in the place of honor at his dinner table. The American ladies also were far from backward in asserting position.

Soon John Quincy Adams would set about the task of reducing protocol and precedence to a mathematical formula—unofficially but precisely as grand marshals of royal courts had done long before in European capitals.

So here was a new century, a new Capital and a new society, although the people elsewhere in the United States were a long time realizing it. And in the political newness, reflecting in some parts the backwash of the French Revolution but more likely the normal evolution of the United States, certain figures stood out as daring prophets.

Thus, Thomas Jefferson, more important in his role as prophet than as President, was the new man of the new day. Moving in his shadow, trailing compliments and gossip with equal disregard, was the new archetype of "lady," the free-speaking, uninhibited Dolly Madison. She was yet eight years removed from her own occupancy of the White House but social arbiter of Washington from the day Jefferson became President.

No one quite knew as yet how to act before the President. And that upset all ideas of normal social customs. The "court manners" prescribed in the Administration of General Washington and Adams were out of date, but formality persisted in people's minds. No longer did women curtsy, as they had in Philadelphia when the President and Lady Washington held levees.

The styles in dress had taken a turn from the formality that marked the close of the Eighteenth Century—when Martha Washington wore a lacy cap over her curls, lace mitts, with a shawl that half concealed her laced and pointed bodice of dusty rose beige, and clasped in her hands a brown satin square bag, with "Mrs. M. Washington" embroidered within a circlet of flowers. This type of dress, and those worn by Abigail Adams, with slashed puff sleeves and innumerable bits of lace showing here and there, had given way to smoother styles.

And as for the costumes worn by the men . . .

There was a row of barber shops along Pennsylvania Avenue a year after the Capital moved to town, and most men left in them their soiled wigs, emerging with freshly powdered ones. But Mr. Jefferson did as much to change the styles in men's wear as movie stars have accomplished in more recent years. In fact, he carried the new democracy in clothes so far as to be revolutionary. He would not wear a wig after 1800, although most men still did. He wore "pantaloons," not breeches and stockings. The New York and Philadelphia merchant princes, considering his trousers, called him a dangerous radical.

The first group of ladies from Georgetown who appeared at the White House on "levee day" waited an hour for the President to return from an outing, and then were received by him in riding clothes! When Mr. Merry, newly arrived as British Minister, put on his dress court uniform to pay his call he found himself:

"Introduced to a man as the President of the United States not merely in an undress, but actually standing in slippers down at the heels, and pantaloons, coat and underclothes indicative of utter slovenliness and indifference to appearance, but in a state of negligence actually studied."

How Jefferson loved to shock people with such displays! But he was not all studied carelessness. He dressed in his best, with clubbed although unpowdered hair, to sit for his portrait by Gilbert Stuart when the young artist set up shop in Washington. Anyone identified with culture soon found an invitation to dine at the Mansion. Father Serra, the Brazilian Minister and naturalist, became a crony in a threesome completed by John Quincy Adams.

Jefferson dined with some formality in company every day, usually with twelve at table and often only men. His plainness was belied by records showing that he spent $10,000 for wines in eight years, when wine was cheap; he left the White House in debt, largely because of hospitality, despite his salary of $25,000 a year.

Nevertheless, it was Dolly Madison who from her first appearance, when James Madison was appointed as Jefferson's Secretary of State, started to make the public life of Washington a thing apart. Until her arrival, Washington was a Southern city, in customs, styles and speech. She adopted it all, and overlaid it with a Northern breeziness that came straight from Philadelphia —a breeziness combined with a toughness that she accentuated by taking snuff with the men and, in later years, being about the only important person to keep her head in the day of the new Capital's greatest crisis.

Dolly Madison was an immediate link between Georgetown society and the Palace into which Jefferson drafted her. His own daughters, Mrs. Jefferson Randolph and Mrs. John Wayles Eppes, both wives of Congressmen from Virginia, disliked official life. Therefore he turned to the next "ranking lady" in the government to act as hostess. Dolly Madison ate it up.

If the Vice-President had been married, his wife would have outranked Dolly, but Aaron Burr, Vice-President from 1800 to 1804, had no wife.

Dolly dropped the lines of her gowns to reveal her round, white shoulders and laced the bodices of her dresses to give the fullest effect to a bust already richly endowed by nature. In eggshell satin, embroidered with pink roses, with luxurious underskirts peeking through the slashed front of her skirts, she was the best and most richly dressed lady of her day. She wore short puffed sleeves to display her round arms and, until she adopted a turban as her uniform headdress, she wrapped her head in a rich band. Curls bounced above and below it when she nodded her head in sprightly conversation.

Some of her friends wished Dolly would be more circumspect, but all of Washington aped her. She and the new government group almost smothered the older, less active local society, but there was a quick blending.

By July 4, 1801, when Jefferson held the first Independence Day Reception at the Palace, the conflicts and feuds were fairly well resolved and all the public officers, most of the respectable citizens, and distinguished strangers trooped to the White House. The total company made about 100.

Of course Congress was not in session and its members generally were at home, but not many members of Congress were considered social. For the most part only a few of the wealthy ones from the Southern States took part in "society," which then was synonymous with "influential."

The 100 persons who formed the government "society" in minikin were invited for 12 o'clock noon. They remained until 2 P.M., standing in little groups surrounding the more distinguished guests—Dr. William Thornton, architect of the Capitol and new Commissioner of Patents, a pet office of Jefferson; Gideon Granger, Postmaster General and connoisseur of champagne; a scattering of Fairfaxes, Custises and Lees; old General Henry Dearborn, Secretary of War.

The Marine Band played martial music and periodically marched through the state rooms. The guests filled plates heaping high with refreshments from the buffet tables spread in the State Dining Room. Well-trained house slaves from Monticello constantly passed glasses of pale yellow and deep red wines from France. Through it all, five Cherokee Chiefs in full regalia, in Washington as guests of the President to celebrate a new treaty of friendship made by their tribe, stood as solemnly as painted statues behind the President's chair.

This party broke up at 2 P.M., and the perspiring members hurried home by carriage or on horseback. They must change the broadcloth and satin clothes which they persisted in wearing even in midsummer, when the temperature often approached 100 degrees, then rest and don fresh linen and outer clothes for the second big event of the day.

This was a subscription dinner at Conrad's served to 50 persons—the top 50 among the 100 who earlier had gone to the President's House. It was served from 4 until 6 P.M. The ladies retired afterward to parlors to loosen their bodices and gossip while the men got down to a little serious drinking and patriotic conversation that lasted for two or three hours.

About 9 o'clock the company had tea and a cold supper and broke up.

When one speaks of eating in Washington in its earlier days, one should approach the subject with some reverent regard. No man with a poor digestion could hope to enjoy political success.

Breakfast was a meal brought to Washington homes by men who for the most part had lived on country estates. This breakfast was designed to strengthen a man for a hard day in the saddle, either supervising his property or riding in a hunt. The noon "snack" was a comfortable meal. Dinner at 4 o'clock was a genuine test of strength, and "tea" or supper in late evening was almost equally as large.

This food came for the most part from local sources, since virtually every type of game was available within a day's walk of the Capital. Waterfowl were easier to shoot in most seasons than chickens to tend. There were deer and game birds in plenty. Furthermore, the Indians long ago had acquainted the natives with the peculiarly excellent qualities of oysters, dredged by fishermen from Chesapeake Bay and sailed in shallops up the Potomac.

Cooking was not very good; the meat almost invariably was overdone. But Mrs. Thomas Law helped to improve its quality when she found in Baltimore, and introduced to many of her associates, a new cooking invention that still was based on the fireplace but improved it in a revolutionary manner.

Before this discovery all meat was broiled on a spit, fried in a pan suspended over the fire, or boiled in a kettle. But Mrs. Law's new contraption had an oven with a door constructed in the chimney on one side of a 6-foot-wide fireplace. There was a large boiler opposite it. This made possible the better distribution of heat and a consequent even quality in browning.

Ham, fish and game would appear, likely as not, on the same table four times a day, surrounded by potatoes, beets, puddings and pies. But these coarser vegetables and pies soon were to go out of fashion, to be superseded by celery, spinach, salsify and cauliflower.

After all, there was little more to do than eat. And eating remains today the primary social activity of Washington, where people eat friends into town and out, do their most important business over lunch and use dinner as the prime machine for "contacts."

Eating does require, however, good places to do it. This means gracious houses, good cooks in the kitchen and an "atmosphere." All of which were growing rapidly, considering the small number of persons involved.

Not that Washington was blooming into a metropolis. It was one of the slowest-growing cities in America, seldom increasing in population by more than 1000 a year until the Civil War. The members of the Congress and the Executive Establishment abandoned it, if they could afford to, from Independence Day until October. It was in effect a winter Capital, and when the higher officials hied to their other homes there was little left indeed. Washington was not yet by any means a Capital as we know it today.

The Constitution to the contrary, Washington was at the beginning of the Nineteenth Century little more than a visible and partially completed meeting ground for representatives of the States. There were no regulatory agencies, and as yet no sense of the jurisdiction of the Federal Government over "inter-State" affairs. The government of the Capital City was anomalous: there was a board of Commissioners to plan and ask Congress for money to make improvements in Federal buildings, but no government of the District as such. For many years crimes committed in the District of Columbia were tried under the laws of the States of Maryland and Virginia, according to the side of the Potomac on which they occurred. Civil suits were settled in the same manner.

The man who stole a pig found wallowing on Pennsylvania Avenue or in the woods on the heights above Georgetown was taken to Montgomery Court House, at Rockville, to be tried. And he might be flogged for it. When an Arlington farmer sued his neighbor, even though both lived in the District of Columbia, the case was tried in Court at Alexandria. No police officer patrolled the streets of Washington for many years, although elections finally were arranged for a marshal to serve legal writs and a sheriff to serve warrants on complaint.

That was, however, the way that people liked it. And in its little way Washington started to grow.

Chapter Three

TAP ROOTS

IT WAS TOO BAD that Colonel Tayloe, whose house was and is one of Washington's most beautiful, hated the place. Perhaps he had a prescience that this home would be tragic—that 30 years after he built it a young lady in his family would kill herself by jumping down the great stair well because of a broken romance with a young English naval officer.

But if Octagon House was proceeding rapidly toward abandonment long before the Madisons gave it fame as the longest-occupied "temporary White House," other houses were blooming.

The Greenleaf-Morris project failed to materialize into the hundreds of planned houses, but many other residences were built at scattered points. A fairly large grouping of these surrounded the hill on which stood the Capitol. The others meandered off in all directions—that is, in all directions except to the east, where the city was supposed to develop. Georgetown blossomed into the largest development, largely because its relative altitude gave some protection from the river mists.

Often unremarked is the fact that Washington, growing as it did in the midst of a revolution in architecture, was a new city in more senses than one. It was a pacemaker, and its older buildings are quite unlike those of other American cities of its period.

It has become the fashion to laugh at early American designs, but there were real students of architecture in those days, and not alone Thomas Jefferson.

The development of building in Washington coincided with the birth of American interests in Adam styles. James Hoban designed the White House (without the porticoes) as an archetype of this design. Dr. William Thornton sprinkled it through his many Washington designs. Charles Bulfinch, who was employed as an architect early in the designing of the Capitol, used much of this school of design. It is characterized, among other things, by slender-columned porticoes, rich doorways, Palladian windows, tall pilasters on exteriors, spiral stairways and oval or octagonal rooms with delicate ornamentation—in combination or all together.

Benjamin Latrobe was the dissenting architect in general, being a worshipper of the Greek lines, such as are in the White House porticoes. So Latrobe may be termed (and some people would damn his memory for it) the father of the solid blocks of mock-Greek temples that today line Constitution Avenue.

Fortunately for Washington, the "natives" did not all feel as did the good colonel of the Octagon House about settling in Washington. There were within a day's riding distance perhaps 500 families of Maryland and Virginia with incomes of one thousand or more pounds a year—very good incomes for the day. In fact, such fortunes were comparable with Jefferson's own before he married a wealthy woman and more than George Washington had, prior to Martha Custis.

Robert Sewell began in 1799 to build Sewell House, now called Belmont House and located at 144 B Street S.E. His was one of the few homes located where Major Pierre Charles L'Enfant, surveyor of Washington, hoped that wealthy persons would build. Sewell's house obtained some fame, in his absence, in 1814, when the only soldiers to resist the British invasion took a stand there. One of them fired a shot that killed the horse under General Ross, second in command to Admiral Sir George Cockburn. In reprisal the house was burned. It was rebuilt in 1820.

In the Georgetown area are three houses of the period which give perhaps the best flavor of the aspirations of residents of the Capital. Incidentally, these reveal the tight interlocking of family interests in the feudal country where the government was established. It only carries out the pattern to point out that two of the three were developed with Martha Washington's money. These two were Arlington House and Tudor Place, seats of the aristocracy. The third was Dumbarton House, a monument to the fact that even in the Eighteenth Century a man might make something of himself, starting from scratch in this new country.

But Arlington House and Tudor Place are the real symbols of the interlocking power of the "Virginia Aristocracy." Their power was so carefully preserved that it controlled Federal affairs almost exclusively in all important things until democracy began to assert itself in the wave that swept Andrew Jackson into the Presidency.

When visitors to Washington look across the Memorial Bridge toward the National Cemetery they see through groves of trees a house crowning the highest hill in this great acreage. It is Arlington House, and the guide books explain that it was the home of Robert E. Lee, until he left Washington to lead the Confederate Army. That, however, is only the end of the story.

George Washington Parke Custis, only grandson of Martha Washington, built the house between 1802 and 1804, completing it with a broad-sweeping portico whose heavy pillars are almost hidden by magnolias. It is palatial in size but chopped into small rooms. Fireplaces would not warm large rooms. Custis built it sturdily of brick, covered with stucco.

The land where the house stands originally was part of a 6000-acre tract, including much of Alexandria, granted by the

Virginia patent holders in 1669 to a ship captain named How-sing for transporting colonists to Virginia. In later years a pro-prietor named Alexander bought it for 6000 pounds of tobacco. It remained as forest land, with a few scattered tenants, until a village on the south edge grew into an important port—Alexandria.

In 1778, John Parke Custis, son of Martha Washington and stepson of the general—in the midst of the Revolution—bought 1100 acres of the northern part of the grant for an investment. He continued, however, to live at Abingdon, his estate south of Alexandria which then adjoined Mount Vernon.

J. P. Custis died in 1781 (here it gets confusing) and Martha Washington took over the property, while also taking John's son George Washington Parke Custis and his daughter Nellie into her home and legally adopting them as the children of herself and George Washington. When Martha Washington died in 1802, which brings us to the early Washington city period, George Washington Parke Custis inherited the land, now known as Arlington. And when he had his house partially fin-ished in 1804 he married Mary Fitzhugh Lee, a connection of the family of General "Light Horse Harry" Lee, who was George Washington's most intimate friend among the Revolu-tionary generals.

These Custises had a daughter, Mary Ann Randolph Custis—the Randolph name recognizing kinship with the family into which one of Jefferson's family married. And in 1831 this daughter married her cousin, Robert E. Lee, then a young Army Lieutenant and the son of "Light Horse Harry." The Lees lived in the house for 30 years, until April 20, 1861. Then Colonel Lee, after two days of silent meditation, wrote a letter regret-fully declining the proffered command of the whole Union Army and mounted a horse to ride to Richmond, accompanied by his wife and such of their seven children who still were at home.

Arlington was one of the first "enemy" points occupied by the Union forces. General Lee never saw it again.

Across the Potomac River, in Georgetown, on a hill now comprising the large block bound by Q and R and Thirty-first and Thirty-second Streets, is a mansion more graceful in its lines but less beautiful in its setting than Arlington. It is the Peter House, generally known as Tudor Place. It, too, is yellow stucco over brick, with porticoes front and rear. Unlike Mount Vernon, Arlington, Octagon House and most of Washington's other celebrated residences, it is not a public trust or maintained by an organization. The house was built by the Peters and in the 1940's it still was occupied by Peters.

This graceful house was designed by Dr. William Thornton for Martha Parke Custis, a granddaughter of Martha Washington, when the young lady married Thomas Peter in 1805. She also had inherited a sizeable slice of the Custis-Washington fortune when Martha Washington died in 1802. Mrs. Peter bought the property from Francis Loundes who had started to build a house in 1794 but had completed only the wings, not the central portion. Dr. Thornton designed a completely new house, embracing the wings, but although the Peters moved in right away, the whole building was finished only in 1815. In the meantime, Mrs. Peter and Mrs. Thornton had stood one day on the hill of Tudor Place and watched the Capital burn, when it was fired by the British in 1814.

In the other American tradition was Ninian Beall who came to this continent as an indentured servant, and in 1703 was awarded for gallantry in fighting the Indians a farm of 795 acres, less than a mile to the southeast of what later became Tudor Place. Beall became wealthy in trade and his family married into the aristocracy. The Beall descendants built an impressive house about 1790 or 1795, and called it Dumbarton, but in 1796 sold it to Peter Casanave, a speculative investor, who almost immediately sold it to General Uriah Forest. It was a bad-luck

33

house until 1813 when Charles Carroll, grandson of the signer of the Declaration of Independence, bought it for a home. Aping his famous grandsire, Charles Carroll of Carrollton, he named the house Bellevue and thereafter signed his letters "Carroll of Bellevue."

So, if Washington was not yet really a city, and had no paved streets or water pipes or sewers, a number of persons at least were conceding that it had some semblance of permanence.

Recognizing the city, however, required a sense of humor. When Gouverneur Morris visited Washington to attend Jefferson's Inaugural, he commented:

"We only need here houses, cellars, kitchens, scholarly men, amiable women, and a few other such trifles to possess a perfect city. In a word, this is the best city in the world to live in—in the future."

Chapter Four

CAPSULE DEMOCRACY

If Washington had never been founded a great many humorists and "human interest" writers, including the smugly self-assertive Charles Dickens, would have had one less background against which to hang their personal and profitable whimsies. Early Washington was crude in many ways.

Nevertheless, even before the War of 1812, there were enough town and enough politics and enough social intercourse, drawn from the seacoast and the rapidly extending inland highways and waterways of the United States, to give Washington an individual character. Wherever one scratched Washington, he uncovered a little bit of Americana.

The broad divisions of American politics were here in capsule form. There was the dying party, the old Federalist, whose standard was carried for years by Aaron Burr and John Marshall, most enigmatic of Virginians. Jefferson hated Burr but had to tolerate him as his Vice-President for the first four years. John Marshall, tall and tight-lipped, was as much a Virginian as any man, but he had aligned himself with the Northern coterie under aging John Adams, now sulking in retirement at Braintree, Mass. On the last night that Adams was President, he named John Marshall Chief Justice of the Supreme Court as his final "Lame Duck" gesture of derision at Jefferson. The Senate, also "Lame Duck," confirmed the appointment.

Not even John Adams, let alone Jefferson—each in his own spite—could foresee that in 40 years as head of the third branch of government John Marshall would make a reputation never equalled by another Chief Justice as an interpreter of the Constitutional rights of man.

It was hard for any man to make a great reputation in the shadow of Jefferson, whose gift of self-press-agentry was as great as his other talents. This man with equal facility hoodwinked Congress into approving the purchase of the Louisiana Territory before it quite knew what it was doing and wrote the *Manual* for guidance of parliamentary debates. He took the *Manual* in manuscript as clear as copperplate to Mr. Smith at the *Intelligencer* for printing. It still governs the Congress and thousands of debating societies.

Now, lest Jefferson get out of hand, let us take a quick glimpse at what was going on around town toward the end of Jefferson's Administration.

Everything seemed to be developing and changing, except the oyster pie.

The Smiths, reflecting the prosperity of the *Intelligencer*, despite competition from the *Washington Gazette* and the *Times and Potowmack Packet*, built a country house, out north of Georgetown, to use in the summer. The farm at Sidney, close to the Capitol and the business district near it, was their "town" home. Living, however, was rather dear. Mrs. Smith, a Northerner and an "abolitionist" who would not own slaves, paid 12 shillings and sixpence a week to a servant who was not very good. On the other hand Dolly Madison, living in the Southern tradition, had to pay $400 for one of many house slaves. Add that price to upkeep and the slave was not cheap either, in days when common workmen often got only two shillings a day.

The male birds of brightest plumage in Washington were Mr. Merry, the already mentioned British Minister, and André Pinchon, the French Chargé d'Affaires who stayed from 1801 to 1805. Their court uniforms were dazzling, particularly alongside the revolutionary clothes popularized by Jefferson. The

French really reached the height of "color" in the dying days of man's sartorial resplendency when Napoleon sent in 1808, as his Minister to Washington, General Turreau de Garambonville, Marshal of France. Marshal Turreau was all but smothered in gold lace and diamond-studded orders.

Robert Smith, "a man of wealth and fashion," moved to Washington in 1804 to become Secretary of the Navy under Jefferson and to remain as Secretary of State under Madison. John Peter Van Ness arrived in Congress as a member from New York, and became a permanent resident under the prevailing pattern. A year after his arrival he won a beautiful bride and a fortune (it seems that all women who figure in older accounts are beautiful) by marrying Marcia Burns. In any event, he left Congress in 1803 to become major of the local militia, had Latrobe build him a large house, and settled down to enjoy life.

Conrad and Suter, a well-regarded innkeeper in Georgetown, picked up considerable competition in the boarding-house business, particularly by Mrs. Doyne, who soon became known as far north as New York. When Joel Barlow, the wealthy poet and later a diplomat (his fame rests on immortalizing hasty pudding in a poem), moved to Washington, he stayed with Mrs. Doyne. Room and board for Barlow, Mrs. Barlow and two servants, with stabling for the horses, cost $40 a week.

Soon Barlow bought Kalorama, an estate north of Washington about a mile and a half from the White House, where today are located more embassies and pretentious homes than in any other section of Washington.

All in all, it was a hodgepodge, which people liked or not according to their tastes. Take, for instance, Sir Augustus Foster, an attaché of the British Legation while Jefferson was President. He did not particularly like all of Washington, but conceded that it was for the most part an agreeable place to live. Here are some of his impressions:

"There were a number of rich proprietors in the State of

Maryland. In the district around Washington, I was assured there were 500 persons possessing estates which returned them an income of 1,000 pounds. Mr. Lloyd, a member of Congress on the Eastern Branch, possessed a net revenue of between six and seven thousand pounds, with which he had only to buy clothes for himself and his family, wines, equipage, furniture and other luxuries. Mr. Tayloe also, whose whole income exceeded 15,000 pounds per annum, held 3,000 acres of land which his father bought for 500 pounds. He possessed 500 slaves, built brigs and schooners, worked iron mines, converted the iron into ploughshares—and all this was done by the hands of his own subjects."

Sir Augustus reported that he saw relatively few members of Congress. (They probably could not afford the social pace.) But, much more pleasing, he never saw prettier girls, or more of them, anywhere. They were the flowers that bloomed at the candlelit balls given in the Georgetown houses. Unfortunately, too many reports verify the fact that bathing was not a universal custom, which perhaps accounts for the fact that dancing figures were designed to keep partners at a distance from each other.

But as for the girls, there was competition. So Sir Augustus confirmed, continuing:

"As there were but few of them, however, in proportion to the great number of men who frequented the places of amusement in the Federal City, it is one of the most marrying places in the whole continent—a truth which was beginning to be found out and became by and by the cause of vast numbers flocking thither, all round from the four points of the compass. Maugre the march of intellect so much vaunted in the present century, the literary education of these ladies is far from being worthy of the age of knowledge, and conversation is apt to flag, though a seat by the ladies is much coveted.

"Dancing and music served to eke out the time, but one got to be heartily sick of hearing the same song everywhere, even when it was, 'Just Like Love Is Yonder Rose.' No matter how this was sung, the words alone were the man-traps; the belle of the evening was declared to be just like both—and people looked around as if the listener was expected to become on the instant very tender and to propose—and sometimes such a result does in reality take place; both parties when betrothed use a great deal of billing and cooing."

Obviously Sir Augustus was a wary young man, but he got around. "In going to assemblies one had sometimes to drive three or four miles within the city bounds, and very often at the great risk of overturn, or being what is called 'stalled,' or stuck in the mud, when one can neither get backward nor forward, and either loses one's shoes or one's patience . . . Cards were a great resource of an evening, and gaming was all the fashion, at brag, especially, for the men who frequented society, who were chiefly from Virginia, or the Western States, and were very fond of this, the most gambling of all games. Loo was the innocent diversion of the ladies, who when they were 'looed' pronounced the word in a very mincing manner."

These parties were the ones to which "society" was invited. Already, however, there was one place to which any man might go—the President's Palace. Curious visitors might walk into its doors any time of the day with a fair chance of seeing the President. Very soon the crowds became so relatively large that special hours were set aside for the President's daily "receptions." So closely was this custom allied to the White House—the people's house in fact—that President Coolidge still was shaking hands with whatever persons gathered at noon each day. President Hoover at long last decided this was too great a drain on the time of a busy man. He stopped the practice. It is dead forever.

The other open meeting ground, almost from the opening days of Washington, was the Capitol. Of course it hardly need be noted the building was not finished. The great central rotunda, provided in the plans from the beginning, was only a hole in the ground for many years, but Congress found the money to build the two original wings housing the Senate and the House of Representatives.

The Senate chamber was the large semi-circular room that later became the meeting place of the Supreme Court, until the court got its own building in the 1930's. The House chamber was the somewhat larger room south of the rotunda that for many years has been known as Statuary Hall.

The Congress ordinarily met in the evening after dinner, as Parliaments still customarily do abroad. And here from the beginning democracy was slightly qualified. There were divisions in the galleries—and still are—separating the common voters from the families of members, from distinguished guests and from the diplomats.

Off the galleries are numerous committee rooms and offices for the officials of the House and Senate. These rooms, little changed from the original, often are used for the serving of private luncheons and small receptions. In the early years of Washington the Capital City was so small, and "society" and politics were so much the same, that the small, bored group heading both made debate evenings as much social occasions as the balls in private homes.

Hence the conclusion that probably more than one law was written, not in formal committee or in debate on the floor but in semi-social drinking and conversation in the anterooms.

It was in these rooms that James Lyon got the firsthand material for his political and biographical writings in the *National Magazine*. Here Major Vermonnet, by making himself agreeable, could find the occasional commission to do a portrait. The young ladies about to be introduced in society practiced the manners and conversation taught by Miss Ann Vidler in her day school at Greenleaf's Point. Sir Augustus already has indicated, however, that the interest of the young ladies was less than might be desired in syntax and politics than in mating. For the intellectual, bored observer of debates it already was possible to fetch along a book from a lending library which the *Gazette* announced on June 1, 1801, was "opened this day, first door west of President's Square, on Pennsylvania Avenue."

In other words, Washington socially was exactly what one would expect of a thriving town, with perhaps a few more wealthy persons than the average. It was Charleston or Baltimore without the commercial population, and it was somewhat the cross section of every port on the Eastern Seaboard. A little city, it had its periodic "lions"—such as Captain Zebulon Montgomery Pike, when he returned in 1808 from exploration of the Louisiana Territory.

There were, too, the usual small-town amusements, not the least of which was the oval track, known as the National Race Course, located north of the town. Here meets were held in summer and fall, with no Puritan restraints: ladies made up possibly a third of the audiences; the biggest crowds gathered on Sundays, and betting was heavy.

The track was exactly a mile in length and 50 feet wide. There were booths crowded into the enclosure where refreshments were to be had. The roofs of the booths were made of planking stout enough to hold the weight of persons who clambered upon them to see the matches, in which owners or jockeys rode in the stiff-backed style of the day.

As many as 3000 or 4000 persons would crowd the enclosure. There was no color bar. The only touch of class distinction was in the reservation of ground, on the western side outside the circle, for the coaches and carriages of the wealthier patrons, who made a day of it, sending along staffs of servants to prepare and serve refreshments.

But in the Jefferson development one thing was lacking—a Palace hostess. How different it would be, said many a lady, if the beautiful mansion could be used as it was intended. Of course Mr. Jefferson had turned out to be a good President and he was a great scholar, and Mrs. Madison was helpful. But if only Mrs. Jefferson had lived or there were a married President. . . .

Chapter Five

RUIN

DOLLY MADISON wore two gowns on her Inaugural Day. The *her* is deliberate, for this day ushered in the *Dolly Madison era* of Washington. The fact that James Madison was elected President was a fortuitous incident. The President, already characterized by Washington Irving on an earlier visit as "a withered little Apple-John," was content and perhaps relieved to take a spot in the shadow. He gracefully gave up the head of his own dinner table to permit his hearty, heady, voluptuous wife to preside.

In a manner far different from the queenly aloofness of Martha Washington—now dead and her era dead with her— Dolly Madison became the First Lady in society as well as in politics, in sports as well as in the drawing room. Her clothes were copied assiduously, her menus aped. Jean Pierre Sioussat ("French Jean"), her cook, became as well known as Henry Clay. The weekly levee was restored in the White House. More dinners were given than by any hostess since residing there. When Dolly went calling it was in a coach that cost $1,500. She patronized the races and set an unexcelled record for parties in the mansion.

"Ah, why," wrote a friend in her diary, "does she not in all things act with the same propriety?"

The friend referred to the so-proper manner in which Dolly entered on her stewardship of the President's Palace. Mistress

43

Madison was the completely formal lady at the Inaugural Reception. She wore plain black cambric in her gown. It had a long train. A bonnet of purple velvet and white satin, crowned with white plumes, topped her costume. She wore no kerchief over her shoulders, revealing—unusual for the day—the full white roundness of her shoulders and bosom, but her deportment made it all right.

The act of Dolly's that won the left-handed compliment was the fact that she did not herself dance at the Inaugural Ball. This was the first Inaugural Ball held in Washington. Dolly was the charming hostess, dressed in pale buff velvet, with a turban to match, and on the turban two bird-of-paradise feathers. Her jewels were pearls, worn on neck and arms and in her ears. The hostess outshone the splendor of Marshal Turreau.

The spring of the Madison Inaugural was the gayest Washington yet had known. For a year there had been extraordinary tension between the United States and Britain and, even greater, between Washington and the greater Eastern cities. The British crisis was due largely to the impressment of American sailors by British warships at sea. But the greater tension at home was due to Jefferson's own iron hand used in the last year of his Presidency to enforce an embargo on American trade, lest the crisis at sea precipitate a war.

As if to give Madison, his protégé, a lift in popular esteem as an inaugural gift, Jefferson lifted the embargo three days before Madison was nominated in 1809. So trade resumed, debates in Congress became less bitter, money flowed freely and— although war may seem in retrospect to have been inevitable— no one believed it then.

When Jefferson left Washington, trailed by a string of wagons carrying his scientific specimens, and his library (original letters from Cortez to the King of Spain, a 1650 folio copy of *Piers Plowman*, Roman maps, and Greek romances in French, Latin and Italian translations), he left it for all time, and the neoclassical tradition of government gave way to another form of life.

An epidemic of yellow fever and a romantic introduction reminiscent of a Dumas plot combined to place in the White House the first true "social leader" of Washington. There simply was nothing unpicturesque about Dolly Madison.

Approximately one sixth of the population of Philadelphia had been killed by an epidemic of yellow fever which scourged that quondam Capital of the United States from August, 1793, until stopped by the frosts in November. One wealthy young man, John Todd, fearing for his pregnant wife and their young son, sent his family to the country, near Gray's Ferry, Pennsylvania. When he joined them, utterly exhausted from work as a volunteer nurse in the city, the young man himself fell ill. His wife, now mother of a second son, nursed him until she caught the fever herself. When she became conscious, after a long illness, she learned that she had been widowed.

In the winter Dolly Todd returned to Philadelphia, to settle into expected quiet retirement in the home of her mother, Mrs. Payne, who ran a boarding house. She was 25 years old, and well to do. In fact, she could well have afforded a house of her own, but young widows living alone at that period were classed socially alongside madams of houses of call.

Aaron Burr may or may not have been a paying guest in Mrs. Payne's House. The stories differ. But he knew the widow Todd, and had paid court to her. James Madison saw the young widow on several occasions and, being already 42 years of age and extremely proper, he sought the means of a formal introduction. His friend Burr arranged it. So one evening, Madison, Burr and a Miss Elizabeth Collins Lee sat in Mrs. Payne's parlor exchanging polite nothings in conversation—Dolly in mulberry silk with a tulle handkerchief tied chastely over her curls.

45

Madison made slow progress, so slow by his now love-quick-ened standards that he asked Martha Washington to write a note of commendation for him. She did.

Madison hired fiddles and banjoes to supply the wedding music when he and Dolly Todd were married on September 15, 1794, and he carried her off to Montpelier for their honeymoon.

Dolly Madison entered society with the entrenched position of wife to a man already famous. Madison got a beautiful wife and a second fortune. Aaron Burr faded from their lives except for one dramatic reappearance yet far in the future.

Eight years of assisting Jefferson had given the new chatelaine of the Palace, one of its youngest hostesses, ample time to prac-tice and to plan. Her first action in setting the pace of styles was to re-upholster the formal furniture in the newly fashionable yellow satin, to hang damask draperies at the windows, install mirrors over mantelpieces and to purchase a piano and a guitar.

Thus Washington bloomed overnight into a full-fledged Cap-ital. The definition includes good oratory in the Senate Cham-ber. Full living saw the levees and balls mounting to the satura-tion point in the winter season, with good cooking now an essen-tial for any hostess who wished to be popular.

The pioneer days of Washington were over; it was the central city of the country because the United States, bursting the seams of its colonial jacket, was becoming a large country. No longer was American business controlled exclusively by New York, Bos-ton and Philadelphia; it had an internal economy, made up of areas containing no cities of their own. These regions sent their statesmen or politicians to Washington. The residents visited the Capital as tourists. They began to look upon it as a focal point more than a century before the Eastern cities yielded face to Washington.

Paving had not yet been introduced, but Pennsylvania Ave-nue now was bordered by trees. There were enough houses to fill in most of the vacant spaces between the Capitol and the

Mansion to dot the area north of the Palace grounds and to make the highway to Georgetown through Q Street less a country lane and more a city street.

Politics naturally was still the only trade commodity in Washington. Charles J. Ingersoll, of Philadelphia, orating in the House, was a temporary rival to Clay and Calhoun.

For the ladies, in the new prosperity fed by reopened foreign commerce and rich river trade on the Ohio and the Mississippi, there were gowns imported from London and Paris, or made by skilled seamstresses over designs imported on ornately dressed dolls. Food was served in the finer houses on plate imported from Europe. The political leaders boasted of a government that in nine years had reduced its debts by half. Albert Gallatin, the French-American, favorite of Jefferson and of Madison, was toasted for his stewardship of the Treasury.

There simply was more and more of everything—more slaves in the baronial houses of the Southerners, more amusements, more gambling and more promises.

Washington became in the first four years of the Madison regime the fountainhead of national pride. It seemed almost routine in June of 1812 when Madison asked Congress to declare war on Britain and the Congress agreed. No one evidenced worry that this gesture held two threats: one that of defeat of the United States, the other the greater threat of rebellion by the Northern cities, already jealous of the power and disdainful of the assumptions of the little city on the shore of the Potomac River.

The gentlemen formed volunteer companies and drilled in Judiciary Square. The members of Congress were pledged to join with them in defending the city, if necessary. General Armstrong and Colonel Monroe, who as boys had fought in the Revolution, were the commanding officers. Monroe, Secretary of War as well as a militia officer, was particularly handsome in the saddle, an indefatigable rider. The worst worry was about a possible insurrection by slaves if the threatening British moved through Maryland.

There was considerable official concern in the spring of 1814, but no person of note fled Washington. Commodore Perry had secured Lake Erie on the north.

There was still an atmosphere in which to note that John Forsyth, a young Representative from Georgia, was the handsomest beau in Washington. Here was a man destined to become a Senator, Minister to Spain and Secretary of War under Jackson. Girls swooned when they gazed at him in drawing rooms—but he was married.

William Pinkney, citizen of Maryland, just resigned from the post of Attorney General, drew packed houses to the Supreme Court when he argued a case, so brilliant was his oratory. Everybody seemed to love a good speech. Witness the crowds of 200 and 300 persons who customarily attended the Congressional debates, veering back and forth between the Senate and the House, according to which side was exhibiting the greater forensics.

All in all, Washington in the spring of 1814 was the center of the loudest, bravest, hardest-eating and hardest-playing political group imaginable. It was ready for any eventuality, and daring the British to show their faces. Then Admiral Sir George Cockburn landed down the Potomac on the Maryland shore.

The only combat officer whose unit distinguished itself on that awful, sticky, hot Wednesday, August 24, 1814, was Captain Joshua Barney, of the Navy, whose battery, mounted on land astride the Bladensburg Road, kept firing until entirely overrun and largely massacred by the vanguard of 4,000 battle-seasoned British Regulars.

Was this the end of the pride and dreams and hopes, of 20 years of planning and building?

Long and arduous campaigns give people time to readjust themselves, to study their next steps. Yet Washington heard only on August 22nd, that the British had landed at the little wharf at Benedict, Maryland. A great number of Washington and Georgetown families left the town but quite a number remained. Word was passed to the city that the British would not harm any civilian or his property if the citizen remained in his house and refrained from warlike acts.

The eager militia, armed with family guns, many of these old when the Revolution was fought, without training and un-uniformed but cheering General Winder when he rode among them, assembled in Bladensburg, through whose main street the British must march to reach Washington. A few of the men recognized and cheered President Madison when, early on the morning of August 24th, he went out to inspect the defenses. With him rode Colonel Monroe.

The mixed feelings in town on this morning reflected the choice of partisans who had divided the city for the past two years or more. Little Jemmy Madison was not at all sanguine about the war. At this moment there was a meeting in Ghent of Commissioners from the United States and Great Britain to talk terms for ending the war, with Albert Gallatin, French-American Secretary of the Treasury, acting as chief emissary for Madison.

Many of the calmer folk of Washington were the old Southerners who thus far had escaped the fighting—the British held New York—and most persons of property.

The confident ones, although possibly not as confident as they seemed, were the followers of Henry Clay, Speaker of the House and absolute boss of the Twelfth Congress, who had helped more than a little to precipitate war by his speeches. Clay had put on the highly influential House Committee on Foreign Affairs his special warhawk cronies—Peter B. Porter, of New York; John C. Calhoun, of South Carolina; and Felix Grundy, of Tennessee.

Few people slept on the night of August 23rd. They followed the pattern of Dolly Madison who at dawn was atop the White

House "turning my spyglass in every direction" and, in coolly
writing the events of the day in a letter to her sister, reporting
"alas, I can descry only groups of military wandering in all directions, as if there were a lack of arms or spirit to fight for their
own firesides."

By noon Daniel Carroll's picked forces of 100 Mansion guards
were summoned to the battlefield, and "French Jean" suggested
that his mistress order the blowing up of the Mansion. But
Dolly was too busy to listen to him. She wrote, "I have pressed
as many Cabinet papers into trunks as to fill one carriage; our
private property must be sacrificed, as it is impossible to procure
wagons for its transportation."

Dolly's story that day was the story of Washington in its first
hour of trial. Few people were there who had not a double sense
of feeling—for their own and for the government. Many probably appreciated fully the meaning of the city for the first time
when the heavy atmosphere was shattered by the noise of gun-
fire from Bladensburg, and when the stench of burned powder
mingled with the river smells in the heat.

Dolly wrote:

"Three o'clock.—Will you believe it, my sister? We have had
a battle, or skirmish, near Bladensburg, and I am still here
within sound of the cannon! Mr. Madison comes not, may God
protect him! Two messengers covered with dust, come to bid
me fly; but I wait for him . . . At this late hour, a wagon has
been procured; I have had it filled with the plate and most valuable portraits belonging to the house; whether it will reach its
destination, the Bank of Maryland, or fall into the hands of
British soldiers, events must determine.

"Our kind friend, Mr. Carroll, has come to hasten my depar-
ture, and is in a very bad humor with me because I insist on
waiting until the large picture of General Washington is secured, and it requires to be unscrewed from the wall. This proc-
ess has been found too tedious for these perilous moments; I
have ordered the frame to be broken and the canvas taken out;

it is done—and the precious portrait has been placed in the hands of two gentlemen from New York for safekeeping. And now, dear sister, I must leave this house, or the retreating army will make me a prisoner in it, by filling up the road I am directed to take. When I shall again write to you, or where I shall be tomorrow, I cannot tell!!"

With the gentlemanly leisure of their profession, when it prospered, Admiral Cockburn and General Ross, the latter on a new horse, rode up Capitol Hill at the head of their re-assembled troops. Their losses had not been sufficient to worry about; the resistance had hardly given exercise to their seasoned forces.

As the first business of a long summer afternoon, the British troops set fire to the Capitol. It burned briskly, and there was just sufficient wind to carry sparks from the Capitol itself to most of the other houses around Capitol Hill. They burned, too, despite the promise to safeguard property. When those fires started, hundreds of Washingtonians who had stayed in their houses, relying on the promise of security, joined the other refugees.

From the Capitol the British procession—it almost was a parade—started northwest along Pennsylvania Avenue, grateful for the shade of the trees which lined it. They broke down the doors of the Palace, from which everyone had fled but whose doors had been carefully and faithfully locked by Jean Pierre Sioussat just before he put Dolly's parrot on his arm and set forth for Philadelphia.

Admiral Cockburn personally visited the Mansion, and gave leave to the troopers with him to eat such food and drink what wine could be found, but quickly. General Cockburn himself looked around. He asked to see Mrs. Madison's chair, sat in it for a bit, and—so reported a contemporary—took for a souvenir the pillow from the chair "adding pleasantries too vulgar for me to repeat."

The yellow damask and polished mahogany burned brightly.

The Mansion was a beacon of fire all night long, while a pall of smoke hovered over the doomed city.

Two days later the British withdrew to their ships, their withdrawal marked by a hurricane that did more damage to private property than the enemy.

The Jeremiahs arose before the embers were warm. Wrote one, "It is not expected that Washington ever again will be the seat of government." Said another, "The people are reduced from affluence to poverty."

Over in Virginia on August 25th, after Dolly Madison had spent one night in an Army tent, an innkeeper wished to evict her because she belonged to the government that had started the war, and would have done so but for the intercession of other guests.

At the cost of a few burned buildings Washington became important in the country because of the controversies that raged about it. . . .

Chapter Six

PHOENIX CITY

WILLIAM WIRT walked around to look at the Mansion. He was one among thousands of visitors. Every Washingtonian did so. It was the center of life in Washington, the symbol, far more than the Capitol, of what Washington stood for. And at the Capitol only the Representatives Hall had been damaged as badly.

"I went to look at the ruins of the President's House," he wrote. "The rooms which you saw so richly furnished, exhibited nothing but unroofed walls, cracked, defaced and blackened with the fire. I cannot tell you what I felt like as I walked among them . . . I called on the President. He looks miserably shattered and woebegone. In short, he looks heartbroken. His mind is full of the New England sedition. He introduced the subject, and continued to press it—painful as it obviously was to him. I denied the probability, even the *possibility* that the yeomanry of the North could be induced to place themselves under the power and protection of England, and diverted the conversation to another topic; but he took the first opportunity to return to it, and convinced me that his heart and mind were painfully full of the subject."

New England was on the verge of secession. An effort to float a war loan of $50,000,000 had failed. There were reports of new invasion threats from Canada. General Pakenham was sailing for New Orleans where none could yet foresee that he would suffer at General Andrew Jackson's hands a bloody defeat, lose his own life, and leave his viscera interred on this alien soil.

Meeting at Hartford, Conn., at the suggestion of powerful Massachusetts, the States of Massachusetts, Connecticut and Rhode Island wrote the "Hartford Convention," inviting all other States to protect themselves from further encroachments by the Federal Government.

In this atmosphere, while Washington residents returned to their homes to patch their lives, and Dolly and Jemmy Madison accepted Colonel Tayloe's invitation to set up housekeeping in Octagon House, the Congress met in special session. Every person who could elbow his way into the main hall of the Patent Office, used as a temporary meeting hall by Congress, listened with hushed breath to see what President Madison would say in his Message to the Congress.

There was no recounting of these things at all, simply the summary statement that, "It is not disguised that the situation of our country calls for its greatest efforts."

The Little Apple-John shut himself up in the library on the second floor of Octagon House to plan the impossible, and Hoban got out his original, yellowed plans for the Mansion to start rebuilding. The Congress could not finance the war, let alone rebuilding of the Mansion, but it authorized him to start planning for the future.

A good cross section of Washington society was gathered in Dolly Madison's informal drawing room on the first floor of Octagon House on the afternoon of February 4, 1815. President Madison was working upstairs. The current topic of conversation still was General Jackson's recent victory at New Orleans. Nevertheless, even such a victory had not stopped the New England secessionists. Even now, three "ambassadors" were en route to Washington to notify the Federal Government officially of the Hartford Convention.

A young man arrived rather breathlessly at Octagon House.

The butler recognized him as Henry Carroll, secretary in the Foreign Service of the United States, long absent from Washington. Mr. Carroll had come straight from Ghent.

He hurried to Dolly Madison, paused in the tradition of his training to bow hurriedly, and then whispered a word to her. Dolly told him to go up and see the President, and then turned to the crowd and shouted, "Peace!"

The peace treaty had been signed on December 24th.

This news echoed through the town, and in a few minutes the voice telegraph had carried it from Georgetown to Bladensburg. Octagon's doors were thrown open for a reception that continued throughout the night. Bonfires illuminated the streets which otherwise were innocent of lights.

By 1816 it all depended on the personal viewpoint whether a Washingtonian jubilated over his life in the Capital City or not. To the chiefs of the government and the Southerners it was a growing capital, with more than 10,000 population, in which gathered representatives of the wit and wisdom of the world's capitals.

To others, like Mr. Law who had lost $250,000 in real-estate investments alone, it was a lost city over which towered the ruins of great buildings destroyed before even being completed.

Two hundred or more ladies and gentlemen paid court to Dolly Madison, still at Octagon House, every Wednesday evening, gossiped perhaps about the contrast between her and Elizabeth Kortright Monroe, wife of the Secretary of State, whose husband was more and more in the limelight as probable successor to Little Jemmy Madison. Mrs. Monroe was frail and delicate in appearance, but a strong Tory to her fingertips. Prominent in what passed for society in New York, she was the daughter of a British Army officer who had held a command in the occupation of New York in the Revolution. Her manners were stately.

Mrs. Monroe fitted into the more stilted edge of society,

which this year gained Hyde de Neuville as the new French
Minister and Sir Charles Bagot as Minister from Great Britain.

Through the winter season of 1816-17, ladies sloshed in carriages through the muddy streets to pay calls every weekday
from after breakfast until noon. Informal receptions marked
the afternoons in the scattered great houses. What evenings
were not ordinarily filled with "at homes" held by official wives,
were given over to balls and banquets. It was a mark of unpop-
ularity to have less than four or five formal evening invitations
a week. Many of the best parties were given in honor of Commodore Stephen Decatur and his handsome wife, new residents
in Washington, who had commissioned Latrobe to build for
them a suitable house on a lot opposite the northwest corner of
the grounds around the President's House.

Mrs. Smith held a party in January at Sidney. She invited 170
persons and 120 attended. There were four musicians from the
Marine Band, with two rooms set aside for dancing, supper in a
third room, and a fourth room arranged as a parlor for those
who wished to talk. General William Harrison was a great beau
of the season, but he was rivalled by James Brown, Senator from
Louisiana, who backed his ambitions with a great fortune and
finally became Minister to France.

In the younger set, the belles of the dances were the daughters of Baron Johan Albert de Kantzov, Minister Resident of
Sweden and Norway, and Louis de Onis, Minister of Spain. The
Spanish Minister himself danced very little. In him, Spain had
sent abroad one of its cleverest diplomats to attempt to circum-
vent infiltration by the United States into Florida.

Indeed, life was very gay, even though persons without carriages must pay as much as $5 to hire conveyances on the wetter
and colder nights and gentlemen usually carried pistols to discourage footpads.

Speaker Clay of the House was the dominant personality of
the day, and a favorite of the scholarly Abbé José Correa da

Serra, Portuguese Minister from the exiled government in Brazil and Jefferson's old crony.

Abbé Serra was the wit of Washington. He amused society by dubbing the Capital, doubtless after a five-mile drive to a party, "the city of magnificent distances," making the first pun on L'Enfant's earlier enthusiastic description of the town as "the city of magnificent vistas."

Maybe it was amusing, if one had plenty of time, a good carriage and horses, and the reasonable certainty of dining most evenings in well-staffed houses with well-stocked cellars and good cooks. But the natives were worried.

Through sixteen years, four Administrations, Washington had not doubled its population. In fact, it was stagnating, not pressing on to rival the cities of Europe, as George Washington had predicted. Abused in descriptions by most visitors, its own people began to feel the sting. The Congress, except for providing funds to restore the President's House and to begin a 45-year program of restoration and enlargement of the Capitol, was not interested.

The Capital lacked pavements, sewers, or any water supply except that coming from private wells. It was without police or fire protection. John Randolph of Roanoke, speaking of this period, said that Pennsylvania Avenue could only be described as "the great Serbonian bog." Mr. Monroe, always a little testy in his speech, called the city a "sheep walk." Fevers were considered routine ailments.

One journalist, writing within the year after the invasion, described the city thus:

"Twelve or fifteen clusters of houses at a considerable distance from each other, bringing to our recollections the appearance of a camp of nomad Arabs, which, however, if connected together would make a very respectable town, not much inferior, perhaps, to the capital of Virginia, and here and there an isolated house; the whole of it, when seen from the ruins of our public edifices, looking more like the place where proud Washington once stood than where humble Washington now stands."

Perhaps, however, the "distances" served one purpose in a day when all cities were primitive. There was ample space to disperse the slops and garbage thrown into the streets, and plenty of mud to absorb the droppings of horses, cattle and hogs that had the run of the streets.

Naturally, if a man permitted himself to get depressed, he would be very depressed indeed. Then, too, the Madison Administration was getting a little tiresome. It was hardly a matter of interest in gossip, so long had people been accustomed to Dolly's extraordinary adventures, when it was whispered about that Aaron Burr, preparing to flee to France to escape the enemies who had grown in number all the years since he had killed Alexander Hamilton, scaled the garden wall at Octagon House to tell Dolly good-bye.

The ladies frankly told each other that you could have knocked them over with one of the feathers from Dolly Madison's turbans. They could not believe what they heard immediately after Monroe succeeded Madison. That Elizabeth Monroe always had been a snob—a British snob, at that—and now this: she would not return calls paid at her residence.

Had the United States, they asked, fought two wars to democratize the United States for this? And the Washington ladies were not alone in their criticism. The wives of the diplomatic corps were equally incensed.

Elizabeth Monroe could not quite understand the hullaballoo. She explained to her friends that she thought the Presidency demanded more dignity than some other persons had given it. All she wished to do was to restore the grace and customs of Martha Washington. Mrs. Washington had not paid calls, but had received at formal levees. Now she, Mrs. Monroe, certainly did not expect callers to address her as "Your Majesty," as many had done to Martha.

The feud just about ruined the season of 1817-18, but it also gave people something to talk about besides politics. By the fall of 1818, however, the Capital had accepted the Monroes and flocked to the reopening of the President's House. Glistening in its new coat of white paint to hide the smoke scars on the stones, it was now and for always the White House.

The White House, too, epitomized the change in feeling toward Britain and France, a feeling being manifested in the new houses elsewhere in Washington. Congress appropriated $50,-000 for the refurnishing of the White House, and left the work to Mrs. Monroe's own taste. She did it in the year and a half between her husband's inauguration and the reopening of the Mansion.

This Presidential wife, herself British and so castigated for it, imported French furniture exclusively for the building, calling on taste cultivated in earlier years when James Monroe had been Minister to France. She imported French china, thin white bordered in orange, and a French chef.

No one boycotted the first invitation reception to the White House, where Elizabeth Monroe, fingering a tortoise-shell lorgnette, holding high on her tiny frame her small head with hair dressed tall and topped by feathers, sat on a raised platform to receive her guests.

There was some more talk about the non-return of calls. But, for the record, no President's wife since has returned calls.

In any event, the squabble was soon forgotten. The country was booming now, and Monroe, rather a nonentity, was a "safe" President and Washington was on its way somewhere. No one quite knew where, but that made no difference.

It was pretty slick of the old boy, people commented in the taverns, to outwit Canning, the British Foreign Minister, and state the Monroe Doctrine, forbidding further colonization in the Western Hemisphere, as a 100-percent American declaration and not an Anglo-American policy. There was also the law setting up Liberia as a free country for Negroes. That should make the blacks happy, and Monroe would be immortalized by having its capital, Monrovia, named for him.

It actually was a little funny to see this Virginia aristocrat become the champion of the common man, and, to give the devil his due, his wife had a good part in it. She might turn the noses of a few of the old busybodies, but everyone was welcome in the White House at the weekly receptions.

A newspaper of the period found that these receptions represented the height of democracy: ". . . In addition to the secretaries, senators, foreign Ministers, consuls, auditors, accountants, officers of the Army and Navy of every grade, were farmers, merchants, parsons, priests, lawyers, judges, auctioneers and nothingarians, all with wives, and some with their gawky offspring; some in shoes, some in boots and many in spurs; some snuffing, others chewing, and many longing for their cigars and whisky punch at home."

Even the friends of Monroe laughed when he was referred to as "James the Lesser," in comparison with James Madison. The Federal Government really became popular. Washington, the Capital, basked in that atmosphere, when in 1820 Monroe committed it to the financing of general public works by approving a law to build a highway, eighty feet wide and paved with gravel, from Cumberland, Maryland, to the Ohio River.

And there was Florida, which became part of the Union in 1819, after a small war in which General Jackson put himself one notch closer to the White House plus a financial settlement of $5,000,000 with Spain. Monroe's re-election, with a majority of electoral votes greater than had been given to any man except George Washington, was an index of the good feeling and generally good life in Washington.

The city was not all White House. There was the Congress, a better show than ever, with John C. Calhoun rising higher and higher to challenge even the President for supremacy as a wit, thinker and statesman. Any speech of his packed the galleries with admirers, mostly ladies, who whiled away the tedium of long speeches by eating fruits and delicacies handed up to the galleries from the floor on the ends of poles normally used to open and close the high windows. In private life, Calhoun was equally distinguished, thanks by half at least to Mrs. Calhoun. His cousin in a remote degree, with the maiden name of Florida, the dark-eyed lady gave to her husband wealth and social prestige far greater than his branch of the family possessed.

Calhoun was the challenger in Congressional popularity polls of Clay, now older, more saturnine, and less glamorous. But they were not political enemies.

The feud that made conversation, and which erupted in 1823 over nothing in particular, was between Calhoun and John Quincy Adams, Monroe's Secretary of State.

Fortunately their political feud did not go so far as that between Commodore Decatur, the highly patriotic but nasty-tempered new resident of Washington, and Commodore Barron. Decatur, who had notched his dueling pistols several times, finally called out Barron. They fought at the Bladensburg Fields. Decatur was mortally wounded and died a few days later. Mrs. Decatur immediately abandoned a house which in the course of time sheltered many of the notables in Washington, including Clay and Calhoun.

There was unusual excitement in August of 1822 when a fever epidemic hit most of the residents of Washington. The doctors first thought it was cholera and there were some deaths. But the epidemic passed without great harm. Of course, sewers and clean supplies of water still were far in the future.

By the end of Monroe's Administration town houses were located as far west as Massachusetts Avenue and Fourteenth Street. There was a law forbidding the free running of farm animals south of Massachusetts Avenue, but no one took it seriously.

Chapter Seven

AN ERA BLOOMS AND FADES

TIME WAS RUNNING OUT for that small band of Easterners who, differ as they might amongst themselves, had held for almost two score years a firm grip on the fortunes of the Republic. And as their power declined, so grew in proportion the prestige—although not the comfort—of Washington.

If it ever is possible to put a finger on a year and say, "This is when it occurred," the year 1824 marked the beginning of the change, of many changes. In that year, the political contest for the Presidency moved openly into the national Capital; in that year the new West found that Washington was the best sounding board for its claims, and in 1824 the "gentlemen" who formerly had run the Federal Government retreated so far as to choose one of the fringe of this group to carry their banner to their last Presidential Victory.

One could not see the picture clearly in New York, which was more preoccupied with trade than politics, or in Philadelphia, cultural center of the United States but a little too preoccupied with generalities to encompass the specific. Washington was the focal point of attack and the reflecting screen, thanks largely to a post service that made the settled portions of the country, except Louisiana, only days apart instead of weeks.

The contest for the Presidency had not, in 1824, yet turned into the scramble that it is today, with candidates attempting to barnstorm the whole country in their campaigns. The elections were run for the most part in "smoke-filled" rooms in State capitals, but they depended mightily on the background built up by the candidates themselves in Washington. This meant not only speeches but the impressions sent to newspapers by correspondents, who mingled in the drawing rooms and boarding houses of the Capital, and in the lobbies of the Capitol itself.

They did not mingle, it may be noted here, in clubs, as did the partisan groups in other cities. It is an oddity of some interest that Washington, for all of its divisions into groups, had no men's club of any sort until after the Civil War. Were the politicos afraid of such exclusive association, because it might not seem to be democratic?

One further word in explanation for the manner in which elections were held then:

The citizens of each State voted in Presidential election years for electors. These electors might or might not be pledged to specific candidates. Later on, before March 1st of the following year, and usually in January, the electors met and actually cast votes for their favorite Presidential candidates. If there was no majority of electors for any one candidate, then the contest was thrown into the House of Representatives, where the Representatives elected a President.

Election by the House of Representatives had put Jefferson into office in 1801, after a contest in which Aaron Burr entered the lists with more votes than Jefferson or John Adams, who was trying to win a second term.

Now, in 1824, the voice of the West was rising, rather angrily and forcefully, and nowhere was it as loud as in the Capitol. There were twenty-four States instead of the original thirteen. The westward migration was so constant and so swift that soon one third of the whole population would be living west of the Alleghenies, in contrast with the fraction of one twentieth counted there as recently as 1800. In all the Western States white men and free Negroes were enfranchised, not limited in voting to freeholders, as was universal in the old East and old

64

South. The voice of the West was the voice of Clay, and of another Senator who in 1824 had not yet reached his political maturity—Andrew Jackson.

Yes, Andrew Jackson was emerging on the Washington scene, a little rough in speech but not the uncouth man so often pictured. He was addicted to shirtsleeves and slippers in private, but he was equally careful to dress in black satin when he attended services at St. John's Episcopal Church.

There were several candidates in 1824. John Quincy Adams, still Secretary of State, was angling both for votes of the old Northern crowd that had turned its Federalism into slightly more liberal tones and for the conservative Southern crowd which was epitomized in the Virginia Gentlemen, of whom Monroe was the last. Henry Clay was ambitious for the Presidency but saw small chance of winning, and he preferred Adams to the fiery Calhoun, another candidate. Then there was egotistical, chess-master W. H. Crawford, of Georgia, Secretary of the Treasury under Monroe. Also, Andrew Jackson.

The upshot of the contest was that Adams won in the House of Representatives, where his majority of a single vote was assured by General Stephen Van Rensselaer, the eighth patroon of his line. There were charges that Clay or Daniel Webster had "seduced" the old general and made him change his vote, but it is more likely that an eighth patroon was trying honestly to save the ways of conservatism in government.

The gallery booed the result, but it stood. A spectator in the private gallery when this vote was taken was an aged man, one of America's greatest heroes and now a penniless exile from his own land—General Lafayette.

About 15,000 people now lived in Washington in the cooler parts of the year. The increase was almost entirely political. There was no industry and little commerce beyond that necessary for the everyday needs of the town. The canal had been constructed up the Maryland side of the Potomac in the hope of opening to trade the rich area above the falls, but little came of it.

The business of Washington was politics, and on politics it would survive or fall.

Mr. Adams became a hard-working and well-intentioned President, even though receptions bored him to death and interfered with his lifelong habit of arising at 5 A.M. He dutifully went through the rounds. Mrs. Adams, English-bred like Mrs. Monroe, carried on the formality established by Mrs. Monroe. Here was the last gasp of dignity in the colonial sense of the word:

"Her doors (the White House) were open to men of every sort of political opinion," wrote an anonymous visitor; "and whatever rancors Congressional debate or executive-office interviews might beget, all were left outside her threshold. Those, too, were the stately days of knee breeches and silk stockings for men; while the women wore Paris gowns of richest material and head-dresses fearfully and wonderfully made."

Louisa Catherine Adams, who had visited most of the European courts with her husband, was the style leader of the Capital, and of the country. Her figure accommodated well the revealing Empire fashion then dominant in France. Here is one example of the elegance of women's clothes of her day:

Mrs. Adams' dress for this particular reception was of white net over eggshell satin. It was banded at the neck, waist and bottom of the skirt with narrow silver-and-black lace, set off by taffeta bows and cording. Lace ran lengthwise up and down short puffed sleeves, and a narrow skirt dropped to the floor from a waistline set as high as possible under her bust. The neck of the dress was low and round. With the dress Mrs. Adams wore gloves reaching the length of her arm to the puff sleeves. Her kerchief, made either to carry or to throw over her shoulders should there be a draft in a room, was a very large linen

66

square banded with eyelet embroidery. In one corner her full name, "Louisa Catherine Adams," was worked into a medallion.

On her feet she wore eggshell taffeta slippers. Atop her high-piled hair was a very tall tortoise-shell comb bearing a picture of Andrew Jackson.

Old John Quincy Adams dutifully pulled on his silk breeches for the receptions and the parties, but he found them dull. On an evening in 1828, he wrote in his diary:

"This evening was the sixth drawing room. Very much crowded; 16 Senators, perhaps 60 members of the House of Representatives, and multitudes of strangers. These parties are becoming more and more insupportable to me."

The "drawing rooms" at the White House became more and more crowded during the Adams regime. One crush was so great that General Scott had his pocket picked of a wallet containing $800. Persons with a taste for going around, and who had the clothes to make an appearance—little else was necessary —had no lack of houses to visit. The Cabinet ladies began in 1825 to hold their own weekly "drawing rooms."

Washington really was becoming a world Capital. In 1825 the United States was the first country to recognize Brazil as an independent nation. President Adams received José Silvestre Rebello as the personal emissary of King Pedro. And Sarah M. Peale painted Rebello's portrait.

Culture came to Washington in formal clothes in 1827 when the Columbia Institute was organized as a cultural society, and the President himself presided over it. Sully painted a portrait of Andrew Jackson. Carusi, a prospering Italian music master, opened a public hall which for a generation was to be popular for meetings and banquets.

An orphan asylum had long since been established, and in 1827 Mrs. Van Ness decided that it needed substantial com-

67

munity support. She organized a fair with 30 tables for exhibitors, and got the Marine Band to play for the occasion.

So there was considerable going out. In fact, high-ranking official hostesses newly arrived learned to their horror that about 500 persons were in the category termed "social." This meant that the 500, merely by leaving cards, could establish a claim to an invitation to a party. The parties got bigger and bigger, with an attendance of 200 becoming average in 1828 for the informal ones.

There were few free evenings in any "official" home for the usual fireside scene. When these could be enjoyed by a few friends, hosts and guests would sit before huge hearths where burned sweet-smelling hickory logs. The men talked and the ladies usually did needlework while clustered, gossiping, around the brightest lamps. There would be fruit and wine on the tables, and coffee or tea for a warming cup before guests started for home. Washington weather never is very cold in the winter, but it bites.

In the waning year of the single administration of the second Adams, Washington began to take form as a city—the skeleton of what it later was to be. The progression always was toward the northwest.

Many families were moving into the fashionable new section centering around Fifteenth and H Streets, northeast of the White House and little more than a block from it. Here the Smiths moved from Sidney, to become neighbors of the Clays, the Cutts, General McComb, the Thorntons, the Wirts and a number of other prosperous "first families." Here, only a mile from Georgetown, life became less strenuous, although it still involved calls almost every morning and parties accompanied by mountains of food in afternoon and evening.

Near this neighborhood was the fashionable New York Avenue Presbyterian Church, in which the Rev. John Nicholas Campbell was winning nation-wide fame for his thundering exposition of Calvinist doctrine. St. John's was located very near by at Sixteenth and H Streets. The Sunday evening preachings in the House of Representatives were going out of fashion.

If there was a single social leader among the official group in the Adams Administration, it was Mrs. Josiah S. Johnston, wife of another Senator from Louisiana. (Wives of Louisiana Senators in those days apparently all were aristocratic and wealthy.) Mrs. Johnston not only was dictator of the *ton,* but she liked to have well-read associates. She bought new books by the dozen— in 1828 *Lady of the Manor* was a reigning favorite—and distributed them amongst her friends.

The friends whose reading tastes were not satisfied by Mrs. Johnston's gifts and loans had two other good sources of serious books, ranging from politics and world affairs to the classics. One was the Library of Congress, recently founded by the purchase, for $10,000, of Jefferson's library. The other was the State Department Library, which is still an important reference library, but no longer a source of popular reading.

No one could consider himself *au courant* in Washington in 1828 unless he read *The American Review,* published in Philadelphia, and subscribed to the *National Intelligencer,* now edited by a cousin of the founder, the brilliant and influential W. W. Seaton.

So, with all its limitations—there was no running water in Washington, even in the White House—the Capital was becoming a community and a center. But in reviewing the well-known names of the period, you will notice the absence of names that were commonplace less than thirty years earlier. Where had the giants gone?

On July 4, 1826, John Adams and Thomas Jefferson had died, the first at Braintree, Mass., murmuring "Thank God that Jefferson still lives," and, a few hours later, Jefferson at Monticello. Now, at Monticello, Jefferson's daughter, Martha Jefferson Randolph, widowed and bankrupt, having sold his library and many of the other personal effects, was preparing to sell the estate, and move to a modest house in Washington. Financial pressure on her was great, with the need to support herself, four daughters, four young sons, four grandchildren, a son-in-law and this youth's grandfather.

Monroe had moved to a small house in New York, never again to return to the South. His estate recently had been made over to the Bank of the United States to compromise his debts.

James Madison, aged 77, still held forth at Montpelier, where Dolly, famously beautiful and vigorous, lived with him, probably not imagining the long future career she would have in Washington.

Even with those of the old crowd living, however, the Virginia Dynasty was dead, as dead as the earlier power of the Federalists.

In everything except a little sentiment, Washington was the new Capital of a new country. Henceforth life and politics would be a little louder, rather more assertive, and typically American.

The Western invasion, the development of isolationism, were about to begin. And Washington, opposing itself to New York, Boston and Philadelphia, was to speak for Ohio, Kentucky, Tennessee and the growing accent of the hinterland.

Chapter Eight

THE WESTERN HORDE

THE NEWCOMERS were a little rude. They drank more than was seemly in the taverns. Occasionally they let off firearms in the streets, and coonskin caps caused people to turn and stare as the wearers rode through ruts so recently marking the paths of gentlemen in violet coats astride the finest Arabian horses.

Those who mourned the "good old days" need turn their minds backward no more than ten years. And yet it might have been ten centuries, so great was the change.

Washington still was an insignificant town, innocent of pavements, street lighting or even a night watch. But it was a barometer. The national picture could not have been as clear in New York or Boston, now occupied with trans-ocean trade. It hardly registered in the doldrums of Savannah and Charleston, where exhaustion of formerly fecund soil already was pushing the plantations westward and leaving little of the former glories. Except for an occasional oratorical voice and the firebrand pitch of gentlemen's debate, the South was finished politically. It would not realize this for a long time, but the tide had shifted.

The picture in Washington was the rise of the common man, the enfranchised democrat who cast his vote and took for the first time a vital role in the political background of his government. In fact, he came to Washington.

Yet the last thing that this new democrat realized was that he was part of a world revolution. It is seldom that Washington, until this past decade, has realized that it is part of the world. And does it now?

The picture at the beginning of the fourth decade of the Nineteenth Century is fairly clear in retrospect. Washington was the pioneer, with universal suffrage for white men coming into full bloom with the abandonment by the last diehard of his knee breeches and peruke.

In 1829, with Jackson's advent into power in Washington, riding figuratively on the shoulders of the mob, France was living its last year under a monarch who presumed to rule by divine right, and Charles X's French satellites already were changing their political coats. In Great Britain in that year the British Parliament enfranchised all Catholics who owned land, a revolutionary gesture, and the movement was far advanced in Britain to enfranchise all members of the manufacturing and merchant classes.

The only difference was that the United States moved a little farther a little faster, and the barometer of change was Washington.

The thin small clan that termed itself Washington "society" was aghast at the change, at the numbers of followers of the new great man who followed his trail up the Ohio River, and across Maryland from Cumberland into Washington. Refreshments were prepared for 20,000 persons expected to attend Jackson's Inaugural Reception in the White House. The food and drink ran out. Jackson, mobbed in friendly but suffocating fashion by his own admirers, climbed out of a window to escape to the sanctuary of his rooms at Gadsby's Tavern, across the river in Alexandria.

The result was that there became two Washingtons, which mingled at the edges but never again were to merge into one— the official Washington and the clique of influential local families later to become known as "cave dwellers." It might have been different if Mrs. Jackson had lived.

Old "Aunt Rachel," it is true, smoked a pipe, but she also had a fine dignity. As White House chatelaine she would have differed from Dolly Madison or Mrs. Monroe, but she would not have been lost. The Hermitage, her own home, was almost as impressive as the mansion, and the company there certainly as keen as at the White House.

But Aunt Rachel had died in December of 1828, and her husband took over the White House as a widower—a widower whose daughter Mrs. Donelson came to keep his house. But Mrs. Donelson had no flair for this life. A stream of children filled her life and mind.

Thus there came into being a political aristocracy, untempered by White House social graces, for Jackson was trying hard to entrench his followers. The pensioners of the older administrations, formerly secure in their jobs from one President to another, found themselves on the street; all the places went to newcomers, under the Jacksonian maxim, "To the victor belong the spoils."

This new version of patronage cut the old-timers to the quick, for hardly a family resident in Washington did not count upon the government as the refuge for its more needy members. What right, they asked, had this new President to take bread from their mouths and to give it to people that no one—absolutely no one—had ever heard of before?

The answer was that Jackson was a politician with the national viewpoint, not a Virginian or a socially ambitious man. He was building a party, not an aristocracy in the Capital. His Cabinet was a scratch lot, and also his associates, but they were chosen for their influence at home, not their prominence in Washington.

So Washington saw Martin Van Buren, the fussy little New Yorker from Kinderhook, step into the office of Secretary of State. Samuel D. Ingham, of Pennsylvania, became Secretary of the Treasury. John H. Eaton, Senator from Tennessee, stepped up into the post of Secretary of War. John Branch, of North

73

Carolina, became Secretary of the Navy, and John H. Berrien, of Georgia, became Attorney General.

Jackson's enemies were delighted with his choice. But the Cabinet members, except Van Buren, had wives, and these wives were the ranking members of Washington society. Then, too, John H. Eaton, on the eve of the Inaugural, had married Peg O'Neale.

Without official rank, but on a par with the formal Cabinet, were a group of Jackson's cronies. This second dominant group was headed by Francis Preston Blair, wealthy friend of Jackson's who at the President's express request moved to Washington to found a newspaper that would express the "party line." Blair did move in, did establish the *Globe* and buy a mansion, a little west of Lafayette Park and hardly 100 yards from the White House. Now known as Blair House, the residence had been built in 1827 by Dr. Joseph Lovell.

No devil with tails and horns was worse regarded in Washington than Blair. None of his detractors, and none of his friends for that matter, could foresee the day when his family would be one of the mainstays of older Washington, or when his house would be purchased by the government as a hostel reserved for visiting heads of state.

On what was this new Washington superimposed? A city which, although small, yet had established a character, had developed its clique of leading citizens and walked with pride along the boardwalks that bordered its wide but unpaved streets.

The social leadership in the diplomatic corps was shared between Charles Richard Vaughan, His Britannic Majesty's Minister, whose invitations to a ball in 1829 brought 400 carriages to the door of the Legation, and the Baron Krudener, who lavishly represented the court of the Czar of All the Russias.

Some of Jackson's quondam rivals might have cut heavily into his political dominance, but it was a bad year for them. Henry

Clay was ill for the time being, so ill that he had to recline on a couch during his interminable political conversations, but yet well enough to get up and stride the floor when he got excited. John Quincy Adams, living in a leased house, was failing fast. He could no longer take his long walks; instead, for exercise, he took up horseback riding. And old William Wirt, who recalled vividly the burning of the White House, was an aging and ill man.

Only Calhoun and Webster were vigorous. The Virginians were out of the picture, their descendants in their houses in Georgetown or across the river a silent lot.

Mrs. Porter, wife of the dashing Commodore, had become the most noted hostess. On alternate Mondays she entertained with a band for dancing and four rooms thrown open to guests. On the other Mondays she merely received her friends informally. In her free time she was assiduous in charitable deeds, because Washington had progressed already sufficiently far in its urban development to have a full complement of poor and needy.

These poor persons, in fact, felt particularly the scourge of weather in the winter of 1829. There was record cold, and the Potomac froze from shore to shore, an event recorded little more than once in a century. Congress voted fifty cords of wood for free distribution among the poor and the Treasury purchased an additional fifty cords for sale at half price—probably the first instance of funds from the public Treasury being used for relief.

But the news, as reported in the *Intelligencer* and the *National Advertiser,* was not all bleak. The Fulton sisters were becoming noted for their amateur singing at social affairs, and they sang in the Italian style. This Italian vogue likewise found Persico, a sculptor, doing all the business he could manage immortalizing the ladies in busts copied after the best classical examples.

Then a blight, invisible but as ominous as an invasion of locusts, fell in the three weeks between February 15th and

75

March 4th. General Jackson came to town in mid-February for his Inaugural on the March date. Some folk whispered of mobs and riots as his followers trooped in to fill the boarding houses and any shanty not otherwise occupied. Whether the whispers were taken seriously cannot be affirmed. But the Porters left town for the time being, as did the Calhouns, the Clays and the Wirts. And old Captain Tingey, whose will purported to dispose of his official residence at the Navy Yard, just died. Jackson's Inaugural Day was warm and beautiful.

It had become the fashion for mothers with marriageable daughters to bring them for the winter season to fashionable, and expensive, Washington. Here was the place to catch a husband.

This background, as much as any other reason, accounted for the shock when Senator Eaton wed Peg O'Neale, fresh from her father's tavern and thus made her a "Cabinet lady."

Jackson might storm as much as he wished, and threaten to fire members of his government who did not call on Mrs. Eaton, but this only made the clamor worse. Only Van Buren, the bachelor and Jackson's political heir, openly espoused Mrs. Eaton's position.

As for the general reaction, what better source than our Mrs. Margaret Bayard Smith, by now a celebrated author, one of the pioneers among the local citizens, and a lady whose reactions seem generally to have been the measure of the norm:

"As for the *new Lady* [the italics are hers] public opinion ever just and impartial seems to have triumphed over personal feelings and intrigues and finally doomed her to continue in her pristine lowly condition. A stand, a *noble* stand, I may say, since it is a stand taken against power and favoritism, has been made by the ladies of Washington, and not even the President's wishes, in favor of his dearest personal friend, can influence them to violate the respect due to virtue, by visiting one who has left her strait and narrow path.

"With the exception of two or three timid and rather insignificant personages, who trembled for their husbands' offices, not a lady has visited her, and so far from being inducted into the President's house, she is, I am told, scarcely noticed by the females of his family."

So much for the girl who had been protégée of General and Mrs. Jackson when they had lived at her father's tavern, the Indian Queen. But there was more to the rancor than simply Peg's background. The gossip went around that her first husband had committed suicide because he found her promiscuous both before and after their marriage. And Senator Eaton himself was suspected of having been rather forehanded in his courting.

But neither Jackson nor Mrs. Eaton surrendered. By 1831, Senator Eaton left Washington, but not his wife. In that year, Jackson forced the recall of the Dutch Minister, Meinherr Huggens, because Madame Huggens refused to receive Mrs. Eaton.

Actually, there probably was more to the Huggens affair than the simple reason ordinarily assigned. It probably was an offshoot of the social campaign being waged by Jackson on his own. The old battler was rattling his social saber as he was organizing his political new deal.

It was Jackson the frontiersman, with iron control over Congress, who set as his first local task the completing of the White House. He built the porticoes designed long ago by Jefferson and Latrobe—and the job was supervised by Hoban who had designed the original house in 1790. Jackson completed the East Room. He refurnished the pantry with china from France, new wine glasses and, accommodating the elegance of the mansion to the times, bought 20 spittoons for the East Room at a cost of $12.50 each. Van Buren, his advisor on design and social etiquette, supervised the first fencing in of the front lawn of the White House.

With his background brought up to date, and with water let into the Mansion through iron pipes instead of the cedar

77

troughs heretofore in use, Jackson set about making some changes in the social hierarchy.

Mrs. Eaton was his first campaign, but soon thereafter he decreed that all Cabinet members outranked the Ministers of foreign countries. That probably accounted for the background of the Huggens affair. It did not faze Sir Charles Vaughan.

But if there were tempests surrounding the social aspects of the White House, there also was a return of political dignity to Washington, acceleration of the forces carried for a while almost alone by the dignified Calhoun and Daniel Webster.

For one thing, Henry Clay, restored in health, returned to Washington in 1831, now as a Senator. And Robert R. Livingston, aristocratic, wealthy and an Episcopal pillar of the Columbia group in New York City, entered Jackson's Cabinet. Mrs. Livingston picked up the reins once wielded by Mrs. Porter and grasped them with firm French hands. For Mrs. Livingston did not forget at any time that she had been, prior to her marriage to Livingston in 1805, Louise D'Avezac, widow of a Jamaica planter and wealthy in her own right.

And Washington was being "improved." For the first time in a generation money was easy, and every city and community was straining to be modern. No less so was Washington. A group of optimistic stockholders, largely Washington and Georgetown businessmen, subscribed sufficient shares to dig a canal along the north side of the Potomac, with locks to lift barges past the Little Falls and the Great Falls of the river, up to its placid surface whence they could move into the rich agricultural country westward.

Pennsylvania Avenue was getting its first paving, not a very permanent job as it turned out, but a coating known as "macadamizing," and named for McAdam, its inventor. Water mains gradually crept through the principal streets and there was a sewer system of sorts, which drained into the Tiber River. This stream flowed in a narrow course between the Capitol and the White House and emptied into the Potomac. Today a visitor to

Washington crosses it at Seventh Street without knowing that the river is underneath, encased in tiling, still the backbone of the sewage system.

All of this building created quite a boom. For the first time there was more work, and more money to spend on public works, than there was local labor, despite the poverty-ridden communities which clustered in the southwestern portion of Washington and in the narrow streets of Georgetown.

More than 1000 Irish laborers were imported from Northern cities with the promise of good, steady wages, to join their backs to those of the local Negroes and white workers. The workmen and their families moved into the already overcrowded quarters of the other poor.

The result was inevitable. Cholera hit Washington in the summer of 1832, sweeping principally through the ranks of the Irish and the Negroes. It raged unchecked until the frosts of fall.

By December of that year the plague was followed, as so often throughout history, by a religious revival. Crowds thronged the House of Representatives again to hear the preaching. Men often left their work to attend weekday revival meetings.

The gay Tayloe sisters joined the Episcopal Church. And there were, unusual for the times, many who joined the Roman Catholic congregation. Principal cause for the Catholic conversion was the Rev. Father Charles Constantine Pise. This pulpit orator and friend of Henry Clay, most eloquent of Senators, soon became through Clay's patronage Chaplain of the Senate, only Catholic priest ever to hold that post.

Thus Washington, without conscious plan, began to find itself a city. True, it still was small, few persons knew each other on the intimate footing of long friendship, all who could abandoned it in the summer, and the forests were rather thicker than before on its borders by reason of the abandonment of worked-out plantations. The tobacco, planted without regard to Jefferson's demonstrated laws of crop rotation and field fertilization, had made most of the surrounding country hard red clay suitable only for nourishing scrub pine.

But the North was thriving and the West was growing. Money and credit flourished in the first great boom to hit the country. A few canny souls foresaw the "bust" in the offing. But this bothered Washington hardly at all.

There was even a little attempt at culture, and Miss Harriet Martineau, the sociologist, visiting Washington in 1835, found much enthusiasm for herself, if not much understanding of her works on political economy. It was a little embarrassing to the local sophisticates when one leader of "society" asked what novels Miss Martineau had written.

President Jackson, however, made no such mistake. The ubiquitous Sir Charles took his countrywoman to the White House to pay a call, and President Jackson gave a dinner in her honor. While Miss Martineau listened, with her deaf ear assisted by the new-fashioned ear trumpet, she heard sufficient intelligent discussion of her theories by statesmen who had boned up hurriedly for the occasion.

Also, the eating was good. The very forests that hemmed in Washington provided in the winter season certainly as good and probably much better varieties of food than could be found on the tables of larger cities.

Mrs. Levi Woodbury provided thirty meat courses for 18 guests invited to dine at 5 P.M. with Miss Martineau. Our old friend, Mrs. Smith, who stood as sponsor for Miss Martineau, served less food, but inscribed in her records the menu of her simple dinner for twelve. This dinner was served by one Henry, a butler who worked by the day. Henry, incidentally, has multiple spiritual descendants—well-mannered and well-trained dignified Negro men who ordinarily work as messengers or clerks in the daytime, and in the social season hire out their services at parties for fees sometimes comparable with the earnings of their hosts.

Henry was a little embarrassed at the simple meal planned by Mrs. Smith, she reported.

The dinner began with boulli, a fish chowder, served alongside a boned fish. It was followed by canvasback duck and pheasants. Then came a "very small" ham and turkey, garnished with partridges, mutton chops and sweetbreads. There was macaroni pie and oyster pie in that order and, for the vegetable course, celery, spinach, salsify and cauliflower. (No such unfashionable things as potatoes, beets, puddings or pies were served at this date.)

The dinner was finished with ice cream and a pyramid of fruit, served in a large tray around whose sides were clustered custards, blancmange, cakes and sweetmeats.

Chapter Nine

MELLOW DAYS

THE NEWNESS had worn off noticeably in 1850 but, as usual, everything was still unfinished. In the lusty little city, where politics was business and there was more leisure than work, there really were only three kinds of people. There were the political ins, the political outs trying to get in, and the minority of non-political native stock, descended for the most part from persons grown rich or tired in office who simply liked to live in Washington.

The great days seemed to be almost dead. The country's interest, it sometimes appeared, had shifted from the national capital and politics to business. Yet in this crossroads of America's main streets any scratching of the surface turned up in minikin some sample of the stuff that made up America.

Washington saloons were notorious, but so were New York and Philadelphia hard-drinking towns. Slavery was a local issue that already had produced a first-class riot, but there was no other city where an American could escape the pros and cons of the avalanche of abolition. The debates over nullification, with Daniel Webster thundering a Northern voice and Robert Y. Hayne of South Carolina and Calhoun bespeaking the South's arguments, had been only the climactic focal points of a thousand local arguments which had eventuated in scores of duels from New York to Charleston and as far west as St. Louis.

The social arguments of Capital officialdom were no more than the upshot of drawing-room conversations everywhere in which a newly wealthy people were becoming conscious of precedent.

In other words, here was an America, boisterous, gambling, ambitious, growing—and all that was America sent its samples, sometimes in exaggerated form, to the little city on the Potomac.

Not even inaugural balls had called forth such a spontaneous crowd as turned out in 1849 to march, with a great display of mourning badges and black stars, behind the beplumed catafalque of a plucky little old lady through the length of Pennsylvania Avenue to the Congressional Cemetery then located half a mile southeast of the Capitol.

Washington felt collectively on that day that it was burying much of the finest of its past. The funeral became for a moment a period of introspection. It was almost inconceivable to think that Dolly Madison and all that she had meant were gone.

This was a thorough closing of an era.

Men and women who were children when their parents took them to the Madison receptions at the President's Palace were middle-aged mourners in the procession. In the later years most of them—whether bankers or waiters in the taverns—had grown accustomed on New Year's Day to going to the White House to pay their respects to the incumbent President and thereafter walking a block north to pause for a moment in the little parlor of the Cutts House and making a bow to Mistress Madison.

Now, Dolly Madison was not the only grande dame who had held forth through these years since Monroe, last of the "gentlemen" in the White House, had bowed his way out. There had been Mrs. Alexander Hamilton, a white-haired and severely coiffed old lady who spent her time visiting the schools. At the age of 90 she walked through the open fields and climbed fences for exercise. There was Mrs. Stephen Decatur, living in retirement in a small house in Georgetown, seldom appearing in public, but a notable figure to those admitted to her salon. And there was Madame Calhoun, who with advancing years became more and more obsessed with a religious fervor, and who seized every opportunity to try to save the souls of her friends.

Dolly Madison exhibited none of these special facets of personality. She simply was a living, sometimes boisterous, open-handed and very much alive old lady who enjoyed every minute of living and had a faculty for passing on the enjoyment to others. She taught her young friends to waltz when the dance still was new. Perhaps she learned the dance herself from the Baron Stackelberg, Minister of Sweden, who introduced it to the Capital. Her friends and the gossips alike noted the perpetual be-rouged bloom on her cheeks and the persistently black-dyed curls that bobbed in animation under her turban while she talked. They loved her for the coloring. She had the courage to be herself. And she wore so well.

It was toward the close of Jackson's tenure in the White House that Dolly Madison came back to Washington. She had gone away permanently in 1817 when "Little Jemmy" had left the White House to retire to his estates at Montpelier. Although years younger than her husband she genuinely loved the little fellow. Careless of money herself she noticed neither the drain that Virginia hospitality put on Madison's purse while he lived or the excessive demands on her own fortune made by Payne Todd, her son. When she returned to Washington she was not wealthy.

There were five Presidents in addition to Jackson at the White House after Dolly moved into the Cutts House—Van Buren, Harrison, Tyler, Polk and Taylor. Hundreds of new faces had come to live in Washington.

The little house on Lafayette Square was seldom empty. Closest among many intimate friends who loved to dine there was Daniel Webster. Everyone really was so nice. Even stiff-necked Mrs. Polk, a leader in the prohibition movement who disapproved of anyone drinking even wine, including Dolly Madison, gave the old lady a special seat of honor at White House receptions while Mrs. Polk stood to receive her guests.

Some of the older families still retained their fortunes. Big and extravagant parties marked the social season in quite a number of pretentious homes within walking distance of Dolly Madison. But one day she woke up to the fact that she was broke —a condition about which most of the country seemed to be aware before she herself knew of it.

There was the old Negro, Paul Jennings, who had been President Madison's body servant. Jennings had bought his freedom and now was Daniel Webster's valet. Dolly discovered that much of the game on her table and the wine she served to her friends was coming into her kitchen in a hamper brought by Jennings directly from Daniel Webster's pantries. She discovered also that Jean Pierre Sioussat, her former White House chef and now a bank clerk, was conniving with her friends and keeping her household accounts for her in such a manner as to make assets appear where none in fact existed.

Daniel Webster apparently talked about his friend's plight in his native Massachusetts because Amos Lawrence of Boston sent down a silk dress to Dolly from one of his mills. Then Robert C. Winthrop of Massachusetts started to take up a subscription to provide an annuity for Dolly, but this she declined with acerbity. Finally the maintenance of Dolly Madison became a challenge to the sporting instinct of official Washington and James Buchanan, in 1848 a Senator, was the one who solved the puzzle.

Matters came to a head when Dolly Madison announced in 1848 that she would hold a "raffle" of some of her effects. The spunky little lady, then 79, made this decision with as offhand a gesture as 35 years earlier she had given $20 and a cow to help found Washington's first orphanage asylum. Nevertheless, announcement of the "raffle" brought a roar of protest.

It was known that in the attic of Dolly's house she kept an old locked leather trunk containing her husband's papers. Here were notes and memoranda that went back to the time when Jefferson and Madison collaborated in publishing the *Federalist* and therein delineated the meaning of the Constitution of the United States. Here were notes dealing with tricky negotiations with England and France at the beginning of the century when Madison served as Jefferson's Secretary of State. And there were sheaves of manuscripts containing the afterthoughts of a political figure whose brilliant record had begun in his teens when, graduated from Princeton at the age of 18, he stayed on for a couple of years to study classical languages including Hebrew.

Certainly not more than a handful of people had studied *in toto* the contents of the leather trunk, but Buchanan and Webster put through a bill appropriating $25,000 to purchase the Madison papers. The buy was a bargain, but at the moment the use to which the money would be put was more important to Washington than the fact that the Library of Congress was obtaining one of its more important acquisitions. The bill appropriating $25,000 was finally passed on Dolly's 80th birthday, in 1848. Twenty thousand dollars of the money was put into a trust fund, $3000 paid off a mortgage on her house held by John Jacob Astor, and the rest went for odds and ends. A silver service pawned for $70 was redeemed and another $20 paid off a pledge against a gold chain.

Dolly died in 1849.

And what had been happening in these years along the straggling streets of Washington—in that town whose center now had moved westward to the vicinity of the White House? Just about what you would find in any little city of its period, except that in Washington more often than elsewhere national figures played the local roles rather than people unknown outside the limits of their counties.

Transportation had changed radically. It was a far cry from the horse and stagecoach days of the first three decades. The steam trains had come to town.

In 1830 there had been ten four-horse stages operated each day between Washington and Baltimore. Other similar equipages crossed the river to Alexandria and proceeded southward or went out the northwest road en route to Cumberland. Travel took a lot of patience.

Take the example of John Quincy Adams back in 1826. He left Washington in his private coach drawn by four horses on July 9th, to make a leisurely visit to his Massachusetts home. On the following day at Baltimore word reached him that his father, the celebrated old second President of the United States, had died on July 4th, at Braintree, Mass. This is the means by which John Quincy Adams hurried home:

At 5 P.M. on the tenth he caught a steamboat plying between Baltimore and Frenchtown at the head of Chesapeake Bay. There he got a stagecoach as far as New Castle. He went on by boat to Philadelphia, there caught another stagecoach to New Brunswick, New Jersey, and proceeded from New Brunswick to New York City by steamboat. This super-speed trip took 45 hours and cost a substantial sum of money. Ordinary travelers who were content to spend four days making a journey now completed in four hours by train, or about an hour by airplane, could do so for a cost of $9.

On July 20, 1835, four trains loaded with one thousand passengers and carrying two bands steamed into Washington. The passengers, flushed with adventure and covered with soot and cinders, divided and went to two dinners in their honor, one at Gadsby's Tavern and the other at Brown's Hotel. This was the new era. Henceforth two trains each way connected Baltimore and Washington daily and cut the travel time between the Capital and its nearest great seaport to two hours and ten minutes.

While the railroad opened up new life for Washington in

trade, because the city never has had factories of its own, it completed the ruin of quite a number of local fortunes invested in the Chesapeake & Ohio Canal and other waterway projects. The canals were completed just in time to collapse in the face of competition by the rapidly spreading railways.

Of course the original village could not turn into a big town without developing certain big-town characteristics, ranging from plumbing to crime and laws to regulate the punishment of crime.

The plumbing came to town in 1832 when a water main on Pennsylvania Avenue was connected with pipes laid down North Capitol Street to bring water from the springs in the hills north of the city.

The crime was self-generated by an extraordinary proportion of riffraff drawn to the city in the train of successive political administrations or fed by the more vicious members among the refugees from slavery who fled north from the Southern plantations. General laws were passed in 1821 to displace the Maryland statutes formerly enforced by near-by courts in Maryland. In 1826 Congress appropriated money for a penitentiary for the District of Columbia to take the pressure off the local jail. By 1830, when the population of the District of Columbia, including Alexandria and Georgetown, had risen to 40,000, enlightened lawmakers decided that the old English criminal laws were too severe. Capital crimes thereafter were limited to those involving murder, treason and burglary—and rape if committed by Negroes. At the same time penalties for gambling were made severe. Nevertheless, seven years later a local newspaper reported that "there is no city in which gambling is carried to a greater extent than in the Metropolis of the country."

Slavery and crime were not synonymous, but it so happened in Washington that the two problems combined to make the first real excitement the city generated on its own. For background, the first abolition society had been formed at Washington in 1827. This society got a lot of support from Southerners as well as Northerners when it was learned that local officials both in Washington and Alexandria actually were selling free Negroes back into slavery as a roundabout way of making money.

It seems that persons confined in jail were forced to pay the cost of their keep, and this keep itself was a contract matter between the government and the jail authorities. The jailers and their assistants would arrest free Negroes on suspicion as escaped slaves, hold them for a year, and then sell them and keep the money as a reimbursement for expenses.

By 1835 this condition had been corrected, but the slave-holding Southerners who dominated life in the Capital were up in arms against what they contended was agitation by abolitionists to create uprisings among the slaves. There was one report that Mrs. William Thornton had narrowly escaped being murdered by a slave turned robber. Then someone started a report that Dr. Ruben Crandall of New York had arrived in Washington to incite an uprising. Dr. Crandall was innocent, a harmless botanist, but a mob started after him and he finally was locked in jail for his own protection.

On August 12th, when the mob was prevented in its plan to lynch Dr. Crandall it decided to get Beverley Snow, a free Negro restaurant owner whose place was "much frequented by the good society of Washington." Reports were spread that he had spoken disrespectfully about the wives and daughters of mechanics. The mob could not find Snow either, but it wrecked his restaurant and burned the homes of some other Negroes.

During all of this excitement the city was "protected" by three constables, this being the entire police force of Washington and Georgetown. There was on paper a force of militia but these so-called troops, backed by a strong pacifist sentiment, were accustomed to report only on one muster day a year, were untrained and had no arms. A company of Marines finally was called from the Navy Yard to protect the public buildings.

If the city was a little rough, nevertheless culture was beginning to be spelled with a capital "C." There were numerous newspapers that came and went, with the *National Intelligencer* the constant stand-by for most people. In 1823 William W. Seaton, editor until 1840 of the *Intelligencer*, and a fellow editor began reporting regularly the debates in Congress; Congress itself did not yet keep a detailed record. By 1824 Andrew Jackson, then a Senator, counted "a dozen or two" correspondents from other cities in the Congress. In 1829 the *Intelligencer* noted that "the letters written from Washington, and published in different parts of the country, are becoming more and more numerous. We occasionally obtain from these sources the first information of what is going on in our neighborhood."

Thirteen churches were built in the 25 years after 1815. On December 7, 1835, the National Theatre, Washington's first "modern" playhouse, opened on E Street between 13th and 14th Streets. Rebuilt many times the National Theatre is still there. The first of the series of National Theatres introduced the new style of putting chairs in the pit and making this the most expensive instead of the cheapest part of the theatre.

Education was probably a little bit ahead of the rest of the country in that part of the District of Columbia north and west of the Potomac River—Washington and Georgetown. There were two free elementary schools in Washington proper known as the Eastern and Western, while Georgetown boasted of its Lancaster Charity School. These schools were available only to pupils whose parents could not afford to pay for their tuition.

For those who could pay there was a wide choice that sprang up in the four decades prior to 1850.

John McLeod, an Irishman, conducted a succession of private schools from 1808 until his death in 1848, which eventually became a wholesale business of teaching. He had at the peak 145 instructors and his Academy yielded him an income of $3000 a year. McLeod made a feature of trading education of children for labor performed by their parents. He was a strict taskmaster, expecting his pupils to attend classes ten hours a day on weekdays throughout the year, except for a two weeks' vacation in August and holidays on July 4th, New Year's Day and every other Saturday.

Miss Lydia S. English founded a fashionable young ladies school in 1831 and there already were by that time two Catholic schools for girls, a seminary founded in 1816 and a convent school dating from 1820. Other enterprising teachers conducted any number of small classes in their homes. Girls were not supposed to learn too much. But those whose parents could afford it had to have dancing lessons given by François Lobbe, as well as suitable instruction in harp playing and album painting.

Nationally speaking, Van Buren's single-term administration was a washout marked largely by the banking collapse resulting from Jackson's fiscal policies. But these were not dull years in the Capital itself. For one thing, there was the scandal that arose when Van Buren and other Federal officials collected their salaries in gold at a time when bank crashes were rendering worthless the money held by most private citizens.

How different this was from Jackson's own personal action when, bankrupt by his expenses as President, he nevertheless gave to the orphans home a lion sent to him by the Sultan of Morocco and permitted the home to sell it to a circus for $3350 instead of pocketing the money himself!

It so happened that Van Buren was the first President not born a British subject, but even this all-Americanism did not keep his more active detractors from referring to him as "the mistletoe politician" and "a perfect imitation of a gentleman."

The bachelor President cut down his receptions to one a year, on New Year's Day. Foreseeing the impossibility of his re-election he simply lived out one term in the White House.

But there was color enough elsewhere in Washington, and not the least of this color was provided by the 50-year-old Bodisco, Minister of the Czar of All the Russias, who entertained lavishly in a large rented house in Georgetown and drove through the streets in a white barouche drawn by four coal-black horses. Minister Bodisco was a bachelor celebrated for the elaborate parties he gave for children.

At one of these parties, attended by the girls from Miss English's school, Bodisco saw Miss Harriet Beall Williams, a large blonde girl, the orphan of a government clerk. He fell in love with her. Her mother, a little nonplussed by this extraordinary turn of the family's fortunes, consented to their wedding.

The custom of the day required that weddings be held in the bride's home, so a wedding party including the President, the Diplomatic Corps and some 500 members of Washington's "society" crowded into Mrs. Williams's little house for the wedding ceremony. The company recovered its breath when the party went to Bodisco's ample house for the wedding breakfast.

In drawing up specifications for his wedding the punctilious Bodisco asked that the bridesmaids include no young women older than the bride. There was a great fluttering in Miss English's school while twenty of the fifteen- and sixteen-year-old girls were being dressed to serve as attendants. Incidentally, the marriage worked out very well.

The gulf growing constantly between so-called official society and the natives broke out into open conflict at the Inaugural of old General William Henry Harrison on March 4, 1841—the Inaugural of a President who was to survive for only one month. Inaugural Balls had become one of the great features of Washington life. There always had been two of these, but in this case there were three. The leading politicians subscribed $10 each for an elaborate ball at the New Assembly, while the run-of-the-mine hangers-on had a $5 ball at Carusi's. But the natives had their own show in the Masonic Temple.

Harrison's death, resulting from a cold caught by the old gentleman when he rode bareheaded through driving rain in his own Inaugural Parade, opened the door to an era which presumably had passed forever with his election. Harrison had been elected as a log-cabin President with John Tyler on his ticket as Vice-President as a sop to the nobs. And now Tyler was President and his wife Julia, more royal than royalty, resumed the social leadership that the White House always gives its Mistress if she chooses to assume it.

For one thing, Julia Tyler drove around Washington in a coach and four. That was all right for queer characters like Bodisco but not for the wife of a democratic President. The comment reached a crescendo when at her first reception Julia Tyler waited until all the guests were present, then entered the drawing room, seated herself on a raised platform and had each guest brought to her individually and announced in a loud voice. She wore a purple velvet dress with a long train and plumes atop a tall hair-do. Shades of Eliza Monroe! More was required, however, than the comments of her neighbors to change Julia Tyler's character. At the last dinner over which she presided in the White House, on March 3, 1845, in honor of James K. Polk, who would be inaugurated President next day, Mrs. Tyler wore on a chain around her neck the gold pen just used by Tyler in signing the law admitting Texas into the Union.

The Polk Inaugural got back to the two-ball procedure, this time with the exclusive affair in Carusi's and one for the common people at the National Theatre. But this time there was a contretemps—somebody forgot to send formal invitations for the Carusi ball to the Diplomatic Corps. This group thereupon decided to boycott the fashionable ball and descended en masse on the National Theatre where the wives of the town's laborers, well laced with whiskey and rum, cavorted through quadrilles and waltzes with ministers and attachés whose uniforms dripped with the gold lace of their official position.

On the night after this most democratic of all Inaugural Balls, while a select audience was watching the Washington *première* of "Beauty and the Beast" the National Theatre caught fire. Not a person was killed in the fire but the theatre stood as a ruin for five years.

So here at the end of a half century was a Washington in which a wag expressed the truism that "in the National Capital the dead are happier than those out of office"—the town which Jessie Benton Frémont termed the drawing room of the Nation.

It was all a little confused but few people yet realized the play of deeper forces swirling around it as a magnetic center. There had been only the first gasps of the issues of nullification, abolition and prohibition.

In 1833 one hundred Congressmen and officials had "signed the pledge" by joining the American Congressional Temperance Society. In 1838 the Senate had barred the sale of liquor on its premises. The House followed suit seven years later. The bars returned later.

The new day in American politics, with the North and the West dominating the government, found expression in 1846 when Congress rather willingly returned to Virginia that part of the District of Columbia lying south of the Potomac River.

But if Washington seemed preoccupied at times with its own little affairs, it was gaining in importance, or at least in size, as a National Capital. The Treasury Building was rising slowly but impressively on a square east of the White House. The Capitol Building, already inadequate, was being enlarged to the form in which we now see it.

In 1840, Thomas U. Walter, an architect, had drawn plans for the wings and the dome to be added to the original structure. The cornerstone for these new works would be laid on July 4, 1851.

For some three years, in Fillmore's Administration, the Secretary of War, Jefferson Davis, not yet dreaming of his own future role as chief of a rebel government, would watch over the enlargement of the Capitol Building with as much care as Washington and Jefferson had lavished on the White House.

Chapter Ten

EVE OF THUNDER

THE CITY HAD BECOME much like a circus tent in which a troupe of acrobats carelessly frolic high up under the canvas roof, all unaware that the safety net has been removed. Never in its lengthening history had Washington served so much as a mirror of the United States.

There may have been, in the early spring of 1857, a few prescient souls who read the handwriting on the wall but, if so, they studiously withheld their prophecies. Any cogent reasoning certainly was buried under the noise of the debate.

The unrecorded thousands of persons, who attended the Inaugural reception of James Buchanan on the evening of March 4, 1857, acted as though this was the beginning of a new and carefree era. No one had been very impressed with Millard Fillmore or Franklin Pierce, and Washington had been quiescent in their Administrations. There had been no glamor about the White House—even though Mrs. Fillmore introduced the style of wearing a lace kerchief suspended by a thin golden chain from a ring—and consequently the trend of living in Washington had diminished.

But this was different. Buchanan had a charming personality. His niece, Miss Harriet Lane, clad in white satin for formal affairs, was a cultivated girl whose charm and manners derived from girlhood association with her father as his hostess in diplomatic assignments abroad.

It was hard to state whether the new President or his niece

attracted the greater attention when at sundown the mob trooped into a temporary pine building, 220 feet long and specially erected for this one occasion in Judiciary Square, midway between the Capitol and the White House. In any event, the food ran out after the guests consumed 8 rounds of beef, 75 hams, 60 saddles of mutton, 4 saddles of venison, 400 gallons of oysters, 500 quarts of chicken salad, 500 quarts of jellies and 1200 quarts of ice cream.

It was a little sobering, but not yet convincing as to the crisis in store, when Mr. Chief Justice R. B. Taney, two days after he had administered the oath to Buchanan, handed down the Supreme Court's decision in the Dred Scott case. The decision simply held that slaves could be possessed in free territories. But what it meant was the shattering of the Missouri compromise under which the Congress had ruled that for the future new States created above an arbitrary line should not be slave States but that in them all men then living or fleeing to them would be free.

One had only to walk through the streets of Washington to see the great gulf that existed between political affairs of high moment and the actual life of the country's citizens. There was talk in abundance, but that is what it was—just talk. In these conversations the drawling and often argumentative phrases of the South virtually surpassed the clipped accents of the North. In its exterior life Washington was a sprawling, overgrown and lackadaisical Southern town.

The part of the city that counted began on Capitol Hill and rambled northwestward to the White House and a small section north and west of it. Georgetown, except for a few well-preserved houses, had become the run-down and ill-kept suburb of the Capital. Here is a bird's-eye view of the city toward the end of the 1850's:

On Capitol Hill two new shiny marble wings of the building,

housing the Senate and House chambers, extended to the north and south. But the Capitol, like most public buildings, was still unfinished. The new hall for the House of Representatives was completed with a brilliant red and gold interior, but the 100 columns which presumably support the roof of the Capitol wings were scattered in sections over the grounds. Only three were in place. The rotunda of the Capitol was a great open space above which workmen were laboriously placing the dome, section by section. Crated on the grounds was the 16-ton bronze Statue of Liberty designed to top the dome. Work had not been started on the terraces or the tall flights of steps leading up the west side of Capitol Hill.

Visitors to the Capitol stopped to look at Persico's heroic figure of Columbus. Many of them gazed with shocked wonder at a likeness of George Washington, done by Greenough in his studio in Rome. The Congress some years back had appropriated $40,000 to pay for a statue of the Father of His Country by the celebrated American sculptor. When the work finally arrived, the disturbed legislators found that Greenough had visualized George Washington as a sun-bathing Roman Senator seated in a chair with draperies around his legs but not a stitch of clothing above his waist.

Walking around the Capitol from the entrance on the east and down the western slope of the Hill, the visitor reached Pennsylvania Avenue. Its boardwalks were well shaded by the elms planted by Jefferson, but the street pavement was so broken that the broad avenue was alternately a sea of mud or a bed of dust. Heavy horse-drawn omnibuses and poor drainage had accounted for the paving. Yet if a man wished to ride from the Capitol to the White House he could take the omnibus at a cost of only twelve and a half cents.

The Mall south of Pennsylvania Avenue had been partially graded. From the Capitol it afforded a view in the foreground of the Smithsonian Institution, marked by tall red-brick towers, and in the far distance one third of the Washington Monument.

The Smithsonian Institution had probably the most interesting history of any building in the Capital. It was an impressive monument, not to the love of a man for his country but to the embittered feelings of an expatriate toward his foreign home. It all stemmed back to James Smithson, an Englishman, who had died in Genoa in exile in 1826.

Smithson left a will stating that if a nephew, his only heir, should die without children his fortune should go to the United States of America. Twenty years later the nephew was dead without issue, and a Congressional committee of inquiry, visiting Genoa, found awaiting it 104,960 golden sovereigns. These sovereigns were about equivalent to $5 gold pieces. So the government accepted the bequest, built a suitable memorial building to Smithson, and made the institution the repository for governmental scientific research.

The completed one third of the Washington monument, almost hidden by the Smithsonian, had been abandoned for the time being for the two usual reasons—lack of money and indecision as to what to do about it.

Now to get along Pennsylvania Avenue.

Anything worth seeing along the avenue was on the north side of the street. Its breadth alone separated whatever was impressive in Washington from slums, open markets and an open sewer that ran between Pennsylvania Avenue and the Mall. The north side was the good side, the south the bad.

Walking westward to Sixth Street the visitor came first to Brown's Hotel and, directly across Sixth Street, the National Hotel. The National catered principally to the Congressional and the Southern trade. Passing scattered shops, livery stables and saloons, a man reached the Kirkwood Hotel at Twelfth Street, where he probably stopped for a drink, and then went on to the new Willard Hotel, show place of the city at Fourteenth Street. All of these hotels were relatively new, the transition

from boarding houses to hotels having occurred virtually overnight.

It was only a step around the corner from the Willard Hotel
to the White House, marked by an ornamental iron fence along
Pennsylvania Avenue on the north, but otherwise not enclosed.
Marshland, which made malaria and dysentery normal occupa-
tional diseases of the Presidents and their families, brought the
brackish backwaters of the Potomac to within a couple of hundred yards of the White House on the south. On the higher land
on that side there was a helter-skelter of barns, sheds, dairies,
shacks for servants and workmen, and all the careless homey
appurtenances of a Southern mansion.

Southeast of the White House was the Treasury Building.
Only a fraction of the building was completed. North of the
Treasury was the War Department Building. Along the western
boundary of the White House grounds were two smallish red-
brick structures housing the State and Navy Departments.

These buildings accounted for all of the Federal establishment except the Post Office and the Patent Office, which occupied opposing corners at Seventh and F Streets, about two
blocks north of Pennsylvania.

North of the White House the city had completed the parking of the block known as Lafayette Square. True to usual practice, it had placed in the center of the square honoring Lafayette
a monument to Andrew Jackson. This monument, created by
Clark Mills, the Charleston plasterer, is the famous, or in-
famous, figure of Jackson waving his cocked hat while sitting
astride a horse reared on its hind legs.

The finer residences and legations were closely grouped,
mostly in row houses despite the great expanses of land, in a
region bounded by Pennsylvania Avenue on the north. Famous
Connecticut Avenue meandered northwest from the White
House, but after a few blocks lost itself in country so wild that
rabbit shooting was a sport that could be enjoyed within walking
distance of the Willard Hotel.

The built-up section was no more than a tiny cell within the ten square miles of the city, but life was lived within it in the fullest sense of the word, literally and figuratively. In the months from November to June, Washington was a hard-talking, hard-drinking, heavy-eating metropolis, and one of the most expensive cities in the world. Government clerks earning $1500 a year were hard pressed to support their families. Many occupied quarters much cruder than those supplied to the house slaves of the wealthy Southern families.

This was one thing that Northern and foreign visitors found hard to understand. The Capital of the United States was a free city, yet under the laws by which it existed slave owning was legal. The Negroes sat stiffly on the boxes of coaches and phaetons, they opened the doors to the finest houses, and when not busy they lounged in groups on the board sidewalks of the streets. No Southerner with any pretensions would be seen in public without his body servant accompanying him. These servants were left at the doors of public buildings or private houses to lounge and gossip throughout all the hours their masters chose to spend away from home.

If a man needed to replace a slave he had to go no farther than the old Decatur House a block northwest of the White House, where another Gadsby ran a weekly auction of blacks in his backyard.

Perhaps so much money was required for living because the business of government was an idle thing. The Congress did not meet every day by any means. Few calls were made upon legislators for the departmental errands that now keep them so busy. The governmental offices opened at 9 and closed at 3 o'clock. Washington was a late-sleeping town in the days when business houses in most cities opened their blinds and their doors at 7:30 in the morning.

In fact, it is hard to see how there was time for anything except eating, drinking and following the convivial routine. Breakfast was served in the hotels from 8 to 11 A.M., with all menus offering such tidbits as steak, oysters and *pâté de foie gras,* in addition to ham and eggs, grits, and the standard Southern dishes. The main meal of the day was dinner served at noon. Supper came at 5. Teas had become an entrenched custom, timed at about 7:30 in the evening and, lest people might not be able to sleep for hunger, hostesses and hotels served another supper at 9 o'clock in the evening.

Maybe the food wasn't very good, because Lord Lyons, a British Minister, pronounced Washington an unfit place to send young men. He noted the lack of clubs or good restaurants and deplored the complete absence of any permanent theatre or opera. But the young men did like the bars, particularly the mint juleps in which all specialized.

The hot humid days of the fall of 1860 were matched in their steaming intensity by a rising crescendo of debate which was adjourned in the halls of the Capitol and government buildings only to be resumed in the bars along Pennsylvania Avenue. The aged General Winfield Scott came from New York down to Washington, despite his aches and pains, to resume actively his role as Commander-in-Chief of the Army. But the fears that prompted Scott's reappearance on the scene were kept carefully hidden beneath the surface. The appearance was given that the talk was just talk, even though people discussed more and more the melodramatic book written back in 1852 as a serial for the *National Era* in Washington by Harriet Beecher Stowe and afterward printed as a volume entitled *Uncle Tom's Cabin.*

There was the odd spectacle of many Northerners wishing out loud that Andrew Jackson were alive. These Northerners asked where was there another man strong enough to assume the Jacksonian role which he had played 20 years earlier when, at a banquet, facing Calhoun, he had shouted down the nullification issue with a toast, "The Union, it must be preserved!"

The elections in November gave little reassurance, because no one in Washington had any idea as to the kind of leader this

Abraham Lincoln, just elected President, really was. The prediction was made freely that he never would live to take office. On top of that, as soon as the election results were announced, South Carolina seceded from the Union.

General Scott, placed in charge of the arrangements for Lincoln's Inaugural, erected a high wooden barricade between the crowd and the portico of the Capitol on which Lincoln stood to take his oath of office from Justice Taney. Soldiers with fixed bayonets surrounded the platform and stood shoulder to shoulder along the route of the Inaugural procession. Cavalry were massed so thickly around the open carriage in which rode Lincoln and Buchanan that spectators along Pennsylvania Avenue could hardly see them.

But no resident of Washington that day precipitated any overt act or disturbance. All of which was surprising in view of the rapid development of events between the election in November of 1860 and the Inaugural in March of 1861.

Virginia had called a conference of delegates from the Southern States in January of 1861, meeting in Richmond, only 100 miles south of Washington. On February 1, 1861, thirty-two days before Lincoln's Inauguration, six other Southern States joined South Carolina in secession and set up a capital at Montgomery, Alabama.

By the time of the Inaugural, most of the leading Southern politicians had left Washington, but a surprising number of the rank and file continued to live in the city.

One Southerner who left caused more grief than anger to his friends. This man was a soldier who as a captain in charge of a company long ago had hanged John Brown at Harper's Ferry. He had been Superintendent of West Point, a former student there who had graduated at the head of his class. This was Robert E. Lee.

On an evening early in 1861, Colonel Lee was invited to dine at the Blair House, across the street from the White House on Pennsylvania Avenue. His host was Montgomery Blair, son of Andrew Jackson's closest friend and now Postmaster General for Buchanan.

Mr. Blair told Colonel Lee that since General Scott was too old for further active service the General and the President would be happy to confer the post of Commander-in-Chief on him.

Colonel Lee returned to Arlington, where he made his historic decision.

Mary Todd Lincoln had social aspirations on a par with those of Mrs. Monroe and Julia Tyler. She entered Washington with great plans.

At her first formal dinner she dressed in purple velvet with a long train. Her hair was done in elaborate curls. A New York caterer journeyed down to Washington to supervise the kitchens.

Hardly a month had passed before Lincoln issued his call for volunteers to defend the Capital. The battle of Bull Run marked the actual beginning of the Civil War. Soon the army of defense in Washington grew to 150,000 men. The Capital itself became a military headquarters. Barracks and hospitals sprang up in all the parks and open spaces.

Martial law was decreed for the city. For four years it was to be only a city existing on the fringes of an armed camp. All that it had been was swept up in the military tidal wave.

There would be another Washington—a bigger and a more active Washington. But the cavalier days were gone.

Chapter Eleven

RECONSTRUCTION

THOUSANDS OF WASHINGTONIANS and visitors from every State danced through the night, oblivious to a blizzard which had raged since early morning. Long after the Marine Band had packed its instruments and gone home the excited and slightly alcoholic crowd rummaged for its wraps in the rooms where they had been piled. This dance was the Inaugural Ball held on March 4, 1869.

Never had there been such a large ball or such a sumptuous one. A small army of bartenders dispensed whiskey and champagne. A corps of waiters carved the joints of meat or ladled out hot dishes that composed the supper provided by the inaugural committee.

The ball was held in the new north wing of the now historic Treasury Building, a structure started by Andrew Jackson. It was completed while the Civil War was being fought. The Treasury itself was somewhat a symbol of victory. Through the long war years, and particularly in those tense days prior to Gettysburg when invasion of Washington was an ever-present threat, the Treasury had been strengthened as a fortress in which Union forces would make possibly a last stand in Washington. Arms and munitions had been stacked high in its spacious offices. Stonework had filled in many of the windows. Flour and pork and water casks had been piled alongside gold and silver in its sub-basement vaults.

The beaming new President, who remained for hours at the

Inaugural Ball and who gallantly led Mrs. Hamilton Fish through a quadrille, was the symbol of the New Day.

Ulysses Simpson Grant was, by the standard which voters so often follow, the ideal President. He was a hero. He was not a politician. He never had run for elective office. He was the great and victorious general of his day. He was the symbol of the new Washington, capital of a country whose divisions—or so it was hoped—had been erased for all time.

Even at this date, almost four years after the termination of the Civil War, the Capital City was just beginning to throw off the atmosphere of an armed camp. Its parks still were dotted with hospitals. The cobbles of its streets were ground into the dust by the iron-shod wheels of cannons and caissons that had poured through it in a flood on their way to the battles fought in Virginia. There was a cemetery in Lafayette Park.

Neither Atlanta, Ga., burned by William Tecumseh Sherman's men on their march to the sea, nor Petersburg, Va., in the bombardment that marked the last decisive battle of the Civil War, had suffered much more damage than had sprawling Washington in its role as headquarters for the victorious troops.

The billeting of 150,000 soldiers as a permanent garrison in the city had left its mark on virtually every building. Even in the Capitol Building itself a regiment of soldiers had camped in the rotunda under the incomplete dome. Committee rooms there had been used for the first year of the war as staff headquarters to supplement the pitifully small War Department Building. The White House had been turned into a fenced and guarded headquarters, but its interior had deteriorated almost to the point of ruin. President Johnson had spent $160,000 on White House repairs alone.

There had been scarcely a private house that had not suffered from sequestration for some governmental purpose, or at least been seized in part for the quartering of soldiery. Many of the trees had been cut wantonly for firewood by the soldiers and hordes of refugees.

Up from the South, funneling through the Long Bridge, connecting the District of Columbia with Virginia, had come crowds of Negroes, freed by the progress of the Union forces and left to find their way to the North. Few of them went beyond Washington. They squatted in the vacant lots in Georgetown and built cabins in the woods near by and oftentimes on vacant lots in otherwise well-developed neighborhoods.

Whatever semblance of urbanity or individualism Washington had possessed as a city had been smothered in this dual invasion.

Within a year after the Civil War, people were speculating on what might have happened had Mr. Lincoln not been assassinated, but this was idle speculation because he was dead, and with him had died almost everything for which he had stood except the single overwhelming fact of Federal unity.

It was hard to believe that so many great ideals could be mishandled to such an extent by a government, simply because the Congress could not stomach Andrew Johnson. This little man, once a tailor's apprentice and renegade Governor of Tennessee, simply was not the man to carry Lincoln's load.

When he entered the White House, frightened half to death by the responsibility, there occurred a political and social disintegration in Washington hardly believed possible after all the other shocking upsets the Capital had experienced. How strong the Union was to survive the squabbles and vicious quarrels that culminated in the impeachment of President Johnson and his acquittal.

Nevertheless, here was the crux of the triumphant story of Washington. This dilapidated city survived its test, because above and beyond the pettiness of the political chicanery being played in it, it stood more than ever before at the crossroads of America.

In its political finagling, in its display of wealth by war profiteers, in the conflict of forces, and above all this, in the underlying feeling that here finally was a government set up to represent all of the people of the United States—this Washington was America!

There was a house on I Street near Twentieth in which lived quietly a sweet-faced old lady who saw on rare occasions a few friends but otherwise felt a stranger in Washington. Even her own exciting past had been forgotten. Very few people knew, and even fewer cared, that Mrs. Peggy O'Neale Eaton still lived as a reminder of a robust but far simpler era of society. And yet she was the one individual who symbolized more than any other the transition from the days of Jefferson, Madison and Monroe to the period of self-willed, self-proud and often raucous Americanism now reaching its fullest flower.

It was a little sad to miss the soft Southern accents, the courtly bows, the broad-brimmed hats and, for that matter, the often demagogic oratory that characterized a Congress and a society dominated by Southerners. Not that demagoguery was dead by any means, but the Northerners were not so charming in putting together the words. Instead of Calhoun and Clay it now was the word witchery of O. P. Morton and other orators that drew spectators to the galleries of Congress.

Southerners were officially welcome in Washington, and in fact in December of 1868 Andrew Johnson had signed the final act of amnesty for the last Southerners still imprisoned for their political beliefs. But the town was cold toward them, and it was the Northerners who set the pace.

There were new names, new faces and, most of all, a new display.

The Willard Hotel, completely renovated, was the center of public life in Washington. New and more imposing houses were being built around the green island of Lafayette Square. More than one visitor remarked that all the people worth knowing lived within walking distance of each other in this sacred part of Washington.

Within a few months after his inauguration, Grant got from Congress an appropriation of $13,000,000 with which to repair and improve the city. Pennsylvania Avenue and the principal streets leading from it were newly paved with cobblestones. Brick sidewalks made their appearance around public buildings and the more fashionable hotels and homes. Perhaps most important of all the improvements was the roofing over of the Tiber River and the transformation of that foul-smelling stream into an honest sewer. The swamp south of the White House was drained.

The civic improvements and the influx of money from the North made the Capital a boom town. There was plenty of money to spend and many willing hands to spend it. Nowhere was the profit of war more evident than in Washington.

No economists yet had been lifted up on the figured columns atop which they now assay the trend of the country to the fifth decimal. So there was no one to point out in Washington the ruin involved in the rise in the public debt during the Civil War from $57,000,000 to $2,758,000,000. Instead, the country was hard at work, and within three years was paying off the debt.

The new railways pushing into the West, the booming industry of the North and the stock manipulations which made millionaires overnight—all these were reflected in the face of Washington. And responsible officials assiduously turned their backs to the South, which began just across the Potomac in Alexandria, washing it out as a business loss.

The Congress raised the President's salary from $25,000 a year to $50,000 to support the White House in its new position. And President Grant—one-time peddler of firewood—became the social arbiter of the day. When Nellie Grant married, in 1874, the young Englishman, Algernon Frederick Sartoris, Grant turned the White House parlors into a bower of flowers for the ceremony, and the menus for the wedding banquet were printed on white satin.

The State Dinners at the White House were the supreme

word in elegance, prepared by an Italian steward named Melah, a fitting successor to Dolly Madison's "French Jean." When Prince Arthur, youthful son of Queen Victoria, visited Washington, Melah presided over the preparation of a dinner for 35 guests which cost a reported $1500.

And yet entertainment in the White House was relatively modest compared to that in hotels and private homes by the political descendants of Clay and Webster, of Monroe and Van Buren. How far away were the days when Mrs. Smith entertained Miss Harriet Martineau with the assistance of her maid and a butler hired for the evening!

The new grading and paving of streets hardly kept pace with the building boom. The shanties came down by the thousands. New and pretentious buildings arose by the score—mostly ornate private homes of a type heretofore unknown to Washington. Plush draperies and Italian carved ceilings, with rooms packed with the newly fashionable mission furniture upholstered in damask and horsehair, filled these stone and brick houses to suffocation.

More than one visitor raised an eyebrow and wondered how the cost of these things accommodated itself to notably low official salaries. A cab for an evening cost $5, if there were no special event; when there was some notable reception—and there were few evenings from November to June when there was not—such an equipage rose to $10. And still the public places could hardly handle the parties for which they were booked.

At Willard's Hotel, the hack line stretched for blocks, while drivers and footmen shouted for the right of way and competed at the entries with the liveried drivers of private coaches. Such coaches now were modest if they cost no more than $2500. Ladies in two-foot trains minced in tight satin slippers up the marble stairs to dressing rooms packed to suffocation.

Not that Willard's was the only fashionable hotel. Even more exclusive probably was Wormley's, at Fifteenth and H Streets, which drew its patronage mainly from well-to-do families and members of the diplomatic corps. The Marquis and Madame Noalles made this their Washington home; likewise Señor and Madame Antonio Flores. Schuyler Colfax and Caleb Cushing lived there in stately simplicity with their families.

The National Hotel, former residence of Henry Clay, still held its quota of official guests, and the new Ebbitt Hotel was in course of planning.

The British Legation moved in the 1870's almost into the "wilderness" of upper Connecticut Avenue, clear out to O Street, into a new official home that all but rivaled the White House in its appointments. In many ways it was more livable, particularly since a chancery provided rooms for offices separate from the living accommodations of the house. The former British Legation soon became another symbol of the way of life in Washington.

Perhaps the gamble of a career in politics put a special fever into men's blood. Or maybe it was the boredom of the routine of so-called official life. In any event, the close of the Civil War found a reputed 100 gambling houses flourishing in Washington. Soon competition reduced this number to perhaps a score, but no small change was involved in the business of the remainder.

Of all the operators John Chamberlain, intimate friend of Senators and Representatives and accepted as a member of "society," was probably the most successful. It was not long after Grant's Inaugural that he paid $150,000 in cash for the vacated British Legation on I Street, a massive gabled house set back from the street and marked by most elegant shrubs and flowers and with ivy climbing the pillars of its portico.

Chamberlain ran a club in which men might gather without ever touching a card or chip. He served dinners up to the finest standards and the many parlors of his house were available to statesmen as conference rooms. But upstairs his croupiers presided at long tables, and here many thousands of dollars changed hands each night. The play was unlimited, except for a house rule that interrupted gambling at midnight for the serving of a supper with the compliments of the host.

One had to be known to gain entry to Chamberlain's, but not to the establishment of John Welcher, where the entertainment began and ended with the food, and ladies were as welcome as men. This Welcher was a little surprised at his own success. A wine merchant in New York, he decided to try his hand at running a restaurant in Washington. So he moved the choicest lots from his cellars to the Capital and undertook to master the mysteries of oyster pie. No man living in Washington now remembers eating in Welcher's but many recall the descriptions given by their fathers and grandfathers.

Of particular importance in the recollection of Welcher's restaurant was the discretion of the host. It was commented after his death that nothing of importance which had happened in Washington from the Civil War to the middle of Grant's Administration had not been the center of some discussion at Welcher's, either at the public tables or in the private dining rooms. But no word of these talks ever "leaked" through gossip by the host or by his waiters.

The same could also be honestly said of Sam Ward, principal competitor among restaurateurs of Welcher. The two men complemented each other. Welcher was the quiet sort. Ward, whose cooking was almost as good, managed a dinner as an impresario stages an opera. There was always some new surprise for the ladies at his tables, and particularly favors for any children who entered his restaurant. It was said of Sam Ward that he could outdo the best storytellers of the Senate with his anecdotes.

If one needed proof that Washington was growing up, that it had arrived as an important Capital in the world, it was necessary only to look in upon the new Legation constructed by

His Britannic Majesty's Minister to Washington, Sir Edward Thornton. True, it was on the edge of a section known as "the wilderness," but there was no skimping in its design or plan. In fact, it started the magnetic pull of exclusive residences northward from the region of Lafayette Square. And it is typical of subsequent and continuing rapid change that the site of this first pretentious legation today is a filling station.

The British Legation had a massive stone porte-cochere facing Connecticut Avenue. From this visitors entered a reception hall through mahogany doors in which was set frosted glass bearing the imperial coat of arms. Up from the hall rose a stairway which merged into a balcony encircling the second level of the hall. At the top of the first flight was hung a life-sized portrait of Queen Victoria.

From the left of the hall doors opened into two salons and a ballroom, whose crystal chandeliers, wall moldings and woodwork were especially designed in England. On the floor was a rug first woven for the express purpose of covering the spot on which Victoria stood in 1851 when she opened the Crystal Palace exhibition at London. The furnishings and draperies in the state rooms were done in rose, silver and gold, and dark-blue velvet.

To the right of the hall were the study and reception rooms for the use of the Minister. Back of the study was the state dining room, with a dinner service of solid silver.

The British Legation was not more than 10 blocks above the heart of the city and the White House, yet in the 1870's this neighborhood contained only some old wooden buildings erected as temporary barracks for use during the Civil War and an abandoned brick building. The boundary of the city, so far as surveys had been carried out, was five blocks farther north, where Florida Avenue now runs. Here began a region of good hunting.

Dupont Circle already was laid out at the intersection of Connecticut Avenue and Massachusetts Avenue, but was undeveloped except in survey maps. South of the Legation were two groups of houses, known as Shepherd's and Phillips', built in rows for speculative renting during "the season."

Connecticut Avenue was paved as far north as Dupont Circle with cobblestones and wooden blocks. A horsecar line ran up it to P Street, two blocks north of the Legation, where it turned west and terminated at a carbarn at Twenty-fourth Street. At Twentieth Street it passed a brickyard. Connecticut Avenue itself runs northwestward from Lafayette Square, intersecting at angles 17th, 18th and 19th Streets and meeting 20th Street at Dupont Circle.

The old brick building that faced the British Embassy built in the 1870's was to have its moment in history when Professor Alexander Graham Bell would take it over as a laboratory to complete his telephone experiments. Soon afterward it would give way in turn to the surge of extravagant home building that came with the boom era.

Nevertheless, there still was a touch of homely modesty remaining in small things. One young diplomat listed the three boarding houses suitable for young bachelors assigned to Washington—Mrs. Marsh's house at 1015 Connecticut Avenue; Miss Somerville's (she was a Scotch lady), first at 1519 I Street and after at 1712 I Street, and Michael Nolan's at 1019 Connecticut Avenue.

In 1876 the little red-brick building had a true headline visitor. This visitor was incognito, but everyone knew that he actually was King Pedro Segundo of Brazil, calling on the United States after a tour of Europe. A dilettante in the sciences, King Pedro had visited in Europe with Gladstone, Charles Darwin and Victor Hugo. Here he assisted at inaugurating the use of Professor Bell's telephone. Before King Pedro left for home he translated into Portuguese a currently popular song entitled "Stars and Stripes."

King Pedro might have had other interesting visits in Washington had it not been for the social ostracism visited on two residents because of their "radical" views. One was Walt Whitman, who eked out a precarious living with a small clerkship in the office of the Attorney General. The other was John Burroughs, the naturalist, with whom Whitman often took long walks through the woods.

More acceptable, but still suspect to the politicians who ruled the roost, was a small coterie of others with various talents. Ben:Perley Poore and Donn Piatt carried the top honors in journalism, and Julia Ward Howe and Gail Hamilton had their circles of friends. Horatio King attempted to maintain a literary circle, centering largely around his friend, Henry Adams, the historian.

John W. Forney, the politico, occasionally opened his house on Capitol Hill for literary evenings. Here one might meet Joseph Medill, of the *Chicago Tribune;* M. B. Brady, already celebrated for his photography in the Civil War; C. L. Elliott, the rising portrait painter, or Thad Stevens. Sometimes also Edwin Forrest would consent to recite lines from the plays in which he was a celebrated performer.

Nonetheless, these were the quiet interludes in a city whose basic life seemed to be made up of endless calls, receptions, dinners and balls—a city in which an official's wife could complain of the excessive cost of dressing in styles requiring a dozen changes of lavender gloves, the price of dinners at Welcher's, or the difficulty of competing socially in circles where Mrs. Kate Chase Sprague had a new gown created by Worth for each public appearance.

Here was a Washington in which pensions for old soldiers already were appearing in appropriation bills passed by each new Congress, with two dollars per month being decreed for holders of the Congressional Medal of Honor won in the Civil War, to assure them against penury. And a Washington in which Senator Zack Chandler gave one dinner, among many in his house on H Street, where the refreshment table was a miniature replica of Peking with candies and cakes tucked into the pagodas.

The old Decatur House—former home of Van Buren and Clay and betweenwhiles a slave market—blossomed into new expansiveness when General Fitzgerald Beale, bulging with gold from California, opened it as his home with a dinner costing $150 a plate.

A daughter of General Beale soon married John R. McLean, who in 1876 founded the *Washington Post*.

At the very heart of this display there was developing a sort of exclusivity, and at the heart of the exclusivity was one woman, endowed beyond normal measure in every way. This figure was Kate Chase Sprague.

Salmon P. Chase was Chief Justice of the United States at the swearing in of Andrew Jackson as President. As Chief Justice he presided over the impeachment proceedings in the Senate where Johnson was acquitted by a single vote. In 1868 he almost became the Democratic nominee for President; some Democrats and Republicans thought that had he been the candidate he would have beaten Grant. A widower, Chase had sired no sons, but his daughter Kate became head of his household while yet a child. By the time she reached her teens her views were treated respectfully by the politicians her father entertained in his home in Ohio.

Chase had moved to Washington first to enter Lincoln's Cabinet, and by the time his beautiful daughter was 21 she was Lincoln's confidante, termed by some well-informed persons the most powerful woman in Washington since Dolly Madison.

There was gossip when she married, at 24, Senator William Sprague, of New Jersey, that this powerful young woman desired most to win control of his great fortune, founded on New England textile mills, as a means of furthering her father's ambition, and her own—that Chase win the Presidency. But at her wedding Lincoln claimed the privilege of a kiss.

By 1865, Kate Chase Sprague had the most exclusive and opulent home in Washington. The biggest diamond yet seen there crowned her headdress. Her furniture and clothes alike came exclusively from Paris. She was undaunted by the fact that her husband usually got drunk at social functions, but after all he was only incidental.

What was important to Mrs. Sprague was the background for her career. It was easy to conceal her husband's habits in the house called "Edgewood," built by her father near the Capital and enlarged after Kate's marriage. It required 40 servants to operate it. Sprague was even less conspicuous in the summer "cottage" at Narragansett, built by Kate with Sprague's money, where eighty rooms were jammed with magnificent furnishings and works of art.

When Mrs. Sprague wished to entertain a politician, or to raise her own stature by some cultural event, such as a lecture by Julia Ward Howe, the invitations were not refused.

When the first baby was born to the Spragues, its layette was a matter of national news interest. The second Grant Inaugural Ball included among its decorations a $1000 floral ornament passed along to the committee by Mrs. Sprague after she had used it for one of her dinners.

Around the focal light of Mrs. Sprague one found the distinguished Mrs. Hamilton Fish, wife of Grant's Secretary of State, who was most complimented for her regal carriage; General Horace Porter and the dashing General William Tecumseh Sherman, and Mrs. W. W. Belknap, wife of the Secretary of War, who later was to resign following proof that he had sold military post traderships for private profits.

There, too, was Lady Thornton, regal wife of the British Minister, and Señora Potesdad, wife only of a Spanish Legation secretary but distinguished as perhaps the most beautiful of the ladies in the Diplomatic Corps. And Catacazy, the Russian Minister, and the fading Madame Catacazy, who in her youth had openly joined this husband as his mistress long before her first mate, an Italian prince and diplomat, was dead. And Mrs. Carl Schurz, disapproving such extravagance.

So it went until September of 1873, when one single event illustrates anew the fact that Washington itself is nothing; that it is a focal point.

Throughout Grant's Administrations there had been growing fears and charges concerning the inter-relationship of government and the moneyed interests. Grave exposures occurred in 1873, irrefutable proof of favored financing given to public figures by banking houses which in their turn were more favored by the government.

There were failures as the result of the exposés, and curtailing of credits. Among the "victims" was Senator Sprague, whose textile empire in Rhode Island collapsed.

No more dinners were served in damask pavilions in the garden of the Chase house. The Narragansett palace was closed.

Washington had experienced its first great boom and hangover.

Chapter Twelve

ORPHAN CITY

THE CONSTITUTION sets forth that no citizen of the United States may be deprived of a vote because of race, creed, color or condition of servitude. As a result of this noble statement all Americans by 1947 could vote for their officials, except convicted felons, a diminishing number of Negroes in some Southern States, and the permanent residents of the national Capital. For this condition, the last-named group of almost 1,000,000 people had to thank the Federal Government during the Grant Administration.

Lest that pin-point the blame more closely than is fair, let it also be recorded that 70 years after the establishment of this oligarchic system, Congress still remained loath to recognize that the residents of the Capital were citizens. Thus the Federal Government permitted them to pay real-estate and income taxes, do jury duty and to be drafted in wartime. But they had no more say in their government than the inmates of San Quentin prison.

The District of Columbia was ruled by laws passed in Congress on the say-so of House and Senate Committees for the District of Columbia. Most powerful voice in these affairs was the Chairman of the Senate Committee for the District of Columbia. The chairman of this committee in 1946, until the Republicans captured the Senate and therefore the Committee chairmanship, was Theodore Bilbo, distinguished only as America's most outspoken Negro-baiter, Jew-baiter and exponent of a type of "white supremacy" already outdated by intelligent persons in Jefferson's day.

True, the President appointed the Commissioners who actually administered the District of Columbia, and the Senate confirmed them. One always was an Army officer of high rank detailed from the Corps of Engineers, with which there was little complaint. The other two usually were political hacks or semi-retired hangers-on who were considered deserving of a sinecure paying $10,000 a year and prerogatives including an impressive limousine and chauffeur for each.

The debate over government of the District always has been a lively one. It excites wondered puzzlement in the minds of foreigners, and most Americans can hardly believe it when the system is explained to them.

This is the brief story of how it got that way: the experimentation that has continued ever since 1805 when a Congressman said that he "never spoke of the inhabitants (of the District) but with pity and compassion."

From 1790 to 1802, when the laws of Maryland and Virginia still governed the original segments of the District taken from those States, there was a Board of Commissioners appointed by the President. In 1802, a new law provided that Washington should be governed by a mayor appointed by the President, a council of twelve elected by all white male residents and a senior chamber of five men elected by the council from among themselves. By 1812, the mayor's office was dignified with a salary of $400 and council members received two dollars for each day they attended meetings. Georgetown and Alexandria continued to govern themselves as free cities within the District of Columbia.

By 1820, when Washington had grown in population to 13,247, election of the mayor by the voters was provided, but property qualifications were set up for voters. This system continued with modifications until 1867 when all male residents were enfranchised.

Now, here was the point where the government of the Capital City ran head on into national arguments. Washington, in case the reader has forgotten, was a Southern city, won by a political deal for that region, laid out and planned up until the outbreak of the Civil War as the political and social center of the South. This location galled the new West more than the North. In the two years after the close of the Civil War Congress seriously considered a petition by St. Louis, Mo., to move the Capital to that Midwestern location.

The petition never had a chance of passage, but it provided the lever for new attempts to "federalize" the whole District of Columbia.

Sayles J. Bowen, mayor of Washington in 1868-69, was an honest and hard-working executive whose one dream was to restore Pennsylvania Avenue to the quiet beauty it had developed before the city became a military headquarters. He pushed through the council a series of plans that eventuated in the paving of the "historic mile" of Pennsylvania from First Street, at the foot of Capitol Hill, to the Treasury, on Fifteenth Street, with wooden blocks. The job cost $2,000,000, incurred as a debt by the city.

Mathew Galt Emory defeated Bowen in a race for the mayoralty in 1870, but he barely had taken office before the Congress passed a law sweeping out the whole form of municipal government and giving the District of Columbia the same type of government as was set up in the Territories. It looked well on paper, eminently fair in its division of control between the local residents and taxpayers and the Federal Government, which necessarily must protect itself against embarrassment by a local political government.

Furthermore, the Territorial plan was sponsored by a native Washingtonian, Alexander R. Shepherd, born during Jackson's Administration. Shepherd, successful businessman and retired at the age of 35, was the go-getter type of new American just emerging in every city. Pugnacious and good-humored, weighing 225 pounds, he was the prototype of the popular public figure. For him there were none of the graces of political rapier work; he used a sledge hammer.

The saloon fronts of Pennsylvania Avenue, always decorated for great events, exceeded their normal flamboyancy on February 22, 1871. Never had the city had such a celebration. This day and the following one were decreed as public holidays because of the concurrence of three great celebrations.

In the first place, February 22nd was Washington's birthday anniversary. In the second place, the paving of Pennsylvania Avenue had been rushed to completion to accommodate a parade dedicating the new street on this date. Finally, Congress had rushed through enactment of the Territorial law to make it effective on February 22, 1871.

Foot races, sack races, lacrosse games and a hundred other amusements had been arranged by a bewhiskered and frock-coated group officially designated as the Committee on Diverse Deviltries. President Grant went personally with a party of gentlemen and ladies to occupy a vantage point from which to watch the parade, replete with marshals mounted on horseback, all the bands which could be assembled, and floats, mostly comic. One constructed by the Butchers' Union portrayed the mock inauguration of a woman President.

The residents of Washington hereafter would have both a body of self-government and a spokesman in the Congress. The Territorial system already was old and well tried. Under it each Territory was represented by a Delegate who sat in the House of Representatives. He could not vote, but he had an office among the legislators, an official position which permitted him to participate in debate and the right of appearing before committees on a plane of equality with Representatives. The check of Federal supervision over Territorial legislatures was provided by a governor appointed by the President.

The separate town charters of Washington and Georgetown ceased to exist. The new Territorial legislation specifically gave the President the right to appoint, in addition to the governor, the members of one of two branches of a legislature, a secretary of the District, a board of public works, a board of health. The residents would elect the second house in the legislature. The Federal Government would pay all officials, and would supervise the tax legislation and collect the revenues. Both chambers of the small legislature must agree by majority vote on all laws for the District. A two-thirds vote by these two houses could nullify a governor's veto of new laws.

Nevertheless, the interests of the Federal Government were finally protected by a section of the new law that stated: "Nothing herein shall be construed to deprive Congress of the power of legislation over the same District in as ample a manner as if the law (establishing the Territory) had not been enacted."

So everyone was happy, and black and white residents alike, equally franchised, put on their holiday attire under heavy cloaks, and made a time of it. To the residents of the District, President Grant was the greatest President yet to sit in the White House. Members of the government won a popularity that displaced the cold and often unfriendly stares given them by the "natives."

The smiles did not last long.

President Grant named as the first Governor of the District of Columbia, Henry D. Cooke. The appointment fell strictly within the legal requirement that the appointee should have resided in the District at least one full year before his appointment.

But what had been the circumstances of Henry Cooke's residence in the District of Columbia? Even the urchins who fought in back alleys for junk knew the answer to that one.

Henry Cooke was the brother of Jay Cooke. Jay Cooke was the head of a financial group with whom Grant was on such intimate terms as to create scandal in gossip circles and genuine concern among his well-wishers, because in 1871 banking and financial manipulation were virtually synonymous. Had not another friendship of Grant's already blackened his record, although he personally was held guiltless, when his pals Jay Gould and James Fisk, Jr. had tried in 1869 to corner the gold market?

There were many who were able to predict that in a short time, as did happen in 1873, the house of Cooke would overstretch itself and carry down many more political reputations.

It was not the fact that Henry Cooke was Governor that excited the most comment; it was this reiteration of the well-known fact that the Federal Government, even the President, had so little moral sense as to carry even into minor appointments the amoral connection of political and money dealings.

Henry Cooke was lobbyist for his brother. He was one of the most powerful men in Washington. His operations included a local branch bank for operations with Treasury connections and the judicious placement of money and financial favors wherever in government they would do the most good.

His appointment was purely one of prestige. Grant was able to give to a treasured friend the position of first citizen of the Capital City. It was a long time since Thomas Jefferson had conferred a comparable honor on Dr. William Thornton.

The House of Representatives then discovered that the new law permitted it to designate such officials as were not specifically to be selected by the President. Within a few weeks it had created 230 well-paid jobs, for distribution on the patronage system. This was a bonanza. Many of the appointees never had offices or saw them if they did. The pay check was the only important thing, and so intended, in the appointment of each one. So, by its own action, the Federal Government created for the District a model form of operation and immediately proceeded to wreck it, as though it had intended to do so from the start.

Washington was ripe for bossism in government, and the "boss" was at hand. Within a few weeks, Shepherd was known universally, in the blunt political jargon of the day, simply as "the Boss." He planned well and skillfully and apparently with Grant's full understanding because Shepherd had made it clear that he did not wish to have one of the higher-sounding titles. Shepherd asked for, and got, one of the five posts on the Board of Public Works. The other four members might as well not have been appointed. From the first day the board was formed there was only one member—Shepherd. He worked carefully in his arrangements, foresaw that the only functioning agency of the new government would be his board. With a governor who was not interested and a Congress concerned only in fattening its patronage within the District, there was none to stop his energetic program to rebuild the city.

Boss Shepherd's idea of modernizing Washington was to tear out everything possible and redo it. True, there were streets in which the grades carried water away from instead of into the sewers—even Pennsylvania Avenue, where the $2,000,000 worth of new paving soon began to buckle and cave. Shepherd was a bear in a china shop when it came to street grades.

Citizens would leave their homes in early morning, according to contemporary reports, and return in the evening to find the streets in front of their houses lowered by several feet, the side-walks and paving torn out, and only the sticky red mud of the subsoil to wade through to reach their doors. The Congress itself was not immune, for Shepherd, secure in Grant's favor, blithely cut away a portion of one side of Capitol Hill to level a street.

The Baltimore and Ohio Railroad crossed Pennsylvania Avenue between the Capitol and the Treasury, and one of Shepherd's pet projects was the elimination of this grade crossing. The B. & O. objected to the expense—stood upon the rights conferred in its charter. When Shepherd became obnoxious in his denunciation, the railroad simply parked a locomotive across the avenue and left it there, forcing traffic to detour.

In one night, Boss Shepherd sent a gang of his bull-necked laborers to the crossing and removed all the tracks and ties of the railroad at either end of the locomotive where they lay on public property. Then he invited the B. & O. to do what it wished—either leave the locomotive as a monument in the middle of the street or cart it away section by section.

The railroad was so impressed with Shepherd that he was offered an important executive post. Shepherd turned it down. He had more fun redoing the city.

The money troubles of the house of Cooke in 1873 prompted Henry Cooke to resign the governorship of the District. President Grant promptly named Shepherd to replace him. To Shepherd the change simply meant a slightly freer hand, if possible, in his grandiose schemes. He continued to wreck and rebuild, to dig up the streets and regrade them.

Only the money panic that hit the United States in the spring of 1874 caused a halt in his operation. Congress, as it sometimes had done, began to wonder where the money was coming from; whether the District could afford the expenses Shepherd was incurring. It feared public reaction if the public learned that public funds might have to be spent on the District.

Committees of the House and the Senate held long hearings on the course of affairs in Washington. They discovered that Shepherd had spent in his three-year plan so much money that the debt of the little city had been increased by $16,500,000.

Further search as to where the money had gone brought out the refreshing truth that Shepherd actually had spent it on public works. Instead of enriching himself as political bosses so often have done, he was a considerably poorer man than when he took public office. In fact, he had so neglected his own private affairs that he was practically broke.

But the Territory was dead. Promptly in 1874 the Congress revoked the law setting it up and placed the affairs of the District temporarily in the hands of three commissioners. The Commission form was made permanent in 1878.

When the Federal Government took the last vestige of self-government from the Capital City, it also wrote into the law the promise that the government would carry half the expenses of operating the Capital. For a long time it did, but now the Federal share of expenditures has been reduced to a small fraction. This is a matter of endless debate between civic spokesmen and the Congress but too dry a matter to inflict upon the reader.

The Federal Government and the foreign embassies and legations occupy just about half the real estate within the boundaries of the District of Columbia. This property pays no taxes, but is policed, protected from fire and provided with water and sewage systems through the local facilities. Many government buildings are protected by special police, but only within their walls. The White House police force, sizeable in itself, patrols the grounds of the mansion but the city police are responsible for protection outside its fences.

The city spokesmen contend that the Federal Government should pay for its share of these services, and say the half portion should be served up, as promised originally. Members of Congress rebut this argument with the contention that the value of city property is so enhanced by the Federal Government that this fact alone offsets the sum the government costs the residents.

Doubtless the argument will extend into another century. What most galls the Washington resident—the simon-pure, bona fide persons who live in Washington as private citizens, who earn their livings there and who call it home—is the "extra-territorial" status given to those government officials and employees who have another "official" home.

The laws are so arranged that two men may be neighbors for 25 years, perhaps have the same incomes and live in identical homes. One, the District resident, has no vote but pays all the local levies. The other, working for the government and maintaining a "voting address" in some State—the address usually consisting of no more than a postal address in a cousin's house —escapes local income taxes and escapes jury duty. Without civic responsibility, this "non-resident" may, if it is cheaper, even get his car license tags from his "official" residence.

Theodore W. Noyes, born in Washington in 1858, and who died only in 1946, was important in the family which founded the newspaper, the *Washington Star*. Noyes was a leading member of the coterie of disfranchised citizens who carried the fight for recognition of the dignity of the District, and at his death, as editor of the *Star*, was wielding a forceful pen in its behalf.

Long ago, in 1888, Noyes testified to a period of amicability, which marked a definite step in development of the city. He wrote in the *Star*, as follows:

"In place of a straggling country village, with zigzag grades, no sewerage, unimproved reservations, second-rate dwellings, streets of mud and mire, and wretched sidewalks, the modern Washington has arisen a political, scientific and literary center, with a population trebled since 1860; a city sustained, improved and adorned by an annual expenditure of more than four million dollars; with surface remodeled; with an elaborate and costly system of water mains; with about 150 miles of improved streets, nearly one-half of which are paved with concrete; with convenient transportation by 33 miles of street railway; with numerous churches and schools, as well as government buildings of architectural pretensions; with broad streets shaded for a distance of 280 miles by more than 60,000 trees, destined to make Washington a forest city; with attractive suburban drives; with reservations and parkings given a picturesque beauty by shrubbery and rich foliage, statuary, fountains and flowers, and with costly private dwellings, rivaling palaces in size and splendor of interior adornment, springing up in rapid succession where Trollope sank knee-deep in mud.

"This wonderful change for the better, effected by certain wise and energetic agents of the general government whom the District delights to honor, is the result, in part, of a reversal of the conditions which hampered the city's growth. Congress, no longer hostile or indifferent concerning the pecuniary needs of the District, has spent large sums not only upon public buildings, but also in the improvement of the city, at first spasmodically, since 1878 systematically.

"The people of the District, encouraged by the general abandonment of the idea of a removal of the seat of government, have also made extensive outlays. But the main public expense of the work of recreating the city is represented by a present debt of more than $20,000,000, nearly all of which has been incurred by officials placed over the affairs of the District by the general government in carrying out those 'magnificent intentions' concerning the Capital, which by the original plan, the nation and not the District was to execute."

There was the snapper. To his dying day, Noyes and his fellow spokesmen for the city denounced this paternalistic system. And the denunciation will long survive him and the other editors who, differ as they may on other issues, are joined on this one.

Chapter Thirteen

BIGGER AND BETTER

Senator William H. Stewart, of California, was a leading exponent of the new American philosophy of "bigger and better" in everything. He combined the characteristics so common in the post-Civil War period in Washington of using his fortune to get high political position and then taking a little more profit out of Washington. The coincidence of his appearance at the time of the Shepherd development was fortuitous.

Quite a number of critics talked openly of charges that the men in favored positions used the "inside dope" on projected improvements to do a little substantial real-estate speculation. Nothing was ever proved, but quite a few tidy fortunes were made. The improvements, combined with a rapid growth of Washington, sent property values in the near-by northwest from low costs per acre to levels measured in numbers of dollars per square foot.

About the time that the British Embassy building got under way, Senator Stewart and a mining partner, Curtis J. Hillyer, bought large tracts of land a short distance to the north. Almost by coincidence, it would seem, Connecticut Avenue soon thereafter was paved, 130 feet in width, all the way up to Florida Avenue, running right through this property.

Stewart sold out his holdings to Thomas Sunderland, another California operator, and then bought back at 50 cents a foot the northwest corner of the intersection of Connecticut Avenue and Massachusetts Avenue at Dupont Circle. There he built "Stew-

133

art Castle," one of the first of the great houses in Washington.

Hillyer built another mansion for himself a little distance west on Massachusetts Avenue, while Senator John B. Henderson, of Missouri, surmounted one of the highest hills on Sixteenth Street, due north from Lafayette Square, with a turreted red-brick castle. The boom was on.

By the middle 1880's the newly fashionable section of Washington to the northwest of old Lafayette Square displayed row on row of houses, abutting elm-shaded walks, which were palatial by any standard.

These were distinguished by mansard roofs, or steep gables. All had elaborate porte-cocheres where visitors might alight from their carriages under cover. Marble and bronze and rare carvings were brought from all over the earth to decorate these residences. Joseph West Moore, the historian, observed "apparently there is no limit to the cost."

In more recent years the Canadian Embassy was housed in a Massachusetts Avenue structure of that period, built by one branch of the Swift packing-house family. When L. B. Pearson moved into the house as Ambassador, he remarked, "I wonder how many thousand pigs went into the woodwork alone."

Now, as Washington approached its centenary, there were at least three distinct communities within the city. These made up its population of close to 200,000, but scarcely ever overlapped within the framework. There was the wealthy top layer, more often than not with official connections, who created the glamor phase of life in the period that died only with outbreak of war in 1917. There was the "government set," dignified by office but too poor to make more than a surface show of its affairs. Finally, there was the poorer level, largely black, representing the spawn of refugees from the Civil War.

If contrast makes up the picturesque life of cities, Washington was as picturesque as its "opposite numbers" among the world capitals—Paris and London. The principal difference was that it was a capital without distractions. There was no industry beyond a flour mill on the Potomac River; no transport other than the railroads barely required to keep open shipments of goods from North and South. The port of Georgetown was all but abandoned to commerce, except for oysters and produce brought up the Potomac from farms along its banks. Georgetown and Alexandria, the latter again a free town across the river, had slid back into the position of run-down suburbs.

There still were vast stretches of unoccupied land within the District of Columbia, but the plan envisioned by George Washington and L'Enfant was taking shape in skeletal form. Here was a city with many broad avenues running at angles to the numbered and lettered streets, and with circles and squares laid off as parks at the principal intersections. A good many tons of statues already had made their appearance in the open spaces—usually monuments erected by subscription of patriotic societies to memorialize heroes of the Revolution or the Civil War. The public buildings included a surprising number among those best known today.

The Capitol at last was fully completed atop Capitol Hill. Naturally, the White House was unchanged. The great Treasury Building was finished. West of the White House was a gargantuan building, covered with every conceivable decorative design, which housed the State, War and Navy Departments, all under one roof. The Navy Yard still was the most important naval construction depot in the United States. The Weather Bureau was functioning. A sprawling soldiers' home had been constructed on beautiful farmland to the northeast of Washington.

Twenty-five foreign countries maintained legations in Washington, most of them on a palatial scale, but none more picturesque than the Chinese, furnished entirely in Mongolian style, or the Japanese. Oddly enough, the only country besides Great Britain which had purchased a residence for its minister was Prussia, which owned a house on Fifteenth Street, Northwest.

All of these legations, as well as the impressive private residences, were within a small area ranging westward from Fifteenth Street and south of Florida Avenue to Rock Creek on the west.

Governor Shepherd had more to do with this development than any other single individual. Before he started his wrecking and grading campaign this entire region was a section of swamps interspersed with small hillocks on which had been constructed barracks for many of the 150,000 troops quartered in Washington during the Civil War. Between the barracks were shantytown settlements of Negroes. Shepherd spent much of the multi-million total of the city debt to drain this whole region and push streets through it. The improvement forced out the Negroes. The barracks came down, and the land went up for sale—often after original title had been secured by politicians.

Conversation in the big houses consisted almost exclusively of boasts about the rapid growth and the achievements of Washington, much the same as that which visitors to Florida in the 1920's encountered from the natives. And there were things to boast about.

There was the Department of Agriculture, functioning in a handsome building south of the Mall, a direct outgrowth of the governmental interest in crops first fostered by Thomas Jefferson. The agriculture department had built two large greenhouses in which flourished 2000 examples of plant life, arranged in precise botanical order. More practical, the Department of Agriculture was distributing more than 2,000,000 packets of seeds a year, as free gifts to farmers in areas where this practice would "improve" crop production. It was relatively unimportant that the free seeds ordinarily went to the farmers with the best political connections.

The Government Printing Office already had set a record which it still holds. It was the largest printing and binding establishment in the world. Employing then between 2500 and 3000 employees it turned out millions of pamphlets a year, as well as printing free speeches by Congressmen for mailing—also free—to their constituents. It still does.

The Smithsonian Institution, scarcely 40 years old, already had become too small to house the scientific collections which poured into it. An annex, known as the National Museum, had been constructed with public funds.

Thomas Corcoran, a conservative Washington resident without official connection, had founded in 1871 the first substantial contribution to art appreciation in the Capital. Corcoran was a collector of rare taste in a day when the country's new millionaires were more concerned with size of canvas and weight of marble than with delicacy of line. His finest piece of art was the "Greek Slave," sculptured in marble in life size by Hiram Powers.

Long before his museum was opened, Corcoran held a special reception to celebrate the acquisition of the "Greek Slave." It almost cost this otherwise conservative gentleman his place in "society," because the "Slave," a pensive, standing and superbly lifelike figure, wears chains on hands and wrists—but nothing else. Among the shocked frock-coated male guests there probably was more than one frequenter of the highly popular, discreet houses that specialized in purveying limpid-eyed quadroon girls.

Socially Washington was a winter resort. This was due partly to the mild climate, partly to the habit of Congress of convening on the first Monday in December of each year and usually remaining in session until the hot weather began in May or June. No crises forced the calling of special extra sessions.

It had become fashionable for Northern millionaires to seek public office, the normal development as the wealth of the country had shifted from the South to the North. Railroad money, textile money and banking had spokesmen in the seats so long dominated by agriculturists from the South. The Middle Western expansion had not yet reached the point where the voice of resurgent agriculture would dominate the thinking of Congress.

Here was the day of—and Washington was the spokesman for it—"infant industry," which asked and received consistently higher tariff laws at every session of Congress. Political futures, if not personal fortunes, were best secured by playing along with the new aristocracy of money.

In Washington, even more than in New York, this was an empire that expressed itself in kid gloves, carriages and gorgeous jewelry. Mrs. Sprague's day was only the curtain-raiser for display.

The social season began officially on New Year's Day and extended to Ash Wednesday, the first day of Lent. Actually, the parties usually were well under way when Congress convened. Despite frowns by churchmen, they continued at a fairly rapid pace through Lent. Protocol had become frozen into a groove as strict as that obtaining in any European Court.

The newcomer to Washington paid the first calls on the older residents, or at the least left cards. By some special alchemy, or the state of their husbands' purses, women with husbands below the "policy level" were supposed to know whether they rated the right to leave cards and to expect the dropping of cards in return. The calling cards, according to the current rule, must be small and plain, "engraved or written but never printed." After the round of calls, a newly arrived hostess sat back to wait for the invitations.

The social procedure was such as to be a full-time occupation, just as it had been in Mrs. Smith's day. A popular hostess never was at home except on the days she received, with the possible exception of Saturday and Sunday.

The success of an official could depend largely on the manner in which his wife capered through her social list, because somewhere in the hierarchy usually was the "boss" who determined whether a Congressman or a Cabinet member was doing a good job.

The afternoon receptions, or "at homes," had become as fixed as the laws of the Medes and the Persians. These were held from 2 to 5 P.M., and were open to all comers. Thus the week opened on Monday with wives of the nine Justices of the Supreme Court, plus those of the General of the Army and the Admiral of the Navy, holding open house. On Tuesday, the prominent families of the West End received their friends or acted as graciously as possible while strangers walked over their Turkey carpets and fingered the brocaded draperies (some had private detectives on duty to protect tidbits from light fingers). On Wednesday the wives of Cabinet members and the Speaker of the House went through this ordeal. Thursday was the mass calling day when all wives of Senators and Representatives must receive visitors. Friday was kept free for special afternoon receptions.

The wife of a new Congressman, outranked by all of these hostesses, was expected to call on each one before she could assume her own place as a Washington hostess. If she made the grade, this Congressman's wife might look forward to a successful season in which she would lunch out every day, spend her afternoons visiting, dine out on all evenings except those when she must give parties herself, and on occasion go to as many as three or four dances in one evening. Not to mention teas and such things as benefit auctions for charities.

The houses themselves were built for parties, with the greater portion of the space being given over to vast reception rooms, even at the expense of small bedrooms. One of the most favored dances of the period was the German, which has since become known as the cotillion. And when Mrs. Congressman really scaled the heights, Mrs. James G. Blaine might invite her to a "kettledrum," which meant the most intimate and informal type of tea held by the social leaders exclusively for their friends. But pity the poor, uninstructed wife of an official who neglected to make a call in person on her hostess within three days after attendance at a formal dinner!

However, all of Washington was not made up of this Cinderella life. The wife of even a senior chief clerk, whose husband technically rated as an "official" and who was paid between $1200 and $2000 a year, could not afford a maid, let alone entertain. Her days were spent in shopping, sewing and housekeeping, except for the occasional clerks' dances in the hotels, where her position of seniority permitted her to be queen for the evening.

Government salaries may have been sinecures, but the clerkships did not lead to riches. The "unclassified" clerks, or common help, were paid between $700 and $1000 a year. The "classified" clerks, or those with special training, got from $1200 to $1800 a year. All of these were men. The only jobs open to women, except menial tasks such as scrubbing, were the copyist type, which paid from $60 to $75 a month, with employment on a sketchy monthly basis, not an annual one.

Butlers and cooks in the fine homes did much better. And, relatively-speaking, in 1947 they still did.

The bottom of the social scale, however, was not white; it was black. Here was a city within a city, some 50,000 persons who constituted a community that was an occasional object of charity but scarcely regarded otherwise. Of course there was Howard University, established as a public school without a "color line" immediately after the Civil War. The university touched, however, no more than a fragment of an uprooted society, still primitive in its understanding of freedom.

The colored Washington was for the most part a happy, shiftless black city that had brought from its more southerly origin the belief that all would turn out well in the end.

Here is a description of that "black society," as it was seen through the sympathetic, understanding eyes of Joseph West Moore in 1884:

"It has been said, apparently with a great deal of truth, that the capital has more intelligent, cultured, well-to-do people (Negroes) than any other American city. They have more prosperous churches, and literary, musical and social organizations, and the thrifty families give very pleasant entertainments during the winter. Excellent public schools, a fine college, opportunities for lucrative government service, are among the advantages provided for the colored people, and a certain number, by no means small, carefully and thoughtfully strive to a good position—to become well educated, well disciplined.

"But, looking at the race as it appears on the surface of Washington life, it must be admitted that many are improvident, unreliable, careless of the future, and are quite content if they have a ragged coat to wear, a crust to eat, and plenty of leisure to enjoy the sunshine. The small, dilapidated cabins occupied by this class in some sections of east and south Washington are really marvels of shiftless contrivance.

"Some of them are scarcely larger than 'sugar boxes' and yet they give shelter to a numerous family. About the doors of these fantastic, wretched abodes a half-dozen little curly heads usually may be seen playing.

"Near Lincoln Park lives a former slave of John Randolph, the haughty 'Lord of Roanoke.' His cabin was constructed by his own hands, and is comfortable in its way, although rudely fashioned and sparsely furnished. The old man, over whose white head many winters have swept, is held in high regard by the people living in his vicinity, and gains a living by telling fortunes and prescribing simple remedies for various ailments.

"He is an odd character, and when in the humor will describe his former life on Randolph's plantation in quaint, vivid and intensely interesting language. His clothes are patched and scarce held together on his bent and tottering form. Usually he sits crouching before his hearth-stone, rubbing his thin hands and muttering to himself, and he leaves his cabin only at rare intervals to hobble a few squares.

"The most ignorant of the colored people are very superstitious, and have great faith in charms and omens, and all of those singular things which came from the South and pass current under the name of voudooism. There are voudoo doctors of their own race, who live well, dress fashionably, and apparently make a great deal of money. They profess to cure everything, from a big wart to a bad case of what they call 'devilish conjuration.'

"They are very mysterious in their practice, and use many curiously fashioned articles which they claim possess cabalistic and astonishing qualities, and utter many strange words. They impress their patients by all sorts of tricks, such as manipulating snakes, whispering in the ear of a dog and pretending to receive an answer, and other silly actions. The credulous Negroes look with awe on these transparent frauds, and do many ridiculous things at the bidding of the 'doctor.'

"Around the great markets one will see among the hucksters whose little stands crowd all the walks a good representation of colored people of peculiar characteristics. The colored hucksters offer for sale twists of tobacco in the natural leaf, warranted to be pure Virginia weed; many herbs, barks and roots, and large quantities of flowers and 'garden sass,' and some have coops of live chickens and ducks.

"There are numerous women in the groups, wearing large bandanna handkerchiefs gracefully entwined round their heads, turban-like, but the colors are not as gorgeous as they were in the days of 'befo' the wa'.' The gaudy red and yellow bandannas are rarely seen, and it is said that the African dames of the markets have resigned to the aristocratic aesthetes these glowing primary tints. They call you 'Honey' in soft cajoling tones, but do not take as kindly to the salutation of 'Aunty' as they did years ago. They are an interesting study, and give a good deal of picturesqueness to the markets.

"On the wharves where vessels that bring oysters to the city from the Virginia bed deposit their cargoes, will be found daily thereabout the winter hosts of Negroes known as 'oyster-shuckers.' They buy oysters from the vessels and, seated in gangs, skilfully 'shuck' or remove the shells, shouting and laughing while they work. Then taking the bivalves in long-tin cans, they go over the city, calling clearly and loudly as they walk, 'Oys! Oys! Here's yer nice fresh oys!' Great quantities of oysters are sold by these vendors every day of the season.

"There are manifold other occupations followed by the black man, diligently seeking the honest penny. The workers have no fellowship with the idlers to be seen on all the thoroughfares—ragged, shiftless sons of Ham, who contrive to live in some unknown way, although they toil not."

Chapter Fourteen

BABY GIANTS—AND A BRIDE

No ONE PLANNED it so, but sometime during the 1880's and 1890's the White House shrank to a small island—important, true, but much less than its former stature—in the Capital and in the country. Washington could not have made it either small or large alone; it was small in Washington simply because the country found it and its occupants mediocre or less.

National policy continued in the name of the White House, but important policy was much more likely to be made in the home of James G. Blaine or of John Hay, the diplomatist and sometimes Secretary of State who began his public career as private secretary to Abraham Lincoln.

In this atmosphere the Diplomatic Corps became important. Weak as were the figureheads of Washington's power, the driving force of the United States was making the country a world power and Washington was its head and heart. This occurred despite rather than because of the accomplishments of the Presidents who succeeded Grant—Rutherford B. Hayes, with his pitiful fear of not being dignified enough for the Presidency; the ill-fated James A. Garfield; pompous Chester A. Arthur; and the 100-percent politician, Grover Cleveland.

The country was bigger than its men in public office, growing faster, swinging more authority in the world. There were foreign rulers who recognized this more clearly than the Presidents. By 1892 Great Britain, Germany and France, the three "world powers," indicated their willingness to accord equality to the capital at Washington by exchanging ambassadors instead of ministers.

This meant considerably more then than it does now, when virtually every country—all the Latin-American ones in particular—are accorded the dignity of ambassadors at Washington.

A minister is the representative of one government to another. In that position in Washington a diplomat deals with the Secretary of State. In the Nineteenth Century he was a messenger of his government, not qualified as a rule to make decisions. But ambassadors had a special position, literally as representatives on the spot of the heads of their governments. An ambassador of Great Britain, for instance, could awaken the chief of a foreign state in the middle of the night, demand to be seen, and there and then in a crisis state policy for his government.

Actually, there was a good deal of distrust in Washington of ambassadors. They suggested kings and royal families. Yet Washington felt the inferiority implied in having only ministers resident there. The ice was broken when the three "great powers" notified Washington that London, Berlin and Paris would be happy to exchange ambassadors with Washington. The change required an act of Congress, which was completed in 1893. Word of the law was cabled simultaneously to the three major European capitals, and new letters of credence started on their way to Washington.

Lord Pauncefoot, bewhiskered, shrewd and jovial minister of Great Britain, received his commission as ambassador one day earlier than his German and French rivals. Presenting his new credentials at the White House, he became the first ambassador in Washington, personal emissary of Queen Victoria to the President of the United States, and first dean of the Diplomatic Corps.

Washington was graduated to the rank of a "Capital of the first class."

If an invitation to dinner at the British Embassy marked the height of social prestige—and many persons counted it so—the Brazilian Legation was to many Washingtonians the most romantic spot among the foreign houses. Brazil was, long after our Civil War, the one country in the Western Hemisphere with a constitutional monarchy. Its legation was royal in every sense of the word—in etiquette, in formality and in its decorations. Furthermore, its ministers—selected to represent the then most important country in South America to the sprawling "Colossus of the North"—carried out the tradition started with the despatch of Father Serra to Washington early in the century.

Salvado de Mendoça, a famous writer in the Portuguese language, visited Washington in 1889 as a delegate to the first Pan-American Conference. At this conference the International Union of American Republics was created. Senhor Mendoça was the one republican on the Brazilian delegation, otherwise made up of royalists.

While the conference was in session word was received that a republic had been peacefully proclaimed in Brazil, following the death of King Pedro Segundo. Blaine, as Secretary of State, personally and publicly congratulated Senhor Mendoça, and it was only natural that in the following year Mendoça should return as Minister of Brazil.

A few years later, in Cleveland's second Administration, Washington rose one notch higher in the scale of international importance when Brazil and Argentina asked Walker Graham, who succeeded Blaine as Secretary of State, to arbitrate a boundary dispute between their countries. The Brazilian Minister was the Baron of Rio-Branco and the Argentinian Minister was Estabislao Zeballos.

Graham decided in favor of Brazil in 1895 after the Baron of Rio-Branco journeyed to Europe to produce an ancient "Map of the Cortes" to prove his point.

Continuing the Brazilian tradition was Joaquin Nabuco, who

became minister in 1905 and shortly afterward ambassador. A tenant of a house on Lafayette Square owned by Elihu Root, President Taft's Secretary of State, Nabuco became dean of the Diplomatic Corps, and intimate friend of Jules Jusserand, French Ambassador and poet, and Lord Bryce, British Ambassador and historian.

When sight-seeing buses drove by the Nabuco residence, the guides would shout, "Here lives the most handsome ambassador."

It remained, however, for tiny Switzerland, only country with a form of government older than that of the United States, to send a fighting veteran of an American war to Washington as its minister. This was Emile Frey, an ideologist who believed in acting on his beliefs.

For no accountable reason, Frey as a young man of 23 years of age journeyed from Switzerland to this country in 1861 to enlist in the Army of the North. In two years he rose in rank through combat from private to major, when he was captured. Released in 1865 from a Southern prison he returned home, entered public life, and in 1882 was sent back to Washington as the first Minister of Switzerland in Washington.

Besides these glamorous figures the occupants of the White House suffered by comparison. Yet Washington was maturing as a focal point of national as well as international interest. It had come into its own as the crossroads of the Main Streets of America. It yet reflected rather than controlled national interests, intrigues, debates and struggles. The time for control by Washington still was far distant.

Very few people slept in Washington on the night of March 2, 1877, only two days before the time when a new President must be inaugurated. No one knew yet who the President would be. True, there had been an election, marked by fist-fights and forensics throughout the country, and by the grimmer spectacle of soldiers with fixed bayonets guarding the polling places in the now completely re-enfranchised Southern States. It was clear to many observers that Samuel J. Tilden, urbane New Yorker and Democratic candidate for the Presidency, had won the greater number of the popular votes. But the Republicans, reluctantly grouped behind Rutherford B. Hayes, bearded, 55-year-old Ohio politician, had raised the cry that, "the Union should be governed by the party that saved it."

Hayes had been a brigadier general in the Union Army in the Civil War, a Congressman and Governor of Ohio. But the Republicans feared him because he was a liberal. In the homes of Washington's political leaders he was discussed in terms indicating that he was desirable as a President only because he had a chance of winning—and was less obnoxious than Tilden.

On the night of March 2nd, while Hayes rode eastward toward Washington, a special Electoral Commission, composed of eight Republican members of Congress and seven Democrats, decided that Hayes had won 185 electoral votes and Tilden 184. Hayes immediately was nicknamed "Eight-to-Seven."

There was nothing really wrong with Hayes, except that many persons laughed at his teetotalism in the day of universal drinking. Oliver Wendell Holmes later called him, in all sincerity, "His Honesty, the President." But the finagling that put Hayes in the White House depressed the United States, and properly brought the politics of Washington into disrepute.

Within his personal sphere, Hayes did not do badly. Nevertheless, it is a commentary on the Washington of his day that 10 years after he had finished his single term he still was trying to refute reports that he had made a profit by saving money from his salary while President.

"When we left Washington," he wrote in 1891 to a friend, "a story was started that I had saved about twenty thousand dollars during my term. This had an appearance of truth, and was perhaps derived from one of the family. But on looking up my affairs at home it turned out that a large part of this reduction of my debts was from collections on real estate sales made before

I left home. I left Washington with less than one thousand dollars."

Such were the issues that excited Washington.

When a green landau, drawn by matched mahogany bays, with carriage, harness and robe all flamboyantly initialed "C. A." deposited the portly, dandified new man before the portico of a completely refurbished White House many persons were reminded of the nationally published exclamation, "Chet Arthur President of the United States! Good God!"

The new President stepped into the White House in 1881 from the Vice-Presidency after his elected chief, James Abram Garfield, had been assassinated a few months after his Inauguration.

Arthur, who was more interested in gracious living in the Victorian sense, than in politics, gave to the White House a new social flare, a brief new leadership in Washington. But it was a limited one because he was a bachelor. Soon the city found in him more things to joke about than to admire. His rummage sale was more talked about than the first Civil Service law, which he signed.

Five thousand Washingtonians gathered on April 15, 1882, to bid eagerly for White House castoffs resulting from a thorough cleaning by Arthur—supervised personally by him—of the attic and the storerooms—some untouched since Buchanan's day. Reports had it that even a pair of Lincoln's pants were included in 24 wagonloads of things dumped into the auction. There was Jacksonian furniture, too, alongside Nellie Grant's bird cage, rattraps and all the moth-eaten furniture of the East Room. The sale netted $3,000 for the Treasury of the United States.

The re-doing of the White House completed, with a highly fashionable colored-glass screen installed in the main hall of the White House, Arthur set up an intimate dining room where he could entertain small parties at dinner. His table was set in what is now the family dining room of the White House. It was decorated, by Arthur's personal selection, with heavy gold paper and draperies of pomegranate plush. Crimson sidelights heightened the glow of the fireplace.

Arthur entertained much as Washington dines today. The dinner hour at last had been pushed back to 8 o'clock in the evening. It was indicative of the leisurely pace that had descended on the country that Arthur and all official Washington could sleep until 9 or 10 o'clock each morning. Frock-coated and bearded Congressmen, themselves often a little dyspeptic from late dinners, dropped into the White House for leisurely conferences any time in the late forenoon until 12; from 12 to 1 P.M., the President shook hands with any casual visitors or tourists who visited the White House. The day closed with the keeping of appointments in the office on the second floor of the Mansion from 4 to 5 o'clock. The leisure persisted for a long time.

It was from this setting that Grover Cleveland, in 1886, drove in his coupé, with Albert Hawkins handling the reins, to inspect on June 2nd the stone house known as Pretty Prospect which he had just purchased for $21,000 in the newly fashionable "summer district" on the Tennellytown Road.

Cleveland now was President, but on this day privacy was more important to him than the office of President. Cleveland had bought a "honeymoon lodge." He was to be married at 7 P.M. In his absence in the afternoon hours the parlors of the White House were packed with flowers, the chandeliers wreathed in smilax, and the mantels in the Blue Room, where the ceremony was to be held, were packed with red begonias, simulating fire.

This romance of the 49-year-old widower President and the 22-year-old Miss Folsom was a romance as intriguing to Washington as the one more than two generations earlier in which the Russian Minister figured. But there was less gossip aroused by it.

Frances Folsom was the daughter of Oscar Folsom, lawyer partner of Cleveland in earlier years. When Folsom was killed in a carriage accident in 1875 he named Cleveland as guardian for his daughter, and the girl "adopted" him as "Uncle Cleve."

The largest bouquet sent to a member of the graduating class at Wells College in 1885 was addressed to Frances Folsom. It came from the White House conservatory. In the fall of the same year, Miss Folsom and her mother were invited to visit the White House at a time when they could be guests of honor at the first of the formal receptions of the season.

The ultra-conservative Cleveland there and then proposed to Frances, but immediately added the suggestion that the girl go abroad with her mother for a year and think it over. She did. The result was favorable. When the Folsoms landed in New York on Memorial Day of 1886, Cleveland sent Thomas P. Lamont, member of his Cabinet, to welcome them and escort them to a hotel there. They remained away from Washington until 5 A.M. on the morning of the wedding day.

Now, however, Washington was in on the secret. There had been so many precedents to establish in order to handle this first wedding of a President in the White House. In a town now built on worship of protocol the groom-to-be, ordinarily the least conspicuous person in any wedding, outranked everyone. It would not do for his future mother-in-law casually to send out cards saying that she was pleased to announce that her daughter would be married on such and such a date to the President, etc. There might even be a political crisis involved.

So Cleveland took the direct line. On May 29th a White House messenger delivered notes to members of the Cabinet and a few personal friends; none went to the members of local "society" among whom Cleveland had few friends, none close. Each note, personally written by Cleveland, read, as follows:

"I am to be married on Wednesday evening at seven o'clock at the White House to Miss Folsom. It will be a very quiet affair and I will be extremely gratified at your attendance on this occasion.

"Sincerely yours—"

The red-coated Marine Band played Mendelssohn's Wedding March. The Rev. Byron Sunderland read the marriage ceremony, and Cleveland's brother, the Rev. William Cleveland, blessed the pair.

Cleveland's plans to spend a quiet honeymoon at his private house were upset by the curious in Washington. He fled to Deer Park, Md., but this visit with his bride was cut short because of the horde of tourists and curious who descended on the quiet town. The Clevelands hurried back to Washington, to a "society" where not one dowager knew the youthful bride.

Nevertheless, the change in the White House was almost instantaneous. Within a single season, disapproval by Mrs. Cleveland of the bustle put it out of fashion.

For a little while these things seemed to be more important than the political empire which Mark Hanna of Ohio had begun to weave for the day when, with William McKinley succeeding Cleveland, he would run the White House from a home next door to the one where Dolly Madison last reigned.

Chapter Fifteen

FROCK COATS AND PROTOCOL

1912.

It seemed now that Washington could, like the Buddhist monk, peacefully contemplate its navel and feel that all was well in the best of all possible worlds. The security of the Capital's position in the country and in the world could be taken for granted. Like the city's modern conveniences, the giant elms that bordered the avenues, or the solidity of the families whose mansions lined Connecticut Avenue and Sixteenth Street, the Capital was complete. Nothing could disturb the Capital's way of life or its established forms. So many thought. . . .

American enterprise, population multiplication and, perhaps most of all, the "man with the big stick" who had been a tumultuous President from 1901 to 1909, had accomplished this. The elderly strollers in Lafayette Park, who took their constitutionals in the hour before dinner, where a Blair or a Beale might be seen seated on a bench with Count Bernstorff, the German Ambassador, could congratulate themselves on quite a job completed by the government.

Washington was now the focal point for so many things that no longer could a single drawing-room conversation encompass the policy of the United States.

Labor and agriculture, each organized strongly, at last had achieved partial equality with the "money interests" that until a decade ago had set national policy. In international affairs,

Washington held its head on a level with London; was deferred to in many instances by Paris, Berlin and Petrograd. For the United States was no longer only a strong country. Washington was in effect the seat of an empire.

The powerful men of Washington had—of course, always with the greatest of good design—made countries and broken them. And if the sun did set part of the time on the American empire, the hours were diminished to very few in the day. One possession, the Philippines, was so far to the eastward that the rays of tomorrow's sun hit it only a few hours after the twilight of each today on the American Continent.

It all had begun with the Spanish-American War in 1898. The war was fought for a good cause, the freeing of Cuba. That had not been a very big war; nevertheless, in it the United States locked horns with Imperial Spain, and beat it in the Atlantic on the land and in the Pacific on the sea. Now, at official receptions, Admiral Dewey wore the gold-inlaid sword presented to him by a grateful Congress.

The hero of the land fighting, as history recorded, was not the winner of a very big battle, but a character whose personality eclipsed that of the generals. This, of course, was Theodore Roosevelt. He had only led a single charge up San Juan Hill at the head of a regiment whose commander, Colonel Leonard Wood, was not even consulted. This act, however, had mushroomed in successive events adroitly handled by its leader into massive history, in which people forgot that the parade of empire had been started by others.

President McKinley had led the country into war with Spain, winning of course freedom for Cuba, but also the annexation by the United States of Puerto Rico, Guam and the Philippines. All this occurred in 1898, coincident with annexation by diplomatic means of the Hawaiian Islands. In the following year, the United States impressed its force on the leading European powers by pushing through the open-door policy in China.

Theodore Roosevelt, succeeding the assassinated McKinley

in September of 1901, capped the foreign-expansion program first by acquiescing in a revolution in Colombia which created the "free" country of Panama, and then within a matter of days negotiating with Panama for the rights to build the Panama Canal.

Washingtonians still talked with pride of a dinner served in the White House on the evening of February 24, 1902. The event was the outstanding symbol of the United States's "place in the sun." It marked the beginning of Germany's effort to court American favor.

Emperor Wilhelm II had sent as a special emissary to Washington his brother, Prince Henry of Prussia. As the first Hohenzollern to visit the United States, Prince Henry carried Imperial greetings.

Secretary of State John Hay sat in the state carriage beside Prince Henry while they drove sedately along Pennsylvania Avenue, from the Union Station to the White House, between the lines of an honor guard composed of 1400 Marines. At the White House, the Marine Band played German music with heavy downbeats by the brass, while the Prince was presented to the Cabinet and the President's aides. Great crowds lined the streets and gathered in Lafayette Park to watch the show through the tall iron fence.

Then the young Prussian, wearing the full uniform and orders of an admiral of the German Fleet, entered the President's office alone, his rank being so high that none could present him to the President. The dinner served later in the day in the East Room was traditional for Washington—oysters, terrapin, canvasback duck and beef, with many wines.

This dinner, more symbolic than important, followed by only a few weeks the first official function given by Theodore Roosevelt, as well as an unofficial affair 24 hours later, both of which were landmarks in Washington life.

The official party was the New Year's Reception in 1902,

when President Roosevelt and Mrs. Roosevelt, who wore a dress of corded white silk, shook hands with 8100 people. The visitors gaped at the new President, at General Nelson T. Miles, Commander of the Army in the Spanish-American War, and at Admiral Dewey. Most surprising, there were refreshments, a new note in White House hospitality in recent years.

For the party on the following night, very limited, engraved invitations and cards of admittance were necessary to pass the portals of a new White House carriage entrance constructed in the east terrace facing the Treasury. This party was purely personal, but "personal" in the lexicon of Theodore Roosevelt meant a new blending of official and "old" Washington society. He was at home in both, a New York politician to the core and, by snobbish reckoning, the first aristocrat to become President since John Quincy Adams.

This was the debut of "Princess Alice," in whose honor there was dancing in the East Room and an elaborate supper in the State Dining Room. Her father toasted his daughter with wine poured into a golden goblet.

It was only four years later that "Princess Alice," standing in the East Room, took the vows of marriage to Nicholas Longworth, a rising young politician, wealthy and with impeccable antecedents, from Ohio.

Thus Washington as a city, smug as Philadelphia had been a century earlier, drifted easily on through the Administration of William Howard Taft. It was a little disturbed at Taft's democratic propensity of slipping around the Treasury to the Press Club on top of the Albee Building, at Fifteenth and G Streets, for an occasional poker game. But this, after all, was no more disturbing than the fumes of the automobiles that had come to make the evening strolls in Lafayette Park a little less pleasurable.

No political hostess could consider that she had "arrived" unless there was a seat especially reserved for her among the hundred or so chairs in the "family gallery" of the Senate for such great occasions as the opening of a new session of Congress, the delivery in person of a Message by the President, or a State Funeral. The highest mark of distinction among the nonofficial families might well be an invitation to occupy Galt's balcony on Pennsylvania Avenue for the great parades.

The distinction of a reserved Senate seat is self-evident. But the Galt invitation takes a bit of explaining, which may help to point up the fact that Washington now was something beyond a seasonal jousting ground for politicians.

In 1802, two brothers named Galt made an undistinguished entry into Washington and took a small shop on Pennsylvania Avenue among the peruke makers and tailors, where they hung out their sign, Galt & Bro. They had a flair for discreet design in gold and silver. As they prospered they developed connections in other world capitals which made them, after a century, international in character.

Galt & Bro. were, and are, the oldest jewelry firm in the United States. At least, no other similar company has seriously challenged their claim, still spelled after the English fashion, "Oldest Jewellers in America."

Long after the fashionable shops had started to move westward on Pennsylvania Avenue and on F Street, a little to the north, they clung to their original address. Their shop, with its easy chairs, was a quiet parlor where ladies might rest in the course of a shopping tour; their balcony on Pennsylvania Avenue was the highest vantage point (socially speaking) from which to view a parade.

By 1912, all of the Eastern American cities had flowered into "first families." They all had begun in the democratic tradition. And they were still democratic. Washington was not unique. It was the average, with probably a little more accentuation of the extremes because it had no middle class in the normal sense of the word. Middle class means business class, but a middle class is not founded alone on retail stores. It implies factories and forges and an assortment of enterprises involving competitive living.

Washington was not competitive, except in politics, and here the city merely got the end result of political enterprise. No native under the age of 60 had ever cast a vote, and the thousands of non-natives were interested only in the political contests in other places.

Washington was essentially political, with scrapings both of the cosmopolitan and the provincial. It was cosmopolitan in winter to a degree that exceeded any other American city, since it drew the brains and wit of every city—and through the diplomatic corps of all foreign countries—to its houses. It was provincial in the fact that no theatrical company, concert orchestra, opera or other type of creative art called Washington its home.

So, having no other primary interest, it made SOCIETY in capital letters its primary interest and wrapped this society around the banner of politics. An anomaly existed in the very fact that the old families who now looked down on politicians as a class of upstarts had shared almost entirely a political background in their origins. No one came to Washington originally for fun; they came because of election or preferment in political office, allowing for the rare exceptions such as the Galts.

At about this time Barry Bulkley, in a privately printed booklet, mentioned as prominent in non-political society such names as the Mays, Riggs, Carrolls, Beales, Hagners, Webbs, Rays, Eustices, Emorys, Goldsboroughs, Addisons, Blairs, Davidges and Campbells. He called them "the untitled gentry, so to speak, whose ancestors laid the foundations of the social distinction which Washington today enjoys."

The Carrolls, Eustices and Addisons, and possibly others, have a pre-Revolutionary flavor in local history. Most of them had been breeding Congressmen and Senators since the beginning of American history. But some of these old names were not really very old. The Blairs began with Andrew Jackson, and the

Beales stemmed from the old general who dug his gold from the soil of California.

For cosmopolitanism it was not necessary to look farther than the Diplomatic Corps, and see how it reflected the penchant of American families for marrying their daughters to proper young foreigners, or vice versa if you like. Mrs. Bryce, wife of the Right Honorable James Bryce, British Ambassador, was the daughter of a Boston merchant. Mme. Jusserand, wife of the French Ambassador, was born abroad but her parents were American expatriates. Countess Bernstorff, wife of the afterward discredited German Ambassador, was an American. Likewise Mme. Bakmetieff, wife of the Russian Ambassador. She was one of the two celebrated daughters of old General Beale, a sister of Mrs. John R. McLean, wife of the publisher. Señora Riano, wife of the Spanish Ambassador, had been Miss Alice Ward, of Washington. The Countess Moltke, wife of the Danish Minister, was the daughter of Nathaniel Thayer, of Boston.

That gives a good idea of the intermingling of political and family interests, to which may be added the fact that three consecutive Belgian Ministers up to this point had had American wives.

"It has been said," wrote Bulkley, "that in no place in the world does money count for so much or so little as in Washington. While it is true that a great statesman may find himself at a social disadvantage without adequate income, and great wealth, if united to official position, is able to attract attention and political following by lavish display and entertainment, yet, at the same time, money, unaccompanied by other advantages, is nowhere so helpless as in Washington, while talent, culture and engaging personality are always at a high premium."

We would express it in shorter sentences today, but that observation still holds good. So do some other things that Bulkley recorded on the days before World War I:

"But while money counts for little in Washington, family for more, and culture and good manners for much, official connection counts for about everything. Official influence is absolutely necessary to social leadership or even great social success.

"The social prominence of a few unofficial houses might seem to contradict this statement. It must be remembered, however, in this connection, that Mrs. Hobson is the sister-in-law of a former Vice-President; Mrs. Wadsworth is the daughter of a former Ambassador to Italy; Mrs. Leiter was the mother of the late Vice Reine to India; Mrs. Pinchot was the mother of Gifford Pinchot, the 'Fidus Achates' of the Roosevelt Administration, while Mrs. Harriet Lane Johnston was the niece of President Buchanan and was for the four years of his Administration the mistress of the White House."

And there you have it—for any year.

But dignify the story as you will with names, Washington also was the typical American town, grown large but nonetheless the average town in its thinking and living despite the exaggerations.

Any city of 25,000 persons in 1912 had its political clique, in which mingled leaders both from the moneyed set and the voters "across the railroad tracks." It had likewise its group of ladies who, applying their own iron-clad standards, attached more importance to the manipulation of a fork than skill in wielding mass influence. And it had, through every strata from the *grande dame* in the house on the hill to the slattern who scrubbed out the jail, its gossips.

The small city had its polite routine of morning calls, luncheons and whist clubs; its "at homes" and protocol for the government of conventions. Likewise Washington.

In the Capital, however, these burgeoned into a routine and mass operation that sometimes frightened the wits out of a small-town social leader who had worked for 20 years to assist her husband get a seat in Congress, and then found herself in

Washington. This woman discovered the end result of a situation in which democracy found its social ideas so confusing that for 100 years it had been piling conventions on the original protocol list drawn up by John Quincy Adams.

The "at homes" had changed hardly at all since 1884, but so much had been added.

Mrs. Newcome got her first thrill, after hiring cabs for a week to drop cards, to learn that there were occasions on which she could walk into any great house as a guest, without invitation, simply by trotting around to the "at homes." The White House hostesses had dropped these weekly receptions, but the leaving there of calling cards—her husband's and her own with right-hand corners turned down—assured at least one invitation during the season to tea.

But Mrs. Newcome soon ceased going, however, to the "at homes," unless she had some special fish to fry politically. She discovered that the hostesses, while gracious, never remembered her name from one week to the next and invariably chatted only with two or three old cronies grouped closely around them. Also, the Cabinet wives had stopped serving tea and cakes—there were no refreshments at all—by an agreement reached on the basis of understanding that since not all Cabinet members could be wealthy men they might as well cut out these fandangos for the crowds of common people.

The only time it really paid a newcomer to call on the Cabinet members was New Year's Day when these august personages, together with the Vice-President and Speaker of the House, held open house, with caviar, champagne, Virginia hams and all the delicacies of the market place loading down their tables. On New Year's Day, Washington en masse, and that included anyone with a clean collar and the desire, stopped first at the White House to shake the President's hand in the morning and then hot-footed it on the rounds of these other houses.

The free parties gave Mrs. Newcome enough to do and sufficient thrill of position possibly to satisfy her first season. By the time that she returned for a second season, her ideas had crystallized into a combination of desires, not to be described as "bigger and better" but "smaller and more select." This program involved, by the time of Taft's Administration, an oblique attack on the White House where, since Roosevelt entered it, social reputations were made or broken in the politest of ways.

Nothing mattered in society to the degree that the type of invitation one received to the White House did. The social hurdle began with the White House. Here matters were determined by a combination of wit and wiles on the part of Mrs. Newcome and the political prominence of her husband. How many speeches have been made in the halls of Congress with one eye on public reaction and the other cocked in the direction of attracting attention among the reputation makers and breakers of Washington? Headlines, won first in regional papers and afterward on a national scale, are as important to the politician's wife as to the office holder.

The assault on the White House began with attempts to wangle special invitations to the receptions. Of course, everyone with any position down to the middle of the office-holding groups automatically rated a bid to one of the receptions, but there was more to it than that—much more. The question was, first, which reception; second, which door of the White House one entered; and third, what came of it all.

There were, until World War II interrupted the routine, five basic White House receptions. These were, in the order of their appearance and importance, the Diplomatic Reception, the Reception for the Supreme Court, the Congressional Reception, and the Army and Navy Reception, and one for the other Departments. Approximately 1500 persons could be invited to each one. The New Year's Day Reception, abolished by Hoover, was a daytime catchall for which no invitation was required.

The Diplomatic Reception included all the members of the Diplomatic Corps and State Department officials. It opened with a fanfare by a bugle, and was in its costuming as gay as a Strauss operetta, with plumes and gold lace cascading down the court uniforms of the diplomats. The Supreme Court Reception was top-hole official. The Congressional Reception has been unkindly referred to as the "cats-and-dogs" occasion to get the rest of the official society, including all the Mrs. Newcomes, out of the way. The Army and Navy Reception found renewed brilliance in uniforms but the guests automatically came from the rank and file of the services: all Army officers on duty in Washington with the rank of Colonel or higher, ditto for the Navy captains and admirals—plus special guests of lower rank, and civilians.

No reception, however, was confined exclusively to the persons indicated by its name. And that was the challenge to Mrs. Newcome. Thus, the more prominent members of each "set" were invited to all receptions, as well as the bearers of distinguished names not in official life. It also became quickly evident to Mrs. Newcome, after attending her first Congressional Reception with her husband, and standing in line in overheated rooms, for an hour waiting to shake the President's hand, that she saw none of the wives of Congressmen with whom she most desired to visit.

These leading members of Congress, surfeited with receptions, probably had turned their cards over to their secretaries or some couple, distinguished at home but unimportant in Washington, who happened to be in town. It is wrong to do this, but the practice always has persisted.

Everyone in Washington except the White House got excited each year that the reception lists were drawn up. There, the job was done by the secretaries and ushers on as cold a basis as a market manager arranges fish and chops in the show case.

When Mrs. Newcome attended the reception, in an expensive hired conveyance, the carriage plodded for an hour through a waiting line to put her and her husband down at the east entrance. Then a corps of coat checkers and attendants hustled them through a long gallery under the terrace to the end of a double line. This line required another hour to wend its way up the staircase to the main hall and around the East Room, in serpentine fashion, to the entrance to the Green Room. While passing through this parlor, ladies pulled up their gloves, fluffed their skirts, took a deep breath and pulled in their tummies.

A minute or two later, at the entrance to the Blue Room, a uniformed aide asked the name, announced it to the President and he, with a smile fixed on his face and his hand cocked to avoid a crushing handshake, said, "Good evening."

Behind the President and his lady stood from 20 to 50 persons. These were the "palace intimates." If Mrs. Newcome's husband remained in office for 20 years, if she never made a social slip, if her husband's party remained in power—if all these things coincided, she might some day stand in that group. Then she could enter the White House receptions through the front door under the great North Portico and never need to stand in line!

But long before that, if Mrs. Newcome were enterprising, she could without too much difficulty wangle an invitation to one of the June garden parties. With a little more energy or pull, she and her husband might get invited to a musicale. But never, never would she sit at any dinner table, either in the White House or in any other home, above the plate irrevocably conceded to her on the basis of her husband's position.

Never were the laws of the Medes and the Persians more strict.

First in the seat of honor at all dinners was the Vice-President, then the Ambassadors, then the Chief Justice of the United States, the Speaker of the House, Associate Justices of the Supreme Court, the Secretary of State, Ministers, other Cabinet members, Senators, Representatives, etc. The President is left out of this list because he never "dines" out, except when the Supreme Court gives its annual dinner for him, or perhaps the Cabinet. Otherwise, even though he eats a meal elsewhere,

he technically is not a guest. The party must be entirely unofficial.

So aspiring hostesses never have tried to get the President for
a dinner party. It would show their ignorance. But an observer
in 1912 reported it thus: "To entertain a Vice President usually
marks the climax in the career of the ordinary social climber."

What happened in the White House after the official receptions? Generally, nothing. President Taft introduced the custom
of serving elaborate suppers, but President Wilson did away
with them, as did all of his successors until Mr. and Mrs.
Franklin D. Roosevelt put ice cream, cakes and coffee on long
trestle tables in the East Room.

Here is an anecdote of the Coolidge Administration, related
by a person who was there.

Mrs. William Vanderbilt was in line for Coolidge's first Diplomatic Reception. She was beautifully gowned, as were the
other ladies, and almost every man wore the gold-laced uniform
and carried the plumed hat marking the diplomatic dress of all
countries except the United States. Mrs. Vanderbilt turned to a
young man beside her, Henry Hopkinson, of the Canadian Legation, and asked if he could fetch her a drink of water. The
heat of the crowded rooms was very oppressive.

Young Hopkinson left and finally returned with a paper cup
filled with water from a cooler in the usher's office. He explained
that President Coolidge had ordered personally that glasses and
silver pitchers not be set out, as had been customary.

This would encourage people, the President thought, to
loiter and to waste time, and he had told the servants that he
simply expected people to shake hands with him and go along
home.

Chapter Sixteen

CROSSROADS

WORLD TRAVELERS were beginning to compare Washington with Paris, adding of course certain qualifications. Tourists arriving by the thousands each day from April to November climbed to the 555-foot tip of the Washington Monument to see the pride of America. This Capital City was the monument to American enterprise, the slightly smug self-created memorial of a country absolutely assured that it was insulated from all the world. . . .

There were faint rustlings from the hinterland of the world, the troublous Balkans, which sometimes kept officials of the State Department poring over reports in locked offices late at night. Henry L. Stimson, President Taft's Secretary of War, spoke weightily on the commitments of an Army which almost had ceased to exist.

But the Atlantic flowed as a broad moat to the eastward, and besides, since amicable arrangements with Great Britain over the Venezuelan quarrel a few years earlier, it was understood that two friendly fleets—British and American—always would keep European troubles from American shores.

Therefore, the visitors to Washington, and the great majority of the politicos and the ordinary residents, sat back to enjoy the city. It was a fair city, a leisurely meeting place. True, the Capital was hot in summer. But almost everyone who was "anyone at all" had the leisure to flee Washington in July and August. And withal it was a formal city, still Victorian and proud of its Victorianism.

Top hats and frock coats had been relegated in most other cities to trunks and closets, preserved in moth balls between Easter wearings and New Year's Day calls. But these were the uniforms of officialdom, *de rigueur* for every daytime occasion. President Roosevelt had been ultra-formal, decreeing formal morning clothes for all male guests invited aboard the Presidential yacht *Mayflower*, regardless of the heat of the day. President Taft had not cared, but fashion persisted.

Formal clothes were obligatory for calls on the President, for visits to the State Department and for daytime receptions. White tie and tail coats for men for dining out were essential. The man with political or social aspirations needed formal daytime and evening clothes far more than business suits.

Policies were made, and the high stakes of politics played, across damask-covered dinner tables, where liveried footmen served in discreet silence. More often than not the laws passed by Congress or the policies enunciated by Cabinet members reflected rather than affected the dinner conversations.

The home of Edward Beale McLean, a great new house on Massachusetts Avenue, covering with its service quarters a whole block, was possibly more important in national affairs than the home of any politician except the President.

McLean's wealth was virtually inestimable, supporting both the palatial city house and a country estate, "Friendship," on the heights north of old Georgetown, bordered by Wisconsin Avenue. He owned many properties, but his prestige and political power rested in the *Washington Post*. Inheritor of part of the vast fortune of General Beale, his father's father-in-law, he had married Evalyn Walsh McLean, the daughter of Senator Walsh, another fabulously wealthy miner.

At her formal parties, Mrs. McLean wore dresses that displayed to the best advantage the Hope Diamond. The McLean parties, most lavish of those given in Washington, recalled to old-timers of their day the "reign" of Kate Chase Sprague, with 250 guests often being entertained at lunch. No President in the White House ever could afford such fabulous entertainment.

In official circles probably the most opulent house was that supported on upper Sixteenth Street by Senator John B. Henderson, of Missouri, who built a red-brick, turreted structure, crowning a large hill and simulating a castle to the extreme degree of being surrounded by a moat. Senator Henderson had a fine taste for liquors and wines and his cellar probably was as valuable as his house. The cellar had a dramatic eclipse a few years later, in 1919. With the coming of prohibition, the Senator's widow, always an ardent dry, employed a large gang of men to break every bottle and pour the vintage wines down the sewer.

Somewhat to the northwest of the White House, in a still sparsely settled part of Washington, Secretary Stimson lived in manorial style on a 40-acre property which had existed in uninterrupted splendor longer than Washington had been a city. This estate was Woodley, created when Georgetown was an infant town with no more apparent future than that of any river port.

Georgetown itself was fallen into decay, its narrow streets and alleys scarcely occupied by any but Negroes and "white trash," with the notable exception of a few great houses. Tudor Place still held its proud position on a hill and Dumbarton Oaks was maintained by the Bliss family in feudal magnificence. But these were exceptions.

Downtown, the Blair family lived opulently but somewhat more modestly in the house their ancestor had bought when he came to Washington with Jackson in 1829. They made a shrine of the library of this house with one of the most valuable collections of Jacksonia in the world. On Jackson place, running up the western boundary of Lafayette Park, the Truxtun Beales perpetuated the spirit of the Decatur House. The former slave market was a high-walled garden. A touch of colonial days lived on in the illumination of its reception rooms and dining room with candles set by the hundreds into gleaming chandeliers.

From across Lafayette Park, the Decatur House was faced by Dolly Madison's last home, now safely preserved for quiet usage by purchase as quarters for the Cosmos Club.

Yes, Washington now had clubs, and a form of club life. In fact, the city which for 70 years had no club at all now had a short list in which membership meant some special distinction for a man.

No politician or millionaire, however well known, could achieve membership in the Cosmos Club simply for those reasons. The prime requisite for membership was distinction in letters, science or exploration. Here was an atmosphere in which Walt Whitman would have felt at home, had he not lived too early for the day when Washington would appreciate the fact that thought, however rebellious, is an achievement.

Two blocks west of the Cosmos Club rose the large brick building of another club where the requirements for admission were rather different. This was the Metropolitan Club, founded shortly after the Civil War as a quiet browsing, eating and drinking spot for men with kindred interests in official life. Diplomats, high-ranking members of the Departments, a handful of Congressional leaders and a sprinkling of native Washingtonians made up its membership. Among its founders were Generals William Tecumseh Sherman and Phil Sheridan. By 1912, this Yankee touch had been ameliorated by inclusion in the membership of a notable number of Southerners. The wounds of the Civil War had healed quickly in the Capital.

Then there was the University Club, patterned after such alumni organizations in all cities. On the outskirts of Washington—up in the region where open fields still divided Washington on the north from Maryland—sprawled the porticoed building housing the Chevy Chase Club, equipped to suit the taste of every type of wealthy sportsman, from tennis to hunting.

The clubs represented a development rather than a change in Washington's peculiar manner of life, the political life and the leisure that accompanied it. While the other cities of America bustled with business and expansion, with development of the "bigger and better" American way of life, Washington resembled Paris in its decent regard for the virtues of leisure as much as in its boulevards.

Here was the home of the two-hours-for-lunch club, of business hours so adjusted that a man could be free for social life by five o'clock and yet sleep late enough in the morning to make up for the rigors of a late dinner.

Clerks worked on more or less regular hours, but those of higher officials and the Diplomatic Corps were regular only in their brevity. A Cabinet member or an ambassador or minister was available in his office from 10 to 12 in the morning and from about 3 to 5 in the afternoon. Such was the pace of the secure old world.

When the Congress was in session, the House and Senate each met at noon and usually adjourned well before 5 o'clock. True, many members had morning chores in their offices and occasional committee meetings to attend but these did not interfere too much with the commonly accepted pattern of enjoyment of life.

Some members of the Congress occasionally indulged in the sport of walking from the foot of Capitol Hill to the Willard. This one-mile walk gave them good exercise, as it was to a great extent uphill. The more sporting members sometimes made a pool of bets based on an agreement to stop in each saloon and have one drink on the way. The survivor, or survivors, who could reach the Willard without becoming so "exhausted" as to require the taking of a cab collected the wagers.

The Congress itself had so few worries that most of the sessions were spent on legislation of pet projects—particularly those involving benefits for their districts. These had become known as the "pork-barrel" bills, because no Congressman dared go home after a session without taking along a metaphorical barrel of pork for his constituents.

A member might get a new post office or two for towns in his district, a special slice of highway funds to be spent on the so-called "post roads," or those necessary to delivery of the mail on which the Federal Government contributed a share of the cost. Or perhaps a bridge, or a new home for old soldiers.

Happiest of all Congressmen were those who were able to obtain legislation defining rivers in their districts as "navigable waters," with the result that the War Department henceforth would be responsible for improving them.

The tariff, "free silver," agricultural benefits and colonial policy usually dominated the debates of the Congress. But most Senators and Representatives counted upon perpetuating themselves in office by the delivery, a bit at each session, of the public patronage that keeps voters happy, and the jobs necessary to support their personal political machines.

That done satisfactorily, a member of Congress or an appointive official could walk the elm-shaded streets and avenues in the serene feeling that all was well in this capital of the best of all possible countries. In fact, the average official seldom was conscious of the seething forces in that world surrounding the North American Continent until some dinner invitation, issued on the mathematically exact basis of protocol, gave him a chance to rub elbows with the outer world in a foreign embassy or legation.

The foreign missions in Washington up to 1914 were for the most part small and inactive, maintained more for prestige than for work. Here was a capital with a minimum of intrigue and the least possible routine in its foreign relations.

The country's leaders held fast, thinking it the best course, to George Washington's injunction against "entangling foreign alliances," and there was little of the *opéra bouffe* atmosphere of intrigue. The "Big Five" in world affairs—for it now was a

"Big Five," consisting of Great Britain, France, Germany, Italy and Russia—sought rather to win advantage by the giving of an opulent and serene impression to the natives. For the most part, they succeeded.

Americans were flattered by invitations to any of these embassies, particularly a card from the Right Hon. James Bryce, British Ambassador and distinguished historian. The tourists gaped at the massive buildings housing the foreign missions. No longer was there debate over the propriety of kings and emperors sending personal emissaries to Washington. The Capital would have been incensed had this distinction not been paid to it.

It was a little impressive, too, to have these lavish bits of foreign lands scattered about the city, flanking the British Embassy on Connecticut Avenue or stringing along the upper reaches of Sixteenth Street. Children looked at them wide-eyed, and adults also, after hearing it explained how each foreign mission was a part of its own country, and not of the United States.

If a criminal fled to an embassy—although none ever did—he could not be arrested by American police without the express consent of the ambassador. A foreign diplomat was immune from arrest, except with the permission of his government. No civil suit could be brought against a diplomat.

Furthermore, the polyglot languages were fascinating, and any housewife doing her marketing might stop for a minute to listen to two Russian ladies speaking their own language to each other, or to a Brazilian and an Italian conversing in French. Incidentally, a social career in Washington made knowledge of the French language more or less obligatory. English had not yet become the common diplomatic language.

Many of the diplomats accredited to Washington spoke only French in addition to their own language, and some had the snobbish feeling that to speak English was a little vulgar. This was the period when a sprinkling of French in English conversation was considered *distingué* and not an affectation.

175

Thus the 40 guests who could be accommodated at the massive black-oak dinner table in the German Embassy might converse entirely in French, rather than in German, the language of their host, or in English, the language of their post. The Russians and Italians felt no offense when this was done, because few Americans ever had an opportunity to learn these languages in schools at home or to use them if they had.

So meandered life in Washington as the quiet Administration of President Taft drew to a close. There were strong political forces tugging at each other in the hustings, with Theodore Roosevelt finally bolting the Republican Party to form his own Bull Moose forces. Europe was boiling up in its old animosities, with France and Great Britain feverishly courting the Czar of Russia in an effort to maintain the balance of power that had existed since the Vienna Conference. Asia was well balanced, so it seemed, with the stalemate that followed the Russo-Japanese War.

Nonetheless, a few persons here and there could smell the new aroma of changing breezes. These knew it was the end of an era. Elsewhere in the United States, the Victorian Age had died some years earlier; in Washington it persisted.

But when it died it did not die gracefully. It expired in the harsh words of broken lines in the Republican Party, a resurgent victory for the Democrats, a new, although scarcely understood, outlook on things foreign.

Washington faced its first revolution since the days of Andrew Jackson.

Chapter Seventeen

POLITICS AND PETTICOATS

THE TALL, slightly stooped man with a beak of a nose brought to Washington its greatest revolution since Andrew Jackson rode in a triumphal procession under arches of evergreens above the Benning Road to take over the Presidency. The Civil War had swept over Washington, leaving it bigger and more important, but there was no such change as this, with the advent of Woodrow Wilson.

For Wilson was the end result of a revolution in the thinking of the United States. There could be no such revolution without the creating of imposing changes in this city. Washington more than ever was the meeting of all the Main Streets of America.

This new Washington won the approving nod of the still vigorous Oliver Wendell Holmes, as he received in his spacious home downtown the intellectual aristocracy of the Capital City. It won the immediate approval of William Jennings Bryan who, failing repeatedly in his own efforts to win the White House as standard bearer of the Democratic Party, bowed to a victor over "entrenched privilege." It won the approval of conservative Robert Lansing, the erudite statesman. It won the approval of the rambunctious Carter Glass, Senator from Virginia, and of Senator Oscar Underwood, spokesman for all that was most conservative in Southern politics. It even won the approval of Tammany Hall.

What was this revolution? More than anything else it was the desire for forward-looking change, something quite different from the desultory, insular feeling that had marked Republicanism for so many years, even in the Administrations of Theodore Roosevelt. Teddy himself had seen the handwriting on the wall, and run on a Bull Moose platform quite similar to Wilson's background, but no party division yet has created a President; as usual, Wilson won over Taft and Roosevelt because his party was solidly behind him.

He won in a manner that made possible more new centralization of power in Washington than had occurred since the Civil War heaped undreamed of authority on the sloping but unbending shoulders of Abraham Lincoln.

For a time, the face of Washington as a city was veiled by the new mantle of political change. Its important people were new figures to Washington, headed by the President himself, and those newly important men who, while they had lived in Washington, had been relegated prior to the Democratic victory to secondary posts. Faces changed all down through the hierarchy of officialdom and bureaucracy. Despite the operation of Civil Service, not many officials or clerks long survived the change in Administration.

The Capital again became, as it had been in the beginning, a Southern city. True, Mr. Wilson had been president of Princeton University and the Governor of New Jersey—a Yankee politician. Nonetheless, President Wilson was a native of Virginia—a historian whose writings stamped him as spiritually a Virginian, descending in a straight line of mental development from Thomas Jefferson.

To put it snobbishly, the Presidency again was occupied by a gentleman of the old school. He held a monumental mine of facts in his brain, and was distinguished by a hard and stubborn core of resistance in his thinking. Withal, these qualities were tempered by a decent appreciation for the flavor of good bourbon whiskey and a taste for the girly-girly shows booked regularly through the season at Keith's palatial new vaudeville theatre.

Washington liked a man like that. Of course the followers of Mark Hanna, retreating in their defeat to the Republican lair of Ohio, considered Wilson a dangerous man. Yet Senator Henry Cabot Lodge, of Massachusetts, senior Republican member of the Foreign Affairs Committee, was in those early days a firm supporter of the President. The great peace schism was as yet undreamed of as was the first World War itself.

Thus Washington had another hero—a President who accepted the vast reforms of Theodore Roosevelt, who in practice although not always vocally was "sound" on the basic idea of "protecting" American industry with tariffs, and who was perspicacious enough to back the hand of Senator Glass in the movement to reform banking by establishing the Federal Reserve System.

Neither was President Wilson obtuse politically. He recognized the need to encourage a younger generation of vigorous embryo party leaders.

Very soon after the Wilson Inaugural one such small politician, known only in New York for his espousal of reclamation as a member of the State Senate, was called to service in the "Little Cabinet." This young man became Assistant Secretary of the Navy, the post by which Theodore Roosevelt also had entered the Washington picture.

Franklin D. Roosevelt and his growing family moved into a large, comfortable house on R Street. This new Roosevelt addition to Washington maintained a cousinly but not close association with Alice Roosevelt Longworth and her husband, Nicholas, the young Congressman from Ohio. Longworth had gone far in the Republican affairs of Congress until the Wilson victory and the democratic capture of the Congress relegated him to a minority role.

As a particular mark of friendship toward Virginia, President Wilson chose a descendant of the cavaliers for his personal physician. To this post he named Dr. Cary T. Grayson, fashionable practitioner and a man of independent means able to maintain one of the finer stables in the near-by "huntin' and shootin' " country centering around Warrenton, Va.

Presidents also have the right to confer military or naval rank on their physicians. Sometimes these are chosen from the Regular ranks, as Herbert Hoover did at a later date when he plucked Captain Joel T. Boone from the Navy, and Franklin D. Roosevelt when he gave this post to Rear Admiral Ross T. MacIntire.

Mr. Wilson chose Dr. Grayson and gave this physician-horseman the reserve rank of rear admiral as a token of intimate friendship.

All of which would have been simple routine but for the sequel.

Like all venerable cities more than a century old Washington by now had its established society which hardly noticed the play and counter-play of political forces. These were the aforementioned "cave-dwellers." Some were very wealthy and some only well-to-do. But like all Southern cities the means behind a name meant little. What mattered was family background, "doing the right thing," and the maintenance of a decent reserve in private life.

Among these "cave-dwellers" was a plumpish, very pretty matron who had been married and widowed within the circle of Washington society. This young matron was a Bolling by birth, a Virginian. Her husband had been a Galt, member of the aristocratic jewelry house. Not wealthy, but comfortable for the day, Mrs. Edith Bolling Galt lived quietly within a close circle of friends. It is unlikely that she ever had met a politician in her life. The White House to her circle was no more than a symbol of the government where ladies left cards at intervals and perhaps attended a reception, but considered it hardly nice to do more.

Admiral Grayson long had been physician to Mrs. Wilson; his wife was a social "protégée" of the youngish matron. Admiral Grayson found himself facing the gravest responsibility held by any physician in America. His new "patient" was not an ill man; rather, he was extremely vigorous. He thrived on hard work. For two years, Mr. Wilson kept his own routine—work varied by an occasional automobile drive—and relaxed within his family circle, over which presided the wife he had married in 1885. But in 1914 the first Mrs. Wilson died.

The last thing on earth that Admiral Grayson proposed to be was a matchmaker. Much less had he any idea that he would promote the first romance in Washington involving a President and a completely nonpolitical member of Washington society. But in the President's new loneliness he suggested walking as imperative to maintenance of the President's health. And since walking alone is dreary routine, he added the suggestion that his friend Mrs. Galt, a lady of charm and reserve, also took daily strolls but had no companion in this exercise.

Wilson met Mrs. Galt and found her a person from whom he did not shrink, as was the case in most of his personal contacts. The diffidence that plagued Wilson through all of his life melted when he, a widower of 58, met this lady who held no opinions on politics and did not try to impress him with flattery. Soon Mrs. Galt was the President's frequent companion both on walks and on drives.

Within a year the President drove quietly on an afternoon to Mrs. Galt's house, and they were married. Both Mrs. Galt and the President wished the affair to be conducted in the strictest privacy. This occasioned a headache for the Secret Service, which must try to follow the President's wishes but above all is completely responsible for his safety.

The honeymoon involved arrangements for a private train to be boarded in the freight yards of Alexandria and a complex series of other arrangements at Hot Springs, Va., where the newly married couple went for a few days.

The time was yet far distant when Mrs. Wilson would become a political issue, as she sought to preserve a broken man from the annoyances of his office, or the sad days when they would move, this invalid and his still-youthful wife, from the White House to a mansion on S Street.

Mrs. Wilson and that house typify still another phase of Washingtonia. Here is a city where one can live privately despite gossip columnists and the impression that all life in Washington is existence in a gold-fish bowl.

The President's widow chose to live privately. One seldom found her name in the newspapers. She was sometimes seen at public gatherings, but she attended only those she had to because of the unwritten laws governing ladies who have once been prominent in official life.

Mrs. Wilson lives within the circle of a mixed group of friends, combining old Washingtonians with others who have simply grown old in Washington. One of her closest friends in later years was Mrs. William E. Borah—"Little Borah"—widow of the late Senator from Idaho who politically was once among Wilson's most implacable enemies.

Another intimate of Mrs. Wilson's once remarked that she liked to play bridge and did play frequently within her own circle. Nevertheless, although her investments apparently prospered, Mrs. Wilson declined to play for a stake higher than one-tenth of a cent a point—hardly a stake at all among avid and prosperous bridge players. Her reason—"Woodrow would not wish me to gamble."

There is, nevertheless, another side of the Wilson romance, without precedent or sequel in the Washington story, which constitutes a small drama unique in history. The city can be as cruel as the gossips of Broadway or the curtained and whispering tongues of any crossroads village.

It would appear at first glance that the union of politics in the form of the President and of the hard, permanent core of Washington "society" would constitute the ideal working arrangement for a country's Capital. It did not work out in that manner.

No sooner had the Wilsons departed on their brief honeymoon visit to Hot Springs, Va., than the gossiping tongues set to work. They played hard on the strain that Wilson had waited hardly a year in widowerhood to marry a young and attractive second wife. It was most convenient to the gossips to overlook the well-known fact that the President and Mrs. Galt had never consciously met prior to the death of the first Mrs. Wilson. They chose to disregard the absolute word of Admiral Grayson as to the facts about the meeting of the Wilsons.

Only guesswork can hint at the possible sequel in social reactions to the relationship between the White House and the old Washingtonians. Very soon the gossip was drowned out by the echoes of the war which began that year in Europe. War, however, was only a temporary deterrent to this contest.

President Wilson won re-election, became by his office the leader of the United States in the first World War and went on through his losing fight for the Peace Treaty to that day, September 25, 1919, when he collapsed at Pueblo, Colo. His private train rushed him back to the White House, where Mrs. Wilson embarked on the trying second chapter of her romance with this highly individualistic character.

Here it is important to note again that the White House, while a single building on a sprawling fence-enclosed lawn, is separated into two distinct parts. The residence and the office wing are connected by a covered terrace, but on some occasions they might as well be miles apart. This was such an occasion.

The office continued its routine, under the stewardship of Joseph P. Tumulty, Wilson's long-time secretary and latterly a nationally known lawyer, who came to the White House with Wilson from the New Jersey Capital. Tumulty ran the offices, seeing the long lists of callers, promising to transmit messages to the President, and either obtaining replies to questions or attempting to molify the more importunate.

At the other end of the terrace a broken old man spent his days in bed, or sitting wrapped in robes in a chair on an upper porch of the White House when days were fine. Occasionally he mustered sufficient strength to be helped into an automobile for a slow drive through Rock Creek Park.

Mrs. Wilson and Admiral Grayson assumed full responsibility that a wife and doctor in any home could and would assume. Nevertheless, the question arose—and it was not quiet gossip but a political shout—as to what line of demarcation existed between the private life of a President and his stature as a public figure. This is an argument that has arisen, in fact, in every Administration, although not in such dramatic circumstances.

Behind this struggle lay, as important background, the fact that no President perhaps had assumed so strongly the role of dictator over what constituted news of his public office and confidential information about his private life. President Wilson, long before his romance, had attempted to lay down the law that no news about his family should be printed in the newspapers.

The intention was understandable, but in a country where freedom of speech and freedom of the press rank alongside the guarantee of freedom of religious beliefs, such a rule is a challenge. President Wilson lost that battle, but he did not lose it gracefully. His attempt left a bitter reaction in Washington—official and otherwise—which quite likely contributed to his later political troubles.

In 1919 his seclusion in the White House led to critical question and serious challenges of his position. Rumors were circulated that he was mentally incompetent, and the question was raised in Congress as to the appointing of a commission to consider Wilson's fitness to continue in office.

These questions were indirect attacks on Admiral Grayson and Mrs. Wilson. The debate split the ranks even of the Cabinet and the group of officials most intimate with the White House.

In the end, Mrs. Wilson won. The argument has long since been forgotten. But it will arise again in some form. It is of interest primarily in the personal phase of the Wilson Administration because the contest lasted so long and became so bitter.

Chapter Eighteen

THE FACE OF WAR

In the early dawn of a summer day in London in 1914, Sir
Edward Grey, British Foreign Minister, stood in the window of
his office looking out on a misty street. Beside him was the Hon.
Arthur C. Murray, his Parliamentary Secretary. Sir Edward
watched the gas street lamps of London being dimmed by lamp-
lighters. Parliament had just approved the declaration by His
Majesty's Government of war against Germany.

Sir Edward turned to Colonel Murray and remarked, in a
historic aside, "The lights are going out all over Europe; I wonder if we shall see them lighted again in our lifetime."

The scene was described afterward by Murray in a letter to
his distant American cousin, and close friend since boyhood.
The cousin was Franklin D. Roosevelt, by now entrenched as
the precocious young Assistant Secretary of the Navy and bat-
tling, as had his predecessor 16 years earlier (Teddy Roosevelt),
for the building of a fleet for defense.

Murray doubted seriously if in his lifetime those lamps
would be turned on again in Europe. Something of his feeling
appeared to be in Roosevelt's mind. Possibly because of this
feeling, Wilson thereafter had no more faithful disciple than
the young Assistant Secretary of the Navy.

While London girded for war, Washington divided into two
camps that fought each other quietly with daggers rather than

openly with clubs. On the surface there was no contest, as for a while social life quickened to a new pace. Attention drew away from Europe to Mexico where a "punitive expedition," led by the dashing youthful Major General John J. Pershing, chased Pancho Villa into the remote deserts and made possible assumption of rule in Mexico by Huerta.

This contest which began in Washington in 1914 was marked outwardly only by the resignation of William Jennings Bryan as Secretary of State and the appointment of Robert Lansing to succeed him. From Texas came the taciturn, lean Col. E. M. House to act as unofficial and unpaid eyes and ears of the President in most of the capitals of Europe.

Nevertheless, these surface changes were not as important as the new forces that came into play when the United States faced its first great decision in the realm of world affairs. The European war of 1914 made Washington the head of a reluctant world power.

Here was the birth and development of another facet of Washington life that is peculiar to the Capital alone. Whether the country likes the fact or not, it exists and probably always will exist. It is the existence of government within government. And if Washington were wiped out in a fraction of a second by an atomic bomb, the same dualism would carry over into the next seat or form of government of the United States.

Sometimes key figures in these factions become nationally known, but they symbolize rather than control; their power comes from some small faculty that makes them trusted by elected officers and by the groups for which they speak. They are the "king's barbers." So citizens have heard from time to time of such men and have scarcely ever understood the relationship that existed—Gallatin in Madison's Administration, James Preston Blair in Lincoln's time, Colonel House with Wilson, and most recently Harry L. Hopkins in the service of Franklin D. Roosevelt.

Each in his day was variously described, according to the

source of description, as the President's wise man or the horned devil of secret negotiations and nefarious deals.

The important thing about these figures is that they happen to be simply individuals who play the political game outside of the ranks of officials chosen by local machines to run for elective offices. They have powerful backing before they achieve prominence. Their actions often are more important than the surface operations of government, because they usually direct the course toward which a bumbling Congress finally marches. On the whole they are no better and no worse than the elected office-holders.

These private leaders loom large in Washington, and it was they, and not the debates in Congress, who directed a long campaign behind the curtain of political secrecy which eventually made the United States an enthusiastic participant in war in 1917. Of course there was the incident of the sinking of the *Lusitania*. But incidents always occur at times of dramatic decision. Without the background there would be no importance attached to any such incidents, with the exception of the monumentally stupid blunder of the Japanese attack on Pearl Harbor in 1941.

Washington invented a new term in 1916—"enforcing peace." This was the idea of leaders who hoped the force of American disapproval could stop the war in Europe. Others among them, however, considered the name a good smoke screen for preparation to conceal participation in the war, while sugaring the plan sufficiently to make it palatable to the country as a whole. There was an organization, cutting through all political ranks, known as the League to Enforce Peace. Such was the interplay for interest in "enforcing peace" that the league, ranged solidly behind President Wilson, had as its president William Howard Taft, the genial ex-President of the United States whose campaign for re-election Wilson had defeated.

The existence of this league, combined with the high-swept interest in the political campaign in which Wilson in 1916 was fighting for re-election, caused all of the United States and much of the world to look toward Washington on the afternoon of May 27, 1916.

The League to Enforce Peace was meeting in Washington that day. Mr. Wilson, already realizing his mistake earlier in saying that the United States was "too proud to fight," grasped the political opportunity to invite the league delegates to the White House. Arranged in seats of honor on the South Portico, these delegates rubbed elbows with a group that included almost all of the leading figures in Washington of that day.

There was suspense in the public mind about what Wilson would say, but the leading members of the league knew quite well what was in his speech. The whole gathering was a masterpiece of timing. It was not the first, or the last, time that the Capital City had been used as the sounding board to suggest high strategy on which political leaders already were agreed, with the hope that the sonorous echoes would call up massed public support.

President Wilson finally walked to the speaker's dais temporarily set up on the portico. He adjusted his spectacles and, in the hushed silence of the waiting crowd, opened the loose-leaf book containing his manuscript. This one was clearly typed, transcribed after he had written and re-written his notes in the shorthand he had used all his life. It was not written carelessly on a sheet of note paper, like the 400 immortal words of the address Lincoln had uttered almost two generations earlier in dedicating the cemetery at Gettysburg.

Wilson started to read and, after a preamble, finally reached the crux of his peace program:

"First, that every people has the right to choose the sovereignty under which it will live. Second, that the small states of the world have a right to enjoy the same respect for their sovereignty and for their territorial integrity that great and powerful nations expect and insist upon. And, third, that the world has a right to be free from every disturbance of its peace that has its origin in aggression and disregard of the rights of people and nations."

The news correspondents, whom Wilson despised, wrote furiously, and messengers hurried with the short "takes," or fragments of their stories, to the telegraph offices. Wilson, standing stiffly erect in the frock coat demanded by the occasion, a historian highly conscious of the history he was making, went on to propose a peace-enforcement method already sponsored by the league itself:

". . . an universal association of the nations to maintain the inviolate security of the highway of the seas for the common and unhindered use of all the nations of the world, and to prevent any war begun either contrary to treaty covenants or without warning and full submission of the causes to the opinion of the world—a virtual guarantee of territorial integrity and political independence."

On that day—that warm, bright May 27, 1916—all the dignity of Washington's broad avenues and its majestic elms, all the political events written into its past, and the good and the evil of its past political history joined as background for one absorbing, overwhelming fact.

Washington became a voice in world affairs.

It was not quite so clear then as now. There was a bitter political campaign still to be waged, and a contest over the Presidency so close in November that a full day and night elapsed after the polls were closed before it was certain that Wilson had defeated Charles Evans Hughes, the Republican candidate. A public, knowing no more of what transpired in Washington than the thin surface of the news, had swayed the narrow margin of victory probably, if there was a single reason, because of the slogan of Wilson's backers, "He kept us out of war."

Slogans generally hold good in politics for about the same length of time required for the weather to fade the brilliant ink used in printing circus posters.

So it was with "He kept us out of war." And here was a reminder of the power of on-piling events in Washington which so often have shaped the destiny of the United States before the Congress, presumably the decisive force in popular government, had cast a single vote.

On April 6, 1917, the Congress—with only six dissenting votes in the House—voted for a declaration of war against the Central Powers. So Congress in the end had the say about going to war. But that decision was inevitable because of the forces clustered in Washington which led up to the vote. The great question of democratic government, as exemplified in the quiet Southern city of Washington, is whether democracies actually make policies or whether policies are forced upon democracies.

Here was a graphic example of how Washington, usually the common denominator of the United States, differs from all other cities. The salesmen of ideas live there.

The Right Honorable Cecil A. Spring-Rice, British Ambassador from 1913 to 1918, was castigated during, and very generally after, the war for having pulled the wool over the eyes of Americans and "dragged" a supine American Government into the European war on Britain's side. Actually, Ambassador Spring-Rice did not need to raise a finger. He was too well trained in diplomacy to do anything that might prejudice the current running in favor of the British Isles.

By the time Spring-Rice attended the second Inaugural of President Wilson, on March 4, 1917, events had almost completely run the course he would have directed them to run had he been able to do so. Washington was war-minded, not because of the President, not because of Congress, but because the United States, moving ponderously, a sprawling giant, was beginning to get its hackles up. The Capital City at last could reflect publicly what had been the confidential conclusions at its dinner tables for the past two years.

On this little stage was being played a succession of acts that burst with renewed dramatic effect on the United States.

On January 16, 1917, von Bernstorff, the once highly popular Ambassador of Germany, handed to Wilson a message from the German Kaiser stating that unrestricted submarine warfare must be inaugurated even if it meant a break with the United States.

Six days later, President Wilson, hoping against hope that he could avoid a fighting war, outlined in a special speech to the Senate a new proposal for mutual collaboration between the major powers that he hoped would lead to peace. The German answer was another message, delivered personally to Wilson by von Bernstorff on January 31st, in which the Kaiser said that unrestricted submarine warfare would be the future course of German action. There would be no more neutral rights for shipping.

Simultaneously, State Department employees working in locked rooms were decoding messages proving irrefutably that von Bernstorff, despite his American popularity and his American ties through his wife, was directing an organization in Mexico with the quixotic idea of mounting there an invasion of the United States.

So on February 3rd—and remember that Congress had not yet voted on any war measures—von Bernstorff was given his papers and orders to leave the United States, and Ambassador James G. Gerard was summoned home from Berlin.

The Inaugural on March 4th was rather an anticlimax. There was the ceremony of administration of the oath on the East Terrace of the Capitol, always the scene of such ceremonies since Chief Justice Taney swore in Lincoln. There was a parade with massed bands and marching clubs from all the cities of the United States.

Little more than a month later, the United States had a Capital City such as no founding father ever had envisioned. There was no comparison possible with anything that had occurred before.

In the Civil War, Washington had become an army headquarters, submerged in the overflow of uniforms of corps marching to war or preparing to defend the Capital itself. Now Washington became the staff headquarters of the greatest mobilization of forces yet undertaken in history—the raising of armies and the equipping of them, with preparations to move millions of men across the Atlantic, so recently considered an impenetrable barrier either to invasion or conquest.

All that was "normal" in the city's life ceased to matter. Dinner-table conversations turned from speculation about the future into cold, hard analyses of plans. General Pershing departed for Europe with a large staff to see how modern wars were fought. General Peyton C. March, as Chief of Staff, began the mobilization of an anticipated Army of more than 3,000,000 men.

Bernard M. Baruch, the youthful and fantastically successful financier, closed his New York house and Hobcaw Barony, his vast South Carolina plantation, and moved to Washington to assume direction of the production of all munitions. Daniel Willard, president of the Baltimore & Ohio Railroad, took over, at Wilson's order, organization for war of all the nation's railroads. Julius Rosenwald took on the job of clothing the Army and Navy about to be created. Herbert Clark Hoover was handed the job of planning for fullest conservation of food in wartime.

In the Navy Department, like the War Department, rapidly sprawling out of peacetime headquarters in the now venerable State, War, Navy Building, a young man got as much responsibility and work as even he, in his ambition, desired.

The older laws that existed in 1917 stipulated that all "procurement" for the Navy should be the responsibility of the Assistant Secretary of the Navy. Of course the admirals heading the various bureaus—Ships, Navigation, Communications, etc. —made the plans and recommended what should be done. But the decisions were made in the end by the assistant secretary.

A far more obtuse man than F.D.R. would have seen in this job the opportunity not only for service but for future political reward. He saw both clearly.

Important, however, as were the personalities, and the jobs they did, the greater fact was that Washington had entered upon a new phase in the history of the United States. It was the Capital of the country with a capital C.

Here was the birth of centralization of authority, the setting of precedents for "emergencies" that would provide the background for revolutionary changes even in peacetime a few years hence. For the first time, government was the supreme force. And before the war should end there would be 900,000 civilians governing, regulating and ordering the affairs of the country in the name of Washington.

Chapter Nineteen

NORMALCY

WARREN GAMALIEL HARDING coined the phrase, and his two successors tried to live up to it—worshipping a god which never existed . . . "Back to Normalcy!"

What is normal? In most men's minds it is the recollection of the most carefree period they have ever known. Nowhere in the United States were more heads concealed, ostrich-like, from the reality of passing events than in Washington. If you could not face a question, you disregarded it. Then everything would be normal. This was the voice of Washington in the 1920's.

From 1920 to 1932, Washington reached a point of political consciousness hardly less high than it was in Grant's Administration, and a social level which represented the last hang-over of plushy Victorianism. It was the overgrown village where a tail coat and white tie were more important than an idea. All but the most robust citizens of the radical States realized that there was no greater risk to political careers than questioning the stability of established things.

Senator Henry Cabot Lodge, leading his Foreign Affairs Committee in the Senate and dominating a large unofficial social group in his opulent home, had won the victory of isolationism. He had proved, to the satisfaction of a solid majority of Americans, that America's primary interest was to withdraw inside America. The test had been the killing of ratification of the Covenant of the League of Nations, in which the great argument revolved around Article X—that statement of principles

197

which Wilson so recently had enunciated with the whole-hearted approval of the League to Enforce Peace, headed by William Howard Taft.

Then there had been the Naval Limitation Conference of 1922, called by Secretary of State Charles Evans Hughes, under the titular leadership of Harding. Rather than limiting, it had apportioned power. Then the Congress, in an economy mood, had withheld appropriations to give this country the "five" place within the 5-5-3 ratio assigned to Great Britain, the United States and Japan.

As a final gesture, the Congress enacted, and President Hoover approved, the Smoot-Hawley Tariff Act which more effectively than any other policy slammed the doors of the United States at its borders against the efforts of American and foreign businessmen to build up friendly trade with our neighbors.

Through all of this Washington had a quiet dozen years, so serene as to suggest the city a century earlier rather than the bustling twenties in which other cities burgeoned with the amplitude of inflation. There were half a dozen impressive buildings erected in downtown Washington, notably the National Press Club Building and the Washington Building. These changed little, however, the general pattern. They merely replaced older structures and, conforming to wise height restrictions that keep private structures from overshadowing government buildings, they did not rank as skyscrapers. The shops never kept pace with the city. Few restaurants were either good or successful.

Where Washington really grew was in its residential district. Transient as is the city—it long ago became known as "the city of good-byes"—it is a city of homes. People live in their houses and in apartments. In the late twenties Washington's theatre, not counting motion pictures, shrank to the plays that could be accommodated in a single house. Tradition lived, however, in the fact that the surviving theatre was the latest in the series of National Theatres.

Supper clubs occasionally essayed their luck in Washington, and while a few that were little more than quiet restaurants survived, the Capital never had a night club on the New York pattern. People simply were not interested in them. The same held true actually for the theatre. Out of so many people, most plays with or without merit usually played to good houses, but on Broadway the Capital was known as a city that "sits on its hands."

On the other hand, should all servants finally go to other jobs, it is a safe bet that the last chef preparing a superlative dinner for a private party will be working in the kitchen of a Washington house. This is the city of private living and private entertaining, and one where private parties frequently equal and often excel the quality of the Embassy parties.

In the 1920's Washington finally reached its height as the tourist's mecca. The tourist coming to Washington found plenty to see, if his feet held out. There were the public buildings existing much as they had prior to 1900; these included the well-known Library of Congress, built shortly after 1880, a monumental structure of stone and pillars in which an effort was made to give due attention to every phase of art and letters.

The buildings now included other institutions built primarily as monuments to the donors. The Corcoran Gallery of Art, having outgrown its original building, was housed in a permanent, graceful building of marble and bronze on Seventeenth Street, across from the State Department. Far to the east, beyond Capitol Hill, was the Folger Library, contributed and built with funds left under the will of Henry H. Rogers, the oil magnate, with its unrivalled collection of Shakespeariana, and within its walls a complete and full-sized reproduction of the Globe Theatre in the London of Shakespeare's day—a setting for annual play festivals.

A sight-seeing bus ride was incomplete without a trip around the Tidal Basin to see the thousands of Japanese cherry trees, presented to the United States as a gift from Japan in the Administration of President Taft. The blooming season for these trees, in April or May, was nationally heralded by the tourist agencies and brought anywhere from 500,000 to 1,000,000 visitors to Washington in the spring season. Washington was a tourist's paradise with individuals and conducted parties arriving literally in droves throughout the year.

To its residents Washington was anything but a paradise in summer. Most of the old-timers welcomed back the routine that enabled the well to do and the higher officeholders to find excuses to abandon the city from the middle of June to October. Until 1930, the British Government officially endorsed this view. It gave to its diplomatic staff in Washington the so-called "hill allowances" paid to public servants in India, special sums to permit the taking of summer homes in the hills.

The joker in the British system was that in 1930, when the embassy site was changed to a hill on Massachusetts Avenue the allowances were cut off, even though every officer except the Ambassador continued to live in the same houses they had occupied before.

In a way, therefore, Washington had changed very little from the form it held when Mrs. Smith was part of the community complaining about the necessity of leaving 500 cards on other residents. There simply was more of it, and the center of gravity had shifted.

No longer were there farms dotting the area north of the Capitol. The famous old farm, Sidney, had become part of the Soldier's Home, and otherwise the farms were divided into a gridiron of streets broken into 50-foot lots occupied by neat, small houses.

Capitol Hill was unchanged from the days when Governor Shepherd had run the streets around it, but the plaza between the Capitol and the Union Station was occupied largely by barracks built of wood and stucco in 1917 to house hundreds of "government girls," or clerks hired in the war expansion.

Westward from the Capitol, there was a green expanse of park, with a massive Civil War memorial dominating it, and flanked by the greenhouses of the Department of Agriculture. But Pennsylvania Avenue on the Capitol end had degenerated to a sorry state.

From Capitol Hill there extended for several blocks a slum known as "Chinatown," but occupied more by bowery-type characters than by the Chinese—junk shops, hotels that let rooms at a dollar apiece and were not particular about nighttime transients, and by shady little stores concealing speakeasies.

The older business section started at Ninth Street, marked by cheaper department stores and general shops, with the exception of Galt's, which still held forth at its original location. Here for a while, too, survived Harvey's Restaurant, where it had been established about 1850, but in the late twenties it moved over to Connecticut Avenue. In the next decade, Galt's surrendered and joined the trek westward to a shop on Thirteenth Street, between F and G.

Dominating the downtown hotels, despite many newer rivals, was Willard's, still in the possession of the original family, and insisting in its name, as it still does today, that it is the New Willard, although its current building dates from 1904. Willard's still held the monopoly on state dinners too large to be held in private homes, although its banquet menus were sadly crippled by a strict observance of the prohibition laws.

The Willard was at that time the exclusive site for the two annual Gridiron Dinners, and the annual dinner of the White House Correspondents Association tendered to the President. Here the Cabinet gave its annual dinner for the President. State societies, made up of residents of the States, held their annual affairs there. The Order of the Caribou elaborately celebrated in the Willard ballroom each year the recollections of the officers who had served with the Army in putting down the Philippine Insurrection.

Vice-President Curtis, who served with President Hoover, once estimated that in his capacity as official diner-out for the Administration he ate at least forty dinners a year in the Willard. The Willard housed Calvin Coolidge when he was Vice-President.

The smaller Washington Hotel, in the same block, opened first as a hotel exclusively for women but soon turned into a general hotel, caught up with the Willard a few years later when Vice-President John N. Garner made it his Washington home for eight years.

East of the Willard had been built on Twelfth Street the very large Raleigh Hotel, but it never captured the traditional Willard business. Neither did the Shoreham, on H and Fifteenth Streets, newer than the "New" Willard, but since razed to make way for an office building.

The building boom of the twenties saw three large new hotels erected along Connecticut Avenue. Most prominent of these was the Mayflower, at L Street, while the Wardman Park and the new Shoreham arose in enormous piles of brick a mile or more farther north. But there is something descriptive of the character of Washington in the fact that, prior to the "modern invasion" of Washington with the New Deal, none of these newer places ever achieved the distinction of a handful of apartment houses so old that in other cities they would have been torn down.

Even in hotels and apartment houses in Washington the distinction of the building depends upon the political position of the tenants. Thus the rambling old structure at 2101 Connecticut Avenue held its head high in the twenties with the reputation that at one time it housed four Supreme Court Justices, plus a distinguished array of Senators including Borah.

Willmott Lewis observed in this period that "everyone worth knowing in Washington lives within a mile of each other." Lewis was qualified to speak—an Englishman, correspondent for the London *Times,* and better informed on Washington than most Americans. Even then he had won the sobriquet he still bears as "Britain's unofficial ambassador."

By the expression "worth knowing," Lewis (in more recent years Sir Willmott) used the understandable snobbish standard of describing people of interest in Washington—officials, diplomats, perhaps writers, and the scientific and judicial personages whose interest brought them to Washington. For Washington now was made up of considerably more than politicians.

A large new building on Jackson Place, just south of the Decatur House, housed the Brookings Institution, a research foundation set up by a St. Louis man which rivals the Carnegie Institute in its factual studies. The Chamber of Commerce of the United States had erected palatial headquarters on the north side of Lafayette Square, only a block from the White House, and the major labor unions had their own establishments here. Dr. Gilbert Grosvenor had built the National Geographic Society into an international organization.

There were more rich homes in Washington than in any other city in the United States, because few persons without private means came to Washington in a political capacity. Men appointed to the Cabinet were expected to live on a scale that made their salaries of $15,000 a year little more than incidental expense money. It was a brave man who would run for a seat in the Senate or the House and expect to make a go of living on his salary.

One "rugged individualist" in the halls of Congress, from a financial standpoint, was Representative Fiorello H. LaGuardia, the holder since of many greater distinctions. While in Congress, collecting a salary of $10,000 a year, he lived in an apartment the writer visited many times, which rented for $65 a month. LaGuardia had to spread his income over the maintenance of an apartment in Washington and one in New York. There were income taxes to pay, political contributions of close to $1,000 a year, many charitable contributions which members of Congress must make as a matter of course, and frequent trips to New York beyond the limit of two a year for which the Government pays.

There were, of course, Congressmen who accepted everything from free merchandise to stock-market tips—anything short of bribes—to help pay the expenses of their office, but never as many of these as one would imagine.

More typical of the officeholder of the twenties was Harry B. Hawes, Senator from Missouri. Senator Hawes made his fortune practicing law in St. Louis and then invaded the field of politics. His salary as a Senator did not pay the cost of his annual hunting and fishing jaunts; it would hardly pay for the porcelains and jade figures he added each year to his notable collection.

Hawes founded a unique society that expired with his advancing age, but which rated at one time as among the most exclusive in Washington. He called it the "Houn' Dog Club" in memory of the Ozarks in Missouri. Only Missouri politicians were eligible. Once admitted to membership, those in the select circle could look forward to three or four evenings a year in which they would sit down among approximately 50 other Houn' Dogs to a superlative dinner, usually of game shot by Hawes. Afterward they spent the evening playing poker under house rules that permitted each one to buy five dollars' worth of chips but required that a member retire from the game if he lost his initial stack of chips.

The "heart" of Washington, from the standpoint of the sight-seeing visitor and the resident alike was that same little area in which Governor Shepherd pioneered by opening the streets— west of Sixteenth Street, from Massachusetts Avenue north to Kalorama Road, running along the boundary of Rock Creek

Park. Most of this triangle is known as Kalorama Heights. At the peak of the rise of the ground, breaking little Bancroft Place in the middle, stands another Octagon House, this one constructed of wood and painted white, the original house dominating the whole wooded estate of Kalorama.

When the British Embassy moved in 1930 out on Massachusetts Avenue, into a Georgian structure of such barracks-like proportions that it was referred to as the "maternity home," it signalled the death of lower Connecticut Avenue, below Dupont Circle, as a residential district. The move was promoted by Harry Wardman, one of Washington's most spectacular boom-time real-estate operators, an American of English background. Wardman traded the new site for the British Embassy, and constructed the great building, facing a private garden covering six acres, in exchange for the old Embassy site, now a filling station.

Very soon thereafter, Ambassador Saito of Japan constructed for his country a new Embassy near the British, one which many persons consider the most beautiful building in Washington. It is of gray stone, two stories high, facing a green lawn on the Massachusetts Avenue side and having a large balcony over-hanging a cliff above Rock Creek Park at the back.

The reaction to the Japanese invasion of Manchuria in the 1930's soon pared down social life there to a minimum, because of ostracism of the Japanese. But this building will sometime find a suitable use after the Mixed Commission, handling Japanese occupation affairs on the Washington end, has finished its task. Its silk-covered walls, tapestries and carved furnishings are memorable.

The French Embassy moved at this period to a great Norman château built by a "copper king" on Kalorama Road. Mussolini in the heyday of his power ordered the erection on upper Sixteenth Street of a pretentious embassy for Italy, including a completely covered and heated garden, copying to a degree the Spanish Embassy, also on Sixteenth Street, which is distinguished by a patio, complete with olive trees, where the flowers bloom the year round. The Germans remained in the old house lower down Massachusetts Avenue where they had been for almost half a century.

These embassies, designed for peacetime usage, all represent the older idea that social contact was the primary responsibility of an ambassador. Attached to each was a chancery, where worked possibly a dozen or a score of people, on a routine in which four hours of office work ordinarily sufficed for a day.

The important part of each embassy was its social side, the idea being that here was the important point of contact. Social secretaries of the embassies laid out a series of small dinners, for up to 50 persons, and used such occasions as independence days of their countries, or royal anniversaries, to invite the mob for mass affairs.

Largest of the mob parties, as would be expected, was that given by the British Embassy in the spring on the birthday anniversary of the king. Naturally, British kings may be born at any time, but by custom the anniversary celebrations are held on an arbitrary date. The British would rather celebrate a royal birthday when the sun is likely to shine and strawberries are in season.

And when the British give a party in peacetime it is all British. Tradition dictates that Lyons, the London caterers, shall provide the delicacies. These used to come by fast boat for special events. In time they probably will be flown. But come hell or revolution, it is a safe bet that the British Empire and Lyons will be socially synonymous as long as either exists.

Perhaps Washington was a happy city, when there was so little to worry it that the Longworth-Gann feud could seem to be important. And do not think for a moment that it was unimportant: the whole structure of precedence and diplomacy was threatened by it, to hear the social leaders talk. To most persons, it provided a good laugh, particularly in the sequel.

Alice Longworth, the "Princess Alice" of Theodore Roosevelt's day who married Representative Nicholas Longworth of Ohio, had become a big girl now. Brilliant, assertive and individual to the point where she calmly carried her infant daughter Paulina around in a market basket, Mrs. Longworth became a younger member of the intrenched "old guard" of Washington. She was both the daughter of a former Republican President in a series of Republican Administrations and wife of the Speaker of the House.

The Speaker is a distinguished personage in his own right. He must be by custom a member of the House, but when the House elects him as Speaker he ascends to a leadership above other Representatives. He gets additional salary and that great badge of Washington distinction, a chauffeur and limousine at the expense of the taxpayers. Some Speakers have achieved more distinction than Presidents, particularly those quick-witted enough and versed sufficiently in parliamentary procedure to make the most of their leadership.

Nicholas Longworth made a more brilliant figure certainly than President Hoover, although his mind was quick rather than deep. Besides a charming personality and a gift for politics, he played the violin well enough to have held his own on either the concert stage or in a jive session. During his Speakership no term of the House was considered closed officially until, after the formal adjournment, Longworth got out his fiddle and led the members in a song fest.

Add to these two personalities the possession of comfortable means to maintain a place in society, and you have a formidable number of the things that go to make up social leadership. By Washington standards, the Longworths "belonged."

Then President Hoover entered office, and with him Vice-President Charles Curtis. The secondary job of the Vice-President is to preside over the Senate. The Vice-President in his dual capacity outranks by one seat at any official dinner table the Speaker of the House.

Had there been a Mrs. Charles Curtis, she automatically

would have been senior to Mrs. Longworth. The Speaker's wife, herself a stickler for correct usage despite her individualism, would have been the first to concede this point.

However, the Vice-President was a widower. Needing a hostess, he brought to Washington his sister, Mrs. Dolly Gann. Mr. Gann retreated into anonymity.

The Vice-President said quite clearly from the start that he expected Mrs. Gann to have the prerogatives given to the companion of a Vice-President. His one-eighth Kaw Indian blood probably contributed to the stubbornness with which he maintained that position. Mrs. Longworth and the Speaker held that there was no such thing as a substitute wife; they complimented Mrs. Gann as a charming lady but let it be known most emphatically that no occasion would be permitted to arise where Mrs. Longworth would be humiliated by having a seat below Mrs. Gann.

You may laugh about it now, but that was a genuine crisis. There are about a dozen dinners a year in normal times where the Vice-President and the Speaker, and their wives, normally are invited together. This simply became impossible, and even the White House schedules had to be revised. Mrs. Gann accepted invitations but Mrs. Longworth declined them. Soon official hostesses accepted the fact.

There was then in Washington a character who might have been invented by a romance author. This gentleman was Sesostris Sidarous Pasha, the Minister of Egypt. Sidarous Pasha was short and rotund, enormously wealthy because he owned virtually a monopoly of the flowers grown in Egypt for the perfume trade. He was a collector of china and world famous in art salons as an amateur photographer.

Sidarous Pasha maintained his legation in oriental splendor. When he drove through the streets of Washington, he appeared in an olive-green Mercedes town car—the longest ever seen on those streets—with chauffeur and footman attired in the same shade of green, seated inscrutably behind the wind screen. No one among his friends credited him with having a sense of humor.

The Egyptian Minister finally reached his turn to have a state dinner in the winter of 1930-31. He invited 48 guests. Unlike the custom at that time, he did not announce the guest list in advance, but his footman quietly left the crescent-crested invitations at the doors of the guests. Only when the dinner party was assembled for cocktails before dinner—prohibition never could touch the embassies and legations—did the guests notice that Mrs. Longworth and Mrs. Gann both were present. For the half hour during which cocktails were served, diplomats and Washingtonians stiffly talked about everything under the sun but the one question consuming all of them was: what would be the upshot of this affair? Would Mrs. Longworth go home? Or would Mrs. Gann?

Then a footman opened the doors to the dining room of the legation. The male guests, all so schooled in protocol that they automatically started toward the ladies who would go in with them, were stopped by the host. He stepped in front of the doors, himself announced that dinner was served, then smiled broadly, and added:

"Kindly sit where you please."

The guests found the dining room dressed, not with the conventional long table, but a cluster of small tables seating four each. Consequently there was no head of the table and no foot of the table.

But life in Washington was not entirely concerned with social feuds.

Robert Low Bacon, a Congressman from New York, and Senator Peter Gerry of Rhode Island, vied for leadership among the political set in Washington—the persons who had the "three graces"—money, family background and popularity.

William R. Castle, Undersecretary of State in the Hoover Administration, and Senator David A. Reed of Pittsburgh, maintained adjoining wealthy homes in S Street, where they gathered parties of senior statesmen around them. These houses were in the same row with the one occupied by Mrs. Wilson, as well as another that had been owned by Herbert Hoover as his Washington house since his Washington service in World War I.

On Massachusetts Avenue and at Friendship, the McLeans continued to give the largest and gayest and most highly mixed parties. Occasionally Friendship turned into the atmosphere of a country club when golf tournaments were organized on the course at Friendship, built by McLean specifically to permit former President Harding, his intimate friend, to enjoy the game in privacy.

At Eighteenth and Massachusetts Avenue was located one apartment to which many persons valued an invitation even more than any White House or embassy bid. Here in a vast building, with only one apartment on each of its four floors, the most distinguished tenant was Andrew W. Mellon, the aluminum king and Secretary of the Treasury. Mr. Mellon, already an old man, entertained very little. When guests were invited to his apartment, they could sit and admire a score of priceless art treasures hanging on the walls as decorations.

Mr. Mellon let no one in on the secret that his will would provide approximately twenty million dollars to build and endow the great museum since erected on Constitution Avenue to house his collection and others which may be considered suitable to hang with it.

Apart from these prominent figures the same families who were named as of 1912, now creeping into another generation, continued to live the quiet "cave-dwelling" lives in big houses where no reporters ever were summoned to be given guest lists, and no news photographers ever were admitted at receptions.

The society-page headlines went mostly to the publicity-seekers—the women who valued the clippings to send "back home" sufficiently to wage long and costly campaigns to gain this type of ephemeral prominence.

This really was not too difficult. There were agencies, run mostly by wives or widows of retired officials, who could deliver anything from a luncheon or dinner party, complete with a Senator or two, to a debut for a daughter at $20 a head, including a suitable selection of white-tied and tail-coated young men from the upper classes of the universities around Washington.

It all took money. But what was money? Washington never seemed to lack it in the twenties. The reason was that, if a politician and hostess bent on making a splash socially in the Capital suddenly ran out of money, he or she did not retire to a small house. The individual went home, and usually another stranger was clamoring at real-estate offices to rent the vacated premises.

The blight struck Washington about 1931. The immediate effect of the Wall Street crash in the fall of 1929 had been ameliorated by the fact that relatively few of the wealthy Washington families lived on speculative earnings. The incomes that maintained the large houses came from solid investments in corporate shares and bonds. Dividends were continued through 1930, while the wealthy individuals waited for the recovery they considered bound to come.

Among the rank and file of Washington there was less hardship than in any other city in the country. The lifeblood of the city, which supports its shops and services, is the Federal Government pay roll. With few exceptions this remained at its normal level. So the clerks ate as usual and the small businesses serving them survived. The bread lines and beggars who began to appear were mostly from out of town—men who had heard that "pickings" were better in Washington than elsewhere.

But 1932 saw the impact of depression reflected strongly. The vast houses for the most part were closed, while their owners retreated to homes elsewhere and cut down their overhead. More than one expressed fear of revolution descending on the Capital.

President Hoover stoutly maintained that "prosperity is just around the corner."

But Mrs. Evalyn Walsh McLean confirmed publicly that she had pawned the Hope Diamond. A Virginia syndicate of money lenders held it as security against a loan of unannounced size to tide Friendship over the financial crisis.

Chapter Twenty

NEW DEAL

THE HOTELS IN WASHINGTON gladly cashed the checks of their guests to get them out of town—to prevent further running up of bills. In some cases, hotel credit was advanced to purchase tickets to send the visitors home.

Washington's "new day" was ushered in with a bank holiday, a lot of fear despite the new slogan, "All we have to fear is fear itself," and a smell of change that pervaded every corner of the Capital. By the night of March 4, 1933, it was clear to every taxi-cab driver that the old order had changed, definitely and perhaps forever.

The façades of the buildings were unchanged, and the traditional lamp glowed under the north portico of the White House, casting over the lawn long shadows from the elms planted by Jefferson. But little else remained the same. Nevertheless, for the most part, Washington manifested hope. It had to, or else the morale of the whole United States would have collapsed.

This hope was to be seen in gatherings of businessmen who had almost forgotten the meaning of the word "dividend." It was also to be seen in gatherings of Democrats who sighed with relief at the ending of their long spell out of favor and patronage. And there was a touch of optimism in the features of the beggars overrunning the town—those beaten men to whom it had long been routine to hand a coin, or perhaps a meal ticket providing dinner, bed and breakfast at one of the charity lodging houses.

This was the new Washington. Possibly in later years Roosevelt took more power into his hands than some of his friends and enemies bargained for. But in the hundred days after his Inaugural in 1933 the only audible general complaint was that Washington did not grasp authority fast enough.

Washington took its first firm step toward becoming the control center of the United States—the complete capital of all the country. The world watched breathlessly and waited, too, for correction of the depression blight that had spread from the United States alike to the Paris Bourse and the Shanghai Bund. The world, all except Germany where a man named Hitler had just become Reichschancellor, waited to see if Washington at long last would take its place in the world.

Within a few hours after the first Inaugural Parade, when Governor Alfred E. Smith, of New York, wearing his traditional brown derby, led the ranks of marchers from Tammany Hall, the new President held a reception for the State Governors and the National Committeemen from the States. The committeemen, like the animals on Noah's Ark, filed in two by two, one male and one female from each State.

This, however, was the service of formality to politics as Washington had seen it for 132 years. These governors and committeemen would get their patronage. There was, nevertheless, a new plan for politics and its devisers already were hard at work in the offices of the White House or in hotel suites scattered around the town.

The caustic wit of the Republican Roosevelts had aimed many a barbed shaft at F. D. R. during his campaign. His remote cousin, Theodore, Jr., had referred to him in earlier years as the "maverick" of the family. In politics he was.

In these opening hours of the New Deal, Washington became the focal point of revolution in forms as well as in activities.

The "bank holiday" itself was the child of the skilled legal brains of the "Brain Trust" who found authority for it in delegation of authority made to President Wilson in the first World War. All of which points up another tradition of Washington, a thing to remember. Not only laws determine what the amorphous machine known as Washington may do and be; it is equally binding as a precedent that some prior Administration has done a deed. If it has, the precedent is set, and there is no challenge on earth for it except perhaps, after a long delay, an adverse decision by the Supreme Court of the United States.

This new Washington can best be viewed by recalling the shift in interest around personalities, because government always is people and Washington is made up of people.

Up to noon of March 4, 1933, the most sought after guests at dinner tables, the lions of Washington who were too remote for any but the most prominent to meet, were political figures whose names were known to most school children. They were old political names, which had become woven into the warp and woof of the pattern of Washington.

Secretary of State Henry L. Stimson and Undersecretary of State Castle were the gods of foreign policy, issuing statements and entertaining discreetly as only millionaires could do.

Senator William E. Borah, the leonine figure out of Idaho, ruled the Foreign Relations Committee of the Senate, and held almost absolute veto over treaties and agreements with foreign countries. These could not become finally operative without assent by two thirds of the Senate. The Senate in all the time from Wilson to F. D. Roosevelt, never cast a decisive vote against Senator Borah on matters of foreign policy.

Senator David Reed, of Pennsylvania, small in stature and a poor orator, was the equally powerful chairman of the Senate Military Affairs Committee, with final power over military appropriations. His, too, was the deciding voice in apportioning patronage when the Congress appropriated some 500 millions each year for development of rivers and harbors by the Engineer Corps of the Army.

Secretary Mellon was the benign guardian of easy credit in the policies of the Treasury Department, while Eugene Meyer, still youthful but long retired and a former power in Wall Street, held the Federal Reserve System in the palm of his hand.

These had been some of the *names* in Washington, the symbols of the authority of government—symbols that were smashed in one of the worst political drubbings in American history when the country decided it wanted some tonic for depression other than the prescriptions issued by President Herbert Hoover and the Republican Party.

The important point is that these and scores of other "leaders" in the outgoing party were political figures, for even Mr. Mellon, who never ran for an elective office, was a power in Pennsylvania politics comparable with Boise Penrose in a slightly earlier day.

Newspapers and hostesses and lobbyists checked a new list of names. They found that it divided itself into two parts. The list was perhaps half "political" in the sense that it was made up of names well known to politics, the former minority leaders. The other half had no political background—in fact, the names were hardly known at all. But this other half, the list of unknowns, comprised the powerful and the important names.

In the Senate, Tom Connally took over the Foreign Affairs Committee from Borah, and the aging Carter Glass fell heir to the Banking and Currency Committee. Senator Cordell Hull, not yet the great architect of reciprocal trade treaties, stepped into the position of Secretary of State. But these were the names of formality.

Washington had a new list of lions, and the names were new.

There always has been a modicum of prestige attached to the job of White House Secretary. To Mr. Tumulty in President Wilson's Administration it meant a great deal. But the position normally has been that of a glorified personal servant, a door opener and telephone answerer.

Louis McHenry Howe, the gnome-like shadow of F. D. Roosevelt was the first of his kind. Many persons believed that, in the circle of disparate men brought to the seat of government by the second Roosevelt, Howe was the most powerful man in Washington. Here at least was no ordinary secretary. Rather he combined in those first years the prestige later divided between Secretary Hull, Harry L. Hopkins and a large group of other men.

Long ago, when the vigorous young Roosevelt was serving a term in the State Senate of New York, Howe, then a youngish newspaper correspondent and editor, decided that Roosevelt was his man. Soon he had tossed aside an unusually good earning capacity and cut all his normal ties—he had no immediate family circle—to become secretary to the young State Senator. He never relinquished that job. Howe stayed through Roosevelt's amazing career as Assistant Secretary of the Navy, a bed-ridden invalid, and Governor of New York.

Roosevelt was not a man to take orders from anyone, not even from Howe. But he had to have an intimate confidant with whom to discuss the things that were on his mind. Perhaps it was the operation of the rule of the attraction of opposites. Such a thing had happened before.

President Jackson, the swashbuckling but actually timid soldier-statesman, found such a man in the courtly, urbane Blair. Retiring and diffident President Wilson used as his alter ego Colonel Edward M. House, of Texas, who enjoyed hugely taking his Texas humor into foreign drawing rooms and measuring his plainsman's common sense against the wit of diplomats. President Coolidge called on Frank Stearns, of Boston, the wealthy manufacturer of paper, to help him through many decisions. All three were "gentlemen of the old school." They could wear tall hats gracefully and make superb speeches.

Roosevelt needed no one to act as his "front." He was the supreme achievement in the creation of self-assured personalities. His need was for a retiring personality, a common-sense artist, against whose blunt comment he could sharpen and refine his own rapier-like mentality.

So Roosevelt, the consummate public politician, turned to Howe, the retiring gnome-like man. Roosevelt, the fastidious eater and dresser, chose for his most intimate companion the little man who was careless of clothes so long as he was covered and who abhorred bathing.

One could count on the fingers of one's hand the Washington houses in which Louis McHenry Howe ate a dinner. He lived in the White House, he worked in the White House, and it was all his life until he died there in Roosevelt's second term.

President Roosevelt wished to honor his friend as much as he could. He assigned to him the great bedroom occupied by Lincoln, whose furnishings included the massive four-poster created to accommodate Lincoln's length.

Howe went to the room, took one look at the bed, and said, "Good God!" He thereupon ordered a footman to set up a small bed, of the type used for emergency guests, in the dressing room of the suite. There he always slept.

Soon all Washington came to know, and see through a long social round, the President's other two secretaries—former newspapermen and both skilled in their jobs: Stephen T. Early, who handled press relations, and Marvin H. MacIntyre, the custodian of the President's engagements. Both were popular, and filled good roles.

But there was no mistaking the fact that actually Roosevelt had one confidential secretary and one only, and his name was Howe. And Howe became almost a man of mystery simply because he kept his mouth shut, minded the President's business, and was so different from all other influential politicians.

We take it all for granted now—that sudden and overwhelming capture of Washington by the New Deal Revolution. This is not a recitation of political events, but here was the first of two vital changes that occurred in Washington—that made the somnolent city on the Potomac into the complete Capital that it is. A war later would make the other change. The year 1933 saw it assume its national stature—and one that, whether we like it or not, promises to remain for all time.

In the hundred days of 1933, from March 4 through May, the power of control over money was taken from New York by enactment of the Securities and Exchange Act. The Social Security Act took from the States basic responsibility for public welfare—the care of the jobless, and the halt, and the indigent. The National Recovery Act (invalidated by the Supreme Court two years later, but only after serving its purpose) set the precedent for Federal control of wages and hours of work. The Agricultural Adjustment Act (also invalidated, but only in theory and not in practice) brought the work of the farmers—how much they raised and when and how—under governmental control.

And many other things were done, including the laws to insure bank deposits, with new and startling controls over the operations of the banks.

All of this was Washington in 1933, and later, and nothing else was very important. It was only incidental that the great houses were closed down on Massachusetts Avenue and Sixteenth Street. The depression had seen to that. Social life on the old pattern almost ceased to exist for a few years, except in the Embassies, where taxpayers somewhere else were paying the bills.

So with change came an unprecedented co-mingling of names and authorities, because no President alone, or no Congress, can do much by himself or itself. Allowing for the fact that the new front-page names almost all were Democrats, the New Deal brought to prominence probably a greater cross section of diverse personalities than any other Administration.

The "Brain Trust" got the most prominence, but a score of names picked from recollection of that hectic period find them not preponderant.

In the Cabinet, Secretary Hull was Secretary of State in every sense of the word, most respected of the coterie of old-line political intimates President Roosevelt gathered around him. Mr.

Hull had been Representative and afterward Senator for half a lifetime—a Tennesseean every bit as tough as his mountaineer father who used a gun to correct a wrong.

To politics Roosevelt made other gestures by naming venerables to high position—wealthy and urbane Homer S. Cummings, of Connecticut, as his first Attorney General; the already failing Senator Claude A. Swanson as Secretary of the Navy (Swanson had been chairman of the House Committee on Naval Affairs in World War I) ; and Daniel A. Roper, of South Carolina, who died after more than fifty consecutive years on the public pay rolls, as Secretary of Commerce.

The "Brain Trust" was more a name than a fact, but its high priest was Raymond A. Moley, lately a professor at Columbia University, shrewd and professorial, who settled quickly into the position of Assistant Secretary of State. A good diner-out and brilliant conversationalist, Moley lasted for about six months—a rather long career for a subordinate who tried to cross swords with Cordell Hull.

Rexford Guy Tugwell, another economist, became Assistant Secretary of Agriculture, but like Moley was more concerned with general policy than the paper-signing routine of his payroll job.

Three full Cabinet members particularly intrigued the "old guard" of Washington to whom development of new faces is a hobby. Foremost among these in point of curiosity was "Madame" Frances Perkins, first woman to occupy a seat in the Cabinet, who brought a curious mixture of social interests to the job of Secretary of Labor, and a tricorn hat that became her banner.

Then there was Harold L. Ickes, to become known in later years by his own self-bestowed title of "the curmudgeon." Ickes, the bellowing and irascible product of a generation of work in reform politics in Chicago, a veritable "Bull Mooser" of the Theodore Roosevelt days, had sought an introduction to Roosevelt before the Inauguration in the hope of getting appointed chief of the Bureau of Indian Affairs. Ickes was not particularly ambitious politically; he was a wealthy man. Roosevelt, with a Jovian gesture, talked to him once and appointed him to a post over a host of bureaus, including Ickes' beloved Indians.

Henry Wallace, the Iowa developer of hybrid corn and experimenter in many life forms, totally unknown to Roosevelt before the election of 1932, dropped into the post of Secretary of Agriculture and became a stormy petrel in politics.

In fact, all kinds of politics was represented in the flow of appointments. Lawrence Wood Robert, Jr., a contractor, of Atlanta, Ga., became an Assistant Secretary of the Treasury and the court jester. He was distinguished as the teller of some of the funniest and many of the dirtiest stories ever recounted at a stag party.

To leaven this assortment, the new President paid his due to the venerable shibboleths of Washington, by filling in the gaps in the State Department with people whom Washington knew and understood.

R. Walton Moore, now dead, of old Virginia stock and a lifelong resident of near-by Alexandria, became the Undersecretary of State. Francis B. Sayre, diplomat and son-in-law of Woodrow Wilson was named as Assistant Secretary of State and later Governor General of the Philippines. And Sumner Welles, career diplomat, was another. Welles returned from diplomatic work abroad to resume a type of living so well backed that the depression made but little dent in his habits. He resided at Oxon Hill, the old Addison estate, and kept a town house on Massachusetts Avenue so large that in 1943 it was leased by the Canadian Government as a dormitory for more than 200 women clerks.

On this stage, too, walked Harry L. Hopkins, of whom more later.

The New Deal was called many things, some not complimentary. But of this it could be said: it made Washington a cosmopolitan Capital. And a powerful one.

Chapter Twenty-One

TYPEWRITER STATESMEN

IN THE MIDDLE 1930's Arthur Krock, the celebrated editorial columnist of the *New York Times,* wrote an article in which he described politicians and newspapermen as perpetual friendly enemies. He pointed out that correspondents and politicos could drink together, play poker together, share the same clubs and have almost every interest in common, but never quite be intimate friends. The time always would come when journalistic ethics or enterprise would require that the conscientious correspondent cross swords even with his best friend in the political ranks.

The general operation of this rule has made the Washington press corps unique. School children are taught that the "fourth estate" is a part of any democracy. In Washington it sometimes seems that the press corps rates in public responsibility somewhere beneath the Supreme Court and above the Congress. In the New Deal period it achieved maturity. The peacetime life of Washington became important.

When Smith founded his *National Intelligencer* he set a standard for exclusive objectivity in political journalism that has held to fairly high standards for more than 150 years. It has changed its form and actually has run almost a full cycle, but in every phase has lived up to a very high degree to the slogan coined in recent years by *Newsweek* magazine, "A well informed public is America's greatest security."

Naturally, newspapers are human institutions and their writers are human beings. So spleen is vented and pet projects are promoted on occasion out of all proportion to their news value. In more recent years the radio occasionally has made the same mistakes. But the fact remains that the reader of any first-class newspaper knows a good deal more about what is going on in Washington than he would if his knowledge were based entirely on what politicians reported to him.

For the first century of news reporting from Washington correspondents as a rule wrote their views rather than what we now consider as news. They served their purpose by setting off their own opinions against those of the politicians. This was the technique developed so highly in the half century prior to 1900 when Ben:Perley Poore became the most distinguished of Washington correspondents and wielded authority greater than any Congressman. From this high point of personal journalism the newspaper reverted to emphasis on straight news reporting, until the last decade when the columnists again are overshadowing the news reports themselves.

In the spring of 1934 the White House doors were thrown open on a starlit evening for the first reception of its kind ever held in Washington. Approximately 400 newspaper correspondents, male and female, accompanied by their spouses or escorts, attended a press reception by means of which the Roosevelts enlarged the formal entertaining list for the first time since the Civil War. Since no precedent existed for this reception it was streamlined to a modern form, without a uniform in the crowd and no formal reception line wending through the Blue Room.

As the guests entered they were taken directly to the President, who wore a tuxedo and sat in a comfortable chair at one end of the East Room. Beside him stood Mrs. Roosevelt. Presentations were made by an aide, but from then on the word was informality. A dance band played in the East Room. Chairs and tables covered the east terrace and guests were welcome to stroll around the grounds. Ice cream and cake and coffee were served as refreshments from a buffet in the State Dining Room. Kegs of beer were broached in the main hall.

In this particular year it seemed evident that a good 98 per cent of the news correspondents in Washington were Roosevelt rooters, as were their papers behind them. Here was the highest point of popularity a President ever had achieved with the newspapers of the United States and it paid off in excellent dividends. But obviously, such is the way of Washington, it could not last. Soon the press corps would be as sharply divided as the Congress itself over the Roosevelt policies.

The press corps in Washington is similar to the political group in that its members almost entirely come to Washington from some other place. It differs in the fact that Washington correspondents, once established, seldom leave and remain to become part of the permanent Washington scene. In a few instances newspaper families are in their second and third generations, even though no member of these families ever has worked for a local newspaper. Thus the newspaper correspondents have become the connecting link in thinking between the old established Washington and the rest of the United States. In 1947 the influence of this corps could best be gauged by the fact that there were more than 600 accredited correspondents for out-of-town newspapers resident in Washington, plus more than 100 special correspondents for radio chains and the periodicals.

Heaven alone knows how many other persons were writing about Washington, because accreditation to the press galleries means that a man or woman devotes his principal time and responsibility to news writing alone. Time was when most correspondents collected government pay checks as a sideline, but this practice was abolished about 40 years ago.

Richard V. Oulahan, who died in the Hoover Administration, came as near as anyone to developing the prototype of the higher bracket of Washington correspondents. He complained in the later years of his life that he had to don white tie and tails so often to keep obligatory engagements that he had scarcely sufficient time to prepare the despatches he wrote almost daily for the *New York Times*. That was part of the penalty of being "Dean of the Press Corps," a distinction not won since by any other individual.

Richard Oulahan was a newspaper correspondent in Washington for about 40 years. He achieved distinction within 10 years after his arrival on the scene, when the New York *Sun,* unable to obtain the news report of The Associated Press, set up its own Washington Bureau with Oulahan as the chief correspondent. This was the first venture by a newspaper in establishing a bureau designed to cover all of the news. After World War I, Oulahan took over the Washington Bureau of the *New York Times.*

It is a tribute to Oulahan, and rather typical of the better type of newspaper correspondent, that he could write objectively about the news and yet enjoy the confidence and friendship of such diverse personalities as the Presidents he "covered." Theodore Roosevelt frequently entertained Oulahan aboard the yacht *Mayflower;* Woodrow Wilson extended his confidences to Oulahan during the trying days of the Versailles Conference. In the latter years of Herbert Hoover's Administration, Hoover invited Oulahan to the White House almost every week to discuss his mounting problems.

That is the type of record Washington correspondents believe is more fair in picturing their achievements than the police-court and spy-scare plots that usually make up motion-picture delineation of their work.

Oulahan, working in the leisurely earlier days and with time to live graciously in a house in Georgetown, never could have conceived, however, the period in journalism in Washington that developed with mounting tones every year after 1933.

Journalistically speaking, Washington became the sounding board for world and domestic political discussion. This created a new era in writing and loosed a flood of reports in which commingle fact, opinion, forecast. News writing from Washington became a profession that spread from practitioners who assume empirical omniscience to relatively unknown specialists who knew more about their special subjects than most officials dealing in their fields.

News from Washington always has been both the reward of the active public servant—favorable publicity—and the bee under the tail of the donkey. It is wholesale reports of all the activities of government—The Associated Press in politics alone employs about one-sixth of the entire press corps—and it is special succinct accounts of little things that make big issues.

When Harry L. Hopkins, as relief administrator, had become the biggest man in the Roosevelt Administration—second only to "the Chief" and White House intimate who had moved into the bedroom vacated by the death of Louis McHenry Howe— one little quotation published by Arthur Krock caused more of an issue than any other New Deal argument.

By that time, as the grip of Washington on all national affairs was tightened, there was no longer that fine community interest between the Administration and the press that had marked 1933. Most newspapers and many newspaper correspondents felt that honest reporting required more emphasis on flaws in an emergency governmental program that rapidly was becoming a new way of life.

Arthur Krock, as successor to Oulahan, had switched, largely because of the Third Term, from ardent supporter to outright critic of the New Deal. Then, on a summer's day, he obtained from sources in which he had the greatest confidence the report that Hopkins had remarked, "We'll spend and spend, and tax and tax, and elect and elect."

Hopkins denied the quotation. Krock stuck to his guns. Eventually, when Hopkins was nominated for the post of Secretary of Commerce, this quotation was the big issue. On a set day the Senate Commerce Committee announced that it would hold public hearings on Hopkins' fitness for the new task. The hearing was moved into the Caucus Room, largest assembly hall in the Senate Office Building. Scores of reporters and hundreds of spectators were on hand. The newsreel cameras were set up, and blinding Kleig lights placed in position to make a perfect picture.

The committee met. Krock was called as a witness. The youngish correspondent, cool as the Kentucky hills of his origin and smooth as the bourbon whiskey distilled there, took his seat. The committee chairman asked Krock for the origin of his report. The correspondent replied drily that he stood on the ethical grounds of his profession to protect the source of his reports. He was excused.

Joseph Alsop, Jr., the brilliant young columnist who later was to interrupt his profession to go to China as a naval officer, suffer capture by the Japanese, obtain exchange and later to return to India as director of Lend-Lease, was called to explain the use of the same quotation. His reply parroted Krock's. He was excused.

Hopkins was invited to testify on his own behalf. He denied making the statement.

So ended a controversy, as most political controversies end. Every conservative opponent of the New Deal believed Krock. Every supporter of the New Deal believed Hopkins. That is politics, and that is the net of much of the journalistic effort. But news reports do stir things up. They make people think. Or do they?

Among the Washington writers, the news columnists have flowered in the past decade to a point where some are the most powerful figures in Washington, not excepting Cabinet members and Senators. In the top category of influence, by universal consent, ranks Krock, who devotes a scholarly pen to editorial interpretation of political events; Walter Lippmann, erudite columnist syndicated by the New York *Herald Tribune*, and an outstanding authority on foreign affairs since he was one of the younger group gathered around Woodrow Wilson, and Drew Pearson, acidulous exposer of those things he considers impure politically or improper publicly.

None of these three compete with each other. They plow separate furrows in the Washington field. Each is praised, damned and feared, according to the political figure discussing him at the moment.

The senior among the columnists is beloved Mark Sullivan, whose articles are Victorian homespun homilies, for which he draws inspiration frequently from his Pennsylvania farm. Another senior columnist, though still a youngish man, is David Lawrence, once a star reporter for The Associated Press. Lawrence writes regularly for a limited group of newspapers, but his Washington influence comes more from his trenchant editing—it has made him a millionaire—of the *United States News,* a weekly of national circulation, and various confidential news services.

Thomas L. Stokes, Joseph and Stuart Alsop, a team of brothers, and Marquis Childs are pressing on the heels of the leaders in the "columning" field.

Out of all this list it would be hard to pick up a daily newspaper that did not print one or more of the names mentioned. Or Paul Mallon, who was almost the first in the race.

Mallon, incidentally, typifies the manner in which reputations are made in the community of Washington. He got his "break" in the 1920's through sheer bravado in overthrowing a shibboleth of politics, while reporting the Senate for the United Press.

The Senate holds two kinds of meetings—open sessions and "executive" sessions to consider and vote on nominations of officers sent to it by the President or to consider treaties or agreements which require ratification by the Senate. Once upon a time the "executive" sessions were held in secret behind doors that literally were locked.

Nowadays there is hardly such a thing as a secret session, but prior to 20 years ago the Senate frequently went into secret executive sessions. It was considered commonplace to hold such sessions, and the injunction of secrecy was a useful cloak to protect members from publicity on their votes on controversial nominations or treaties.

One such session was held on a nomination now long forgotten. Mallon decided it was time to challenge the rule. He printed a list showing how Senators had voted in the secret session. As a result, all reporters were forbidden thereafter to go on the floor. They must remain in the gallery or talk to Senators in the lobby and halls. But the Senate also heard the long echo of public approval of Mallon's action and thereafter shied away from secret sessions.

As a matter of fact, newspapers seldom, if ever, miss a story because reporters cannot wander around the Senate floor. Few Senators long delay in going into the lobby when a correspondent wishes to interview them.

If there is a moral in this illustration, it is that even radar is no more sensitive in its capacity to register reaction than the ear of a politician.

And what do Washingtonians read? The politico normally reads one local paper and his home-town paper. The upper level add to these a New York paper—normally the *Times* or the *Herald Tribune,* sometimes the Baltimore *Sun* and the *Christian Science Monitor.* But the native of the District of Columbia reads his local papers exclusively.

Here again is the essence of the make-up of Washington. One newspaper is owned locally. One is owned by a nation-wide chain. Another is owned by a retired "Wall Street banker." The last is a first cousin of the Chicago *Tribune* and New York *Daily News*—the powerful McCormick-Patterson combine.

In no other city except New York is there such diverse control of reading matter, and few readers elsewhere have the opportunity to "pay your money and take your choice" of the headlined despatches.

In an earlier chapter, the writer quoted Noyes, the late editor of the *Star* who died in 1946. But Noyes was only one of a large and fecund family which started the *Star* and bids fair to have enough descendants to own and operate it for generations to come. The *Star* is a conservative newspaper, its whole history marked by a cautious approach to anything sensational. It is published on afternoons of weekdays and Sunday morning.

For many years it was a standard joke in Washington that the *Star* had only one strong editorial position: it was bitterly opposed to vandals who destroyed the native blossoming dogwood trees or the cherry trees around the Tidal Basin. The Noyes family also laughed at the joke, and they could afford to laugh, with ownership of a paper that in the days of unlimited newsprint occasionally printed more advertising than any other paper in the world.

Actually, the *Star* is a well-rounded newspaper that leans principally on The Associated Press for its reports but buys many special services and in the last war began sending its own correspondents abroad.

Editorially it certainly is not sensational, and it publishes several of the more conservative columns. Noyes was so jealous of maintaining a neutral position that he finally contracted with Lowell Mellett, firm believer in the New Deal, to write a column called "On the Other Hand," to balance the conservative flavor of the editorial page.

Exclusive to the afternoon field alone is the tabloid *Daily News,* which commingles news, pictures, Scripps-Howard editorials and comics into an interesting pocketful of newspaper. The little *News,* while tabloid in character in Washington, is the Capital outlet for features that loom importantly in many other leading newspapers. It is not sensational. This was the paper which politicians once got every day to read the famous

231

columns of Raymond Clapper, who died in the Pacific. And it was the Washington billboard for the unforgettable war reports by Ernie Pyle.

To mention the *Star* and the *News,* however, is only one means of passing on to a battle of titans in a newspaper war that continued only until Eugene Meyer, president and publisher of the *Washington Post,* resigned his active direction of that paper. This ended a ten-year battle for supremacy in the morning-newspaper field between two of the largest private fortunes in the United States and two newspapers so different that one had to look at the date-lines to be sure they were issued on the same day.

It also was a personal battle between Meyer, abetted by Mrs. Agnes Meyer, his wife and a journalist on the old New York *World* before she became Mrs. Meyer, and Mrs. Eleanor ("Cissy") Patterson, co-owner of the Chicago *Tribune* and New York *News,* cousin of Robert McCormick, publisher of the former, and sister of the late Joseph Medill Patterson, publisher of the latter. Don't let the "Mrs. Patterson" confuse you, because after being twice widowed, Mrs. Patterson took back her maiden name while retaining the married title.

Eugene Meyer, partly because of Mrs. Meyer, whom he married in 1907, had wanted to publish a newspaper in Washington ever since he served in the Capital in World War I. In the early 1920's he discussed founding a Washington newspaper with Oulahan as editor, but dropped the idea.

A very wealthy man, who retired 25 years ago from active Wall Street banking operations, Meyer held to the idea through 12 years as Governor of the Federal Reserve System.

In the meantime, the *Washington Post* was declining from the national prominence it enjoyed half a century ago. The depression all but wiped it out, while Edward Beale McLean's income shrank. The reader may recall the story of the pawning of the Hope Diamond. Finally, the *Post* went on the auction block. "Cissy" Patterson and "Governor" Meyer were the most active bidders. Meyer won. His initial investment in his new "hobby," representing both original cost and initial capital was authoritatively reported as being $1,250,000. Another reported million followed this investment. Getting into the newspaper business, even with a failing paper in a moderate-sized city, is not a poor man's sport.

Thereafter the *Post* became the enigma of modern publishing, aside from the fact that it has become a profitable investment. Instead of being content with merely owning a newspaper, as his friends expected, Meyer worked longer hours than any of his employees. His fingers were literally in the editorial and news direction as well as the business office. Through many staff shifts he built up a news organization comparable with that of the greater big-city dailies.

A conservative in every sense of the word, the *Post's* publisher took a broad view of world problems, to the point where President Roosevelt on at least two occasions before the war cited the *Post* for its exposition of the foreign policy of the United States.

This paper, supposed plaything of a wealthy capitalist, became the forum for many special articles by Agnes Meyer, arguing the needs of the depressed classes, which would not have been out of place if featured in an outright labor newspaper.

It long ago became a commonplace to see Meyer seated at luncheons and dinners held by the Overseas Writers, the Gridiron Club and the National Press Club, a reporter among reporters. Many Washington correspondents improved their acquaintance with news sources through repeated invitations to parties tendered by Meyer to newsworthy personages at his palatial home standing behind a walled garden in Crescent Place.

In October of 1945, many of the great of Washington gathered at a large luncheon to honor one of Washington's distinguished citizens. The principal speaker was James F. Byrnes, Secretary of State. The laudatory speech was made by Frank B.

Noyes, president of the *Star*. The guest of honor was Eugene Meyer, whose seventieth birthday was being celebrated. The *Washington Post* was Meyer's great achievement.

One of the few great houses on Dupont Circle still occupied as a private residence—manned by liveried servants and the scene of dinners as lavish in every detail, including the vintage champagne, as those given by embassies—is the home of "Cissy" Patterson. She took the house years ago when it was fashionable for wealthy people to spend the social season in Washington. As the years passed, Mrs. Patterson manifested more and more an urge to emulate her brother and cousin, and have a newspaper of her own.

Finally she took over the failing Hearst newspapers, the morning *Herald* and the evening *Times*. Merging them, she set out to publish a round-the-clock newspaper.

The *Times-Herald* is a little bit of many things in publishing. It prints more comics than any other newspaper. Its news columns reflect the reactionary stand of the Chicago *Tribune*. In it are the gory type of "tabloid" stories that built the giant circulation of the New York *News*. Its society pages have been studded with a passing parade of names and near-names among well-known families. The *Times-Herald* has the largest circulation in Washington.

Maybe in some future year there will be a dinner tendered to Mrs. Patterson by a group of the type which honored Meyer. Washington will know when "Cissy" becomes 70 years of age.

Chapter Twenty-Two

DIPLOMACY: 1939 STYLE

THE BIGGEST MISTAKE that foreigners, and many Americans, ever make is to assume that Washington "rules" the United States. The fact is—and it makes Washington more important rather than less so—that whatever governing is done in Washington is accomplished by agreement among many sections or schools of thought throughout the country. That was President Roosevelt's greatest strength: he knew it.

The great success achieved by Lord Halifax, the wartime Ambassador of Great Britain, was due principally to his courageous and sincere work to get acquainted with the United States. The tall, thin envoy was the Twentieth-Century diplomat. He learned a lot about the United States. In turn, he gave to many Americans some perspective of what Great Britain was doing in the war. Certainly he gave the British viewpoint. That was his job. And he knew he could do it better on the road than in the Embassy.

When Halifax was hit with an egg in Detroit, his graceful remark—"Fortunate people to have eggs to throw away"—did more for good will for Britain than any dinner at which he presided in Washington.

Too many people representing foreign countries in Washington, and the same examples exist among America's representatives abroad, always have thought that anything could be accomplished if enough effort and persuasion were exerted on the "right people."

It will be many years before there occurs again such a graphic example of the crosscurrents of diplomacy that make up Washington as occurred in 1939-40. In those years Washington grew into full stature in the eyes of foreign countries. The hot and expensive city became the prime diplomatic post for foreign ambassadors, the United States the most courted country in the world.

The reason: everyone wanted something. This precipitated the greatest battle of cocktail glasses and dinner services in modern times. And every embassy, in its own way, muffed the ball.

The most coveted invitation in Washington below one from the White House itself was the large, rectangular card surmounted by the British royal crest. Personification of British majesty in Washington since 1930 had been the amiable Scot, Sir Ronald Lindsay, predecessor of Halifax. Jovial, tall—he stood six feet, four inches, and broad as a wrestler, a mountain of dignity in his formal dress of kilt and scarlet jacket—Sir Ronald gave the impression of believing that all that mattered in the conduct of his country's foreign affairs was an intimate acquaintance among the leaders of Washington, New York and Newport. He preferred small dinners in the family dining room of the Embassy, but when long residence made him Dean of the Diplomatic Corps his time was largely taken up with obligatory exchanges of full-dress parties and calls with the other members of the Corps.

This was the year when Lend-Lease was the greatest American political issue. So the British Government played its trump card, according to the views of the British Foreign Office. It decided that this was the time to pay the United States its highest compliment—the King and Queen should pay a state visit to Washington. The visit did create a stir—more than the British bargained for.

Washington was not unaccustomed to receiving visits from distinguished guests. There had been no end to the parade of

236

Prime Ministers to the American Capital. The Prince of Wales had visited Washington in 1924, and King Prajadhipok of Siam in 1931. Prajadhipok was a little king, of course, but royal as could be.

But to have the King of Great Britain and Ireland, Emperor of India, Defender of the Faith, etc.—this was the trump British card, and the playing of it was put into the hands of Lindsay.

The King and Queen arrived in June, which called for a garden party on the six beautifully groomed acres of Embassy lawn. The weather was hot, but it did not reach anywhere near as close to the boiling point as the political and social events preceding the actual procession of Their Majesties through the crowd eventually invited to meet them.

In the Washington *Social Register* are listed approximately 1300 persons. In the Congress, at full strength, are 531 members, plus their wives and, as the *Congressional Directory* puts it, "unmarried daughters in society" and "other ladies with them." Seldom do these lists overlap. In the Executive branches of the Government are about 1000 officials with some pretense to position, and these too have families. The Diplomatic Corps runs to several hundred additional, plus families, but many of these duplicate the *Social Register* list.

The British Embassy garden party was arbitrarily limited to 1500 persons.

If the reader, who probably has some mental picture of the importance attached by officials to position, will imagine which of the members of these groups would voluntarily give up the "distinction" of being invited to the Garden Party he will have a fair picture of the dilemma which faced Sir Ronald, Lady Lindsay and Miss Irene Boyle, the long-time social secretary of the British Embassy.

In the exaggerated atmosphere of place in Washington, the Lindsays and Miss Boyle faced a much harder task than did Barry Wall a half century ago when the reigning Mrs. Vanderbilt asked him to designate the 400 persons who could be accommodated at a reception in her Fifth Avenue Mansion. It seems absurd now, but many persons reasoned that the Royal Garden Party's "1500" would go down in Capital history as importantly as the New York "400."

Yet the list had to be culled, at Sir Ronald's explicit order. The only way a harried British Embassy staff that still thought in the pre-1914 era could do this was to make an arbitrary choice according to position and place. The atmosphere of culling was not helped by advance reports that the Royal ménage had notified the White House as to the type of bed sheets Their Majesties preferred, or the leaking out of such "human-interest" stories as the one that a "plate man" traveled with the royal pair to supervise the silver used to serve them at table. In the atmosphere of 1939, every such story gave rise to criticism of "undemocratic" actions, often by the same people who were determined, come hell or high water, to get to the Garden Party.

There was a press conference at the British Embassy, at which Sir Ronald made an announcement about the Garden Party. He was asked about the handling of the guest list. Replied Sir Ronald, "It's just like heaven. Some are chosen, some are not!"

"Heaven's" original list was well sprinkled with unofficial names from Washington, New York, and Philadelphia. The official list was culled down to the highest State Department officials, the chairmen of committees of the Senate and the House and all the members of the Foreign Relations Committees of each body—except Senator Hiram Johnson. The British Embassy thus undertook to spank the ranking isolationists in Congress. The British would not understand that isolationist votes would have to be changed before even F. D. Roosevelt could amend the Neutrality Act and force a law authorizing Lend-Lease through the Congress.

Senator Johnson commented, "After all, the Senate is merely the treaty-making body of the United States and not the *Social Register.*" The comment of the wives of Senators and Representatives was not so restrained. They bombarded the State Department and the secretaries of the White House with demands that "something be done." High-ranking American officials were genuinely concerned at the omission from the list of ranking statesmen such as Senator Charles L. McNary, the Minority Leader of the Senate.

As for the Diplomatic Corps, the invitation list simply was confined to ambassadors, ministers and embassy counselors. There was little the Corps could do about it; no one cared very much outside of the foreign ranks about its own squabbles.

But there was some smooth footwork to be done to calm other ruffled feelings. Into the predicament stepped Vice-President John Nance Garner, isolationist to the core, but with eyes that saw farther than his own prejudices. "Uncle Jack" called up his good friend, Sir Ronald, and explained to him the importance of a Senator, particularly a Senator's vote, and above all the temper of the aroused wife of a Senator. All the members of the Senate and their wives were invited at the last minute.

Then "Uncle Jack" mended his own political fences by declining an invitation to the dinner given by the King and Queen at the Embassy in honor of the President, the only known instance when anything short of death has caused the declination of such an invitation.

What Britain can almost always count upon, however, in the crosscurrents of diplomatic affairs in Washington, is that while its Embassy can do, and often has done, stupid things, its mistakes are the kind that eventually are passed off as jokes. Britons and Americans finally reach the point where they get a mutual laugh from them. Many other countries do not have this faculty, or this luck, as 1939 so aptly demonstrated.

At a time when the least whisper of diplomatic intrigue was the cause of a new controversy—touched off with equal asperity in Washington or San Francisco or Boston or Dubuque—the representatives of the other major European powers seemed intent on making asses of themselves and enemies for their countries.

The Germans attempted by sheer bravado to face down America; no Nazi had learned anything from von Bernstorff's mistakes. The French seemed intent on being always French in the comic-opera sense of the word. The Russians, both before and after the German alliance that preceded their fighting of a defensive war, acted like characters out of an E. Phillips Oppenheim detective story. The Japanese, diplomatically, were as stupid on their part as was the United States in its military estimate of the armed skill of the Japanese.

The sun was already setting on any prestige the Nazi Government may have had by 1939, due entirely to the Germans themselves. Controversy still scurried around the figure of Hans Dieckhoff, whose name headed the German diplomatic list as ambassador, but who had been recalled by his government to save face, to avoid his actual banishment.

The old German Embassy on Massachusetts Avenue had become an office structure. With amplified funds supplied by Hitler, Dieckhoff had leased for an Embassy residence the home of Countess Gladys Vanderbilt Szechenyi, wife of the former Hungarian Minister to the United States. The house was almost opposite the British Embassy on western Massachusetts Avenue. It was imposing, with a ballroom in a special wing.

The Germans in Washington, following the pattern set by Joachim Ribbentrop, then Ambassador to Great Britain, used two tactics, both equally obnoxious. Had the British planned the German campaign it could not have worked out better for Britain on the local scene.

The old Embassy became the business headquarters for an espionage business that included the transmission of funds to German agents in Latin-American countries, the sending out of anti-American literature, and the organization of pro-German groups in the United States—all carried out under the cloak of diplomatic immunity for the mails and diplomatic freedom from surveillance in domestic operations. But the State Department knew about it. An official protest accomplished Dieckhoff's recall, and perhaps to some extent, stopping of the operations.

The other phase of the German operations, equally futile, consisted of assiduous courting of newspaper correspondents and officials through social intercourse. This went on under the leadership of Hans Thomsen, Counselor and Chargé d'Affaires. Dr. Kurt Sell, prior to Nazi days the well-known Washington correspondent for the Wolff News Agency, gave once a year a formal Bavarian party and in-between-whiles informal *bierabends* in his home. Herbert Sholtz, who left Washington to become Consul General in Boston, courted personal popularity, while little German fry, including the embassy secretaries Herbert Blankerhorn and Herbert von Strempel, entertained out of all relation to their means—and laughed with their guests about the ineptitude of the Nazi leadership.

There was more amusement and curiosity than anything else among the estimated 2000 Washingtonians who crowded the Shoreham Hotel ballroom at a reception given in March of 1940. The guest of honor was His Royal Highness, the Duke of Saxe-Coburg and Gotha. Grandson of Queen Victoria, this little man, who seemed to be bewildered by it all, was in Washington as president of the German Red Cross.

The reception in his honor was featured by plenty of champagne, abundant cocktails, Virginia ham, cold turkey and the usual caterers' trimmings. About the only thing the reception accomplished was to prove that in Washington you can get a crowd together anywhere that refreshments are served. One recalls the little old lady who for years made the rounds of these parties and always filled a large handbag with sandwiches before leaving. Six weeks after the reception the Germans invaded Holland.

The Russian Embassy is an older, massive building on upper Sixteenth Street, dark as a tomb, in which the Czarist envoys maintained a ducal atmosphere of restrained elegance until the Revolution swept them out. Through a dozen years, while a single caretaker paid by the State Department slept in the house, mice ate the stuffs from the upholstered furniture, vandals broke the glass in the windows and exposure completed the job of ruin. The mansion originally built by the Pullman family as its Washington show place fell to pieces.

In 1933, swarthy Alexander Antonovich Troyanovsky had opened the renovated Russian Embassy with a reception to which the Union of Soviet Socialist Republics sent more exotic foods than ever had loaded the tables of the building. Black beluga caviar from Astrakhan, champagne from the Caspian region, whole sturgeons and little jellied fish, plus plenty of whiskey and cocktails. String music came from hidden orchestras, and three floors of parlors hardly sufficed to hold the crowds of the curious who flocked to the first formal party given by the newly recognized Russian Government.

A handful of top Russian officials, impeccably dressed, seemed bent only on demonstrating how "civilized" their country could be. That was what the public saw—or at least that large section of the public which had won admission cards to the affair.

Few saw the other Russia manifested in the old building. That other Russia was on the upper floors where for weeks workmen, hired without regard to cost, had been rushing through a special job. On those floors, formerly devoted to guest suites and elaborate sitting rooms, there had been created a virtual rabbit warren of small apartments—tiny rooms with kitchenettes. These were the living quarters, and among them the sound-proof conference rooms, where worked the real Russia. The confidential employees of the Kremlin were not to appear in public, to be seen or to talk, whether at work or off duty.

The Russian "front" was maintained for several years through the period of Troyanovsky. It finally was abandoned for all practical purposes when Constantin Oumansky, youngest Ambassador ever accredited to Washington, was promoted from his former job as Communist shadow and stool pigeon in the Embassy to the ambassadorship. Some years later, during the war, Oumansky was killed in an airplane accident in Mexico, where he had been sent as Ambassador. In those days Washington could respect Russia as a fighting ally in Europe; but few tears were shed for Oumansky.

His was the task in 1939 of running this Embassy. Oumansky gave his first reception in 1939. His guests included precisely the American officials and journalists who had to go, the entire German diplomatic group, and the hungry horde always waiting for a cocktail-party invitation.

The upper stories of the Embassy had become even more carefully locked quarters. A plumber called to work would see countless faces peering at him from behind partially opened doors. The Embassy so feared contact with Americans that it bought a large house on Kalorama Heights and turned it into a school for the children of staff members. Even the littlest Communists must not be contaminated by Western association.

After Russia and Germany crawled into bed with each other, Oumansky demonstrated his complete lack of understanding of Washington by registering complaints about reports in the American press about Russia, and crying at the State Department that his Embassy was not being treated with proper respect. Sumner Welles, then Undersecretary of State, listened to him with frigid attention.

The Japanese Embassy on Massachusetts Avenue already has been referred to as probably the most beautiful building in Washington. It was built along American lines with the slightest touches of all that is delicate and lovely in Asiatic art. Into it went the understanding of a great Japanese, Ambassador Saito, who retired because of ill health in the 1930's, died in America, and who was so highly regarded personally that his body was sent home on a cruiser. Saito was not part of the "new Japan."

The Nipponese could not find another Saito. Most of his type were dead or imprisoned by the war lords when time came for replacement. They sent to the Embassy the elderly retired Admiral Nomura, surrounding him with a fleet-footed staff of younger men who carried on the real work of the Embassy.

Nomura had virtually no social life. His staff—as we learned at the cost of a fleet of warships—did its work well.

André de Laboulaye, secretary in the French Embassy at Washington in 1916, had been an intimate friend of Assistant Secretary of the Navy Franklin D. Roosevelt. Madame Laboulaye was equally intimate with Eleanor Roosevelt.

Six days after Roosevelt was inaugurated in 1933, Laboulaye, now the new French Ambassador, with Madame Laboulaye, arrived in Washington. Mrs. Roosevelt called on the morning of the seventh day. On the eighth day, Madame Laboulaye was telling her friends that she considered it unbecoming of Mrs. Roosevelt to make such an unexpected call—that the President's wife should act with more dignity.

After that all was anti-climax.

The French Ambassador eventually convinced his government that the old house leased by France on Sixteenth Street was unbecoming to the dignity of his country. He obtained a grant of $450,000 to purchase for France the John Hays Hammond house on Kalorama Road, complete with swimming pool and gardens rolling down to Rock Creek Park.

Laboulaye served for six years as Ambassador in the serene belief that he had learned in his youth all that an ambassador need know about America, never consulting his staff, and seeing even fewer people who might have given him a picture of life as it is in America than Lindsay, of whom he was most jealous.

George Bonnet, formerly a member of the French Cabinet,

followed Laboulaye, and made a point of interpreting the "isolationists" to his government. He believed his own exaggerated interpretations and wound up a brief career by warning France that appeasement was in order.

The French believed Bonnet and acquiesced in Munich, and then sent along to Washington Count René Daynel de St. Quentin. Rich, an authority on wines, St. Quentin attempted to follow the German pattern of influence through entertainment. His contacts and his extravagance alike were useless. France fell.

Any further detail of diplomatic life in Washington in 1939 would be superfluous.

This parade of personalities serves only to point up one facet of the gripping period through which the Capital of the United States was progressing. Cut politics how you would, and slice the arguments down to the last word in Senatorial debates, Britain could not lose.

Chapter Twenty-Three

HOME TOWN: PRE-PEARL HARBOR

LONG BEFORE THE DEPRESSION Washington had been bursting out of its public buildings by the sheer inertia of steady growth. But only the invention of the Public Works Program as a means of making work gave the push to Congress necessary to realize this fact. When billions could be voted for the country as a whole, Congress finally considered it politically expedient to spend millions on the Capital. The coming of World War II found the job half done.

Washington was a mixture of old public buildings, newer blocks distinguished by a uniform similarity to overgrown Greek temples, and a large scattering of "temporary structures" erected in 1917-18 and for the most part kept in service.

Herbert Hoover, in his Administration, was rather sharply criticized for building the vast Department of Commerce Building on Fifteenth Street, between Constitution Avenue and D Street. It was called a monument to his own vanity, because he had been for 12 years Secretary of Commerce. By the end of the second Roosevelt Administration—with Harry L. Hopkins' Works Progress Administration going full speed—the Department of Commerce had become only one end of several blocks of public buildings turning colonnaded faces toward Constitution Avenue and the Mall, and interspersed with gardens, walks and parking areas.

The Interstate Commerce Commission went in one jump from a plaster-board, two-story building, no more than a shack, covering a block, into a marble palace. Secretary Perkins and her Labor Department moved into a new building with bronze elevators and an auditorium as large as a moderate-sized motion-picture theatre. The elderly Victorian Library of Congress grew an annex, carefully concealed in its rear, larger than the original building, and completely air-conditioned.

The Congress, in appropriating the money for these and a hundred other projects, found it could afford to spend between $4,000,000 and $6,000,000 to air-condition the entire Capitol and the adjacent office buildings for Senators and Representatives. One observer remarked that the next project would be to roof over the entire city and air-condition it.

There is, between the Capitol and Union Station, a large plaza covering several blocks. On this there still remained at the start of the government's depression building boom rows of "temporary barracks" built to house the "government girls" imported from other regions in World War I to assist in the clerical work of the war. Typical of government, there never had been an appropriation to tear down the buildings. They simply stood and decayed.

In the new Washington, the money not only was appropriated to tear them down, but the Senate, which is on the north end of the Capitol grounds and thus adjacent to the plaza, appropriated some more money for the building of a great garage under the plaza itself. The garage is completely concealed and sacred to the Senate. Congressmen park outdoors. All that a visitor can see at the site is a parked and tree-planted area, with sparkling fountains.

The building boom benefited for the most part the newer Departments and bureaus. The older agencies, being already housed, were ordered to withhold their own plans until the more pressing needs of a bureaucracy growing by leaps and bounds—in 1940 Federal employment throughout the country almost exceeded the 1,000,000 mark—had been met.

The State Department thus remained in its palatial gingerbread building completed shortly after the Civil War—the most ornamented building in all of Washington, and one about which the legend clings that an architect concerned in its design was already insane when he helped to draw the plans.

The State Department was growing out of its own building, but quarters were kept there—it was known originally as the State-War-Navy Building—for the Secretary of War and Chief of Staff of the Army. One large suite, occupied by a few aides and secretaries, also remained there in dignified segregation, its entrance marked by a sign, "General of the Armies." These were the permanent headquarters of the aging gentleman, by then a permanent resident of Walter Reed Hospital, who led American Armies to victory in the first World War—John J. Pershing.

The Navy long since had left the State-War-Navy Building, its Secretary and Admirals retreating to the "temporary building," a sprawling concrete structure to the south, built in 1917. Later another great naval war was directed from the same building, despite its creaking floors, cracked cement walls and condemned structure.

The War Department was housed through all the peace period, except for the Secretary and Chief of Staff, in the Munitions Building, a twin of the Navy Department Building, equally "temporary" and equally long-used, just west of the Navy Department. The Army, however, did wangle a new building, completed just before the war. This building, permanent and ornate, was designed to meet the needs of the ground and air force headquarters for a century to come. When war occurred in 1941 the entire building was barely sufficient to house the map section of the Army.

The Census of 1940 revealed that Washington proper, within the bounds of the District of Columbia, was a city of more than 700,000 people. There could not be such a spread in government without a comparable rise in population. Generally speaking, each new government employee gave reason for the addition of another person to the non-official population of Washington. And both brought their families. Then both families settled into a form of life characterized by the fact that Washington is the wealthiest city in the world, on the basis of per capita population.

The depression curtailed fantastic entertaining for a while, and caused the closing of many of the great houses. These, in fact, soon were leased in large numbers as overflow for government offices. Once Rexford Guy Tugwell, then chief of the Rural Resettlement Administration, invited Harry Hopkins up to see his offices, installed in one of the abandoned mansions. Hopkins walked into the main foyer. He stared at mirrors rising to the ceiling and surmounted by gilt cupids, the frescoed walls and chandeliers. He grinned and observed to Tugwell, "I'll buy a drink, but I won't go upstairs."

So here was a city in which the average income was listed at $1000 a year, against a national average of $600. Of course, the government clerks were not wealthy, but a surprisingly large number were well to do. They were able to buy food and clothes and to populate the city's boulevards with more automobiles than were operated in any other city the size of Washington. The government paid every two weeks, on the dot.

Now it seemed a little foolish that the Federal Government had restored to Virginia the part of the District of Columbia originally ceded to it. The Yankees were invading Virginia again in numbers greater than the army sent across to fight the Battle of Bull Run. Alexandria and Arlington, still retaining their corporate positions as small cities, were actually suburbs of the sprawling Capital. Their streets were crowded with old houses "restored" to modern form and new houses carefully constructed to look like old ones. To live in Alexandria had become *chic*. Apartments went up in barrack-like blocks.

Then came the Capital Airport. There had been an airport just across the Potomac, long since outgrown with the development of larger planes. Its inadequacy finally was proven beyond a doubt when a chartered airliner, carrying among its passengers a party of Congressmen, crashed before it could get off the ground. The government moved to find another field.

The new airport, also a product of the WPA days, was made on a bog from dirt dredged out of the Potomac. But such are the little distinctions that exist between federal and state authority that the government virtually had to make a treaty with Virginia to regularize usage of the airport.

The biggest bone of contention was not in the operation of the planes but of the restaurant. This threatened for a time to become a major issue. The airport was supposed to pay its own way. As part of the plan, a large restaurant was built along the side of the main building. A long wall of ceiling-high plate glass gives a full view of the runways. The attraction of the restaurant is obvious. The catering concession was rented at a very high fee long before the building was completed.

The hitch, however, was that the building was located in Virginia, which had local option on the matter of drinking. Arlington County, where the airport is located, permitted sale of liquor in bottles but never, never by the drink. And what good was a restaurant as a tourist attraction without drink service!

The problem was solved by a solemn agreement that the airport is part of the federal establishment, that it is under the jurisdiction of the District of Columbia, and that a Martini served in its restaurant is not a Martini served in Virginia.

The ruling of federal authority across the river helped to smooth the way for erection later of the great Pentagon Building, where 40,000 "Pentagon pigeons" labored in the last war. No drinks were served in the Pentagon—nor are they in any government building—but the authority of the District of Columbia over its extra-territorial government buildings was thoroughly established. If anyone ever writes to the War Department high command in the Pentagon Building, the address is Washington 25, D.C.

The people of Washington were the people of the United States, in all their commonplaces and most of their exaggerations. Smart people, gossips, headline seekers, the ambitious and the chiselers. They were cosmopolitan, too, in some senses of the word, particularly among the "smart set," as distinguished alike from the "cave dwellers" and the rank and file.

Washington was in 1940 the only city in the world where the cocktail party survived as a social weapon. It fitted into the peculiar character of Washington, where it might be the usual 5-7 affair for a few friends, or socially grew into a large evening affair with turkey and Smithfield ham to help push down the liquor. In the latter event, it was called a "reception."

Almost all parties in Washington attended by more than eight people, and particularly those announced in the newspapers, have a reason behind them. The reason, however, for the greatest efforts made by the most indefatigable hostesses is not nefarious; it is a form of determined ambition that has flowered into part of the Washington picture. These parties reached their fullest bloom in the 1939-41 era.

This was the period when Washington began attracting more "lions" than ever. Also, the rising national prosperity based on the European war and American "defense" programs started dividends rolling into the pockets of hostesses, or those of their bill-paying husbands.

The high priestess of the headline hostesses, whose only rivals for many years were the Latin-American and Chinese Embassies, was Evalyn Walsh McLean. Lean and vigorous in entertaining, Mrs. McLean determinedly remained in bed most days until 5 P.M. or later to preserve herself for the mass functions where anyone might be invited to eat and drink, as long as his name had made the headlines. One of the oddest characters among Mrs. McLean's guests went to Friendship so often that finally he married a daughter of the house, although he was 37 years older than his 20-year-old bride.

The very fact of Mrs. McLean's ascendancy in the party field, itself an old Washington custom, does point up the fact that Washington had become by 1940 such a big town that one could no longer generalize about its customs.

There were public party throwers and other hostesses who would consider it unusual for their names to get into the newspapers. Thinking at random, the writer recalls Mrs. Charles Carroll Glover, Jr., Mrs. Robert Woods Bliss and Mrs. George A. Garrett, all of whom have homes and chefs among the finest in Washington. But they entertain only their friends, or perhaps the officers of organizations in which they are active. Never are the names of their guests sent in neatly typed columns to the newspapers. Neither do they invite "society reporters" to their homes, with the proviso that these come with notebooks in their handbags. When these writing ladies go to the homes of such hostesses—and all are popular—they go simply as guests.

The more conspicuous party group in Washington is made up of the hostesses who welcome reporters and consider the snaring of a photographer from one of the local newspapers an achievement. These entertain with as much care as Florenz Ziegfeld staged the Follies, and some in a year spend about as much money in doing so. Their reward is a repetition of headlines in the *Washington Times-Herald,* most faithful recorder of who gave what and who was there.

Mrs. McLean, who during the war enlarged her guest list to include masses of service men as long as these were in Washington, made her party name with a courage as spectacular as the 44-carat glitter of the Hope Diamond. All other hostesses in Washington tried to get together groups of "congenial people." They feared scenes, particularly those weighty political dissertations that arise after the fifth cocktail and become serious issues, although the most vociferous participants may not remember them through the headache of the morning after.

The lady presiding over Friendship Heights watched for opportunities to pair off dissident individuals, and enjoyed particularly seating them side by side at more formal affairs, where they were glued in their chairs through at least five courses of food—soup, fish, meat, salad and dessert—and four wines—sherry, red, white and champagne.

Unfriendly commentators termed Friendship a "Washington Cliveden," comparing it with the British meeting ground of the equivalent of the "America Firsters." This was not true. There were plenty of the rugged isolationists on hand, but it was just as easy to find guests such as Senator Alben Barkley, the Majority Leader of the Senate and veteran New Deal Congressional leader, or Senator Connally, Chairman of the Foreign Relations Committee and thoroughgoing internationalist.

The "Cliveden" label more likely stemmed from the extraordinary romance between Mrs. McLean's daughter and Robert Rice Reynolds, large, portly and not-so-young former Senator from North Carolina. Reynolds, whose oratorical training grew out of experience as a carnival "barker"—he once recalled how he and Huey Long worked the same "pitch" in their youth —was the direct result of the seniority system in Congress. This system is so sacred that its bitterest opponents will not support abolition of it.

Reynolds got into the Senate in 1932. A shrewd politician, he won election, and a second term, by campaigning in the back country in a broken-down Model T Ford. He wore ragged overalls as a campaign uniform. He was named to the Military Affairs Committee as a new Senator and eventually became the senior Democrat on it, and therefore the chairman. That made him a "celebrity," and he remained a "celebrity" until 1944, when a series of circumstances brought about his retirement from public life.

As a Senator, Reynolds led the type of life peculiar to one form of politician. He bought a cheap little house in an unfashionable section on Capitol Hill, and made speeches for distribution (free) among his constituents emphasizing the modesty of his life in Washington. At the same time, he became one of the more conspicuous of Washington's party men. This path inevitably led to Friendship.

On October 9, 1941, Miss Evalyn Walsh McLean, 20, was married to Senator Reynolds, who then was 57 years of age. Mrs. McLean gave the wedding at Friendship. The bride was the fifth one whom Reynolds had led to the altar. After five years, this Mrs. Reynolds also died.

While Mrs. McLean was the *doyenne* of the well-known hostesses until her death in 1947, she was not without competition, particularly from two younger matrons who, with the assistance of great fortunes, were making their names as hostesses. These were black-haired, Hungarian-born Mrs. Morris Cafritz, and blonde Mrs. Robert Guggenheim.

The Cafritz fortune is native Washingtonian, founded solidly on enough hotels and apartment houses to have sheltered all of Washington a century ago. Morris Cafritz made his fortune in real estate. The source of the Guggenheim fortune was copper and was set aside for Colonel Robert while he was serving as a Regular Army Officer (he once was the immediate superior of the late General George S. Patton, Jr.) until his retirement before World War II with the rank of colonel.

There probably are not a score of houses in the United States comparable with the modernistic mansion erected in the 1930's by Morris Cafritz on a hill in the western part of the city. It is as large as any of the old houses; its modern decorations remind visitors of the décor of the newest ocean liners. The drawing room, which can comfortably accommodate 200 people standing or a fourth that number seated, has picture windows from which can be seen, across Georgetown, all of the city to the Capitol's illuminated dome. The ends of the room have murals containing heroic-sized women, copied from Egyptian friezes.

In this house "Gwen" Cafritz sparkles through the winter season with a series of small dinners, large cocktail parties, larger receptions, and Sunday afternoon "at homes" patterned after the salons of earlier days. In the spring and fall, when she is not at Hot Springs, there are garden and swimming parties. Supper dances are held in a ground-floor supper club as large as many of the New York night spots, complete with a glass floor illuminated from underneath.

The entertainments by "Polly" Guggenheim have been given in more classical surroundings—the fabulous city estate named Firenze. This house was partially burned in 1945 but was restored immediately along its former lines.

Firenze stands in 20 acres of parked lawn, complete with swimming pool, tennis courts and a corps of gardeners, fenced and guarded by locked gates and watchmen. The property is no more valuable than its treasures.

In the great hall, with a pipe organ concealed in its pickled-oak panneling, there hangs a Van Dyck portrait of an English noble, with the locket worn in the portrait by the long-dead subject encased under glass in the frame. In the house are paintings by Titian and lesser known masters, and rare Italian primitives. The colonel's brandy is almost as old as some of his art objects.

Guests at the balls given by the Guggenheims, when postwar entertaining was resumed, were required to show cards of admission at the door, and after checking their wraps, report to a desk where their names were carefully checked. One could not blame the Guggenheims, gate crashing having developed to a high art in the Capital.

From these impressive parties Washington entertaining tapered off into hundreds of others each season, of every size and type. Some wives of Senators and Representatives, but not many, essayed a busy social life. Very few could afford it. The

"Congressional set" lived more its own life with two circles roughly marked by membership in the Senate Wives and the Congressional Wives, who met periodically for luncheons and had a community social life at the Congressional Club.

The "Cabinet ladies" and the wives of Justices of the Supreme Court dutifully held "at homes" before the war, but the older social custom of trotting around leaving cards and sipping tea was largely discarded. In almost servantless Washington, most "society" housewives were so busy in the daytime that there was little time left between breakfast and evening for anything except appointments with the hairdressers and an occasional lunch, preferably at the Mayflower or the Carlton Hotel.

Dining out in public places was the exclusive prerogative of strangers in town. Washington never supported a restaurant that would be called good by New York standards. Its thousands of apartment dwellers and boarding-house habitués wanted a decent dollar chef's special, not a chef's delight ending with crepe suzette.

When well-established hostesses of the native school had to entertain away from home because of cook trouble or other reasons, they did so in the 1925 F Street Club, the Sulgrave or one of the country clubs—preferably Chevy Chase. Even in the depression, candidates for admission to this venerable country club (by 1940 completely surrounded by suburban homes) waited seven years or more between sponsorship and admission.

There is apparently a law which decrees that just about the time men and cities consider their lives well organized along a familiar pattern something happens. Washington was complacent in 1940, when in some degree it awoke to find that it had problems.

The Capital ran into a financial crisis when it had to face the probable cost of the "defense" program. A horde of lobbyists and "expediters" came to town with all kinds of enticements checked off against expense accounts. The population grew beyond the wildest dreams of even the most optimistic real-estate speculators.

Suddenly, hotels that had been starving to death for years had to set up priority lists for reservations. The spenders demanded so many facilities that cocktail bars and night clubs were crowded into every cranny of dusty old lobbies or vacant stores.

Thousands of new faces, many of them prominent from first-page newspaper publicity, appeared in the lobbies of the hotels, and a sizeable number—the first and luckiest and most prosperous—settled with farsighted reasoning into the community of Washington. And some old faces came back into prominence.

This was a catholic movement. It could not be catalogued as any particular type of invasion. It was, to a degree greater than the Capital had ever experienced, a rebirth of the type of people who made up the important part of Washington.

The threat of war required many and diverse talents. Franklin D. Roosevelt, facing a strongly isolationist trend throughout the country, thrust aside his New Deal and mobilized new lieutenants.

It was more than 28 years since Henry L. Stimson had taken his hat off the stand in the office of the Secretary of War and "retired" in 1912. It was seven years since he had last appeared in public as Secretary of State. In all those years he had been known as a conservative Republican, aloof from everything that might be labeled New Deal. He was the personification of wealthy and entrenched conservatism, living in retirement either at his famous Washington home, Woodley, or on his estate on Long Island. President Roosevelt asked the elder statesman to take over the War Department. He did.

In Chicago, Frank Knox was building up his newspaper, the highly successful *Daily News*, spokesman for Republican conservatism, but not isolationist. The old "Rough Rider" and professional journalist had taken a flier in politics in 1936 as candidate for the Vice-Presidency on the Republican ticket. Most persons had forgotten even his name. Roosevelt asked him to come into the defense picture as Secretary of the Navy. Knox moved to Washington.

In Detroit, William S. Knudsen, who had become a production genius in the automobile industry, was preparing to enjoy retirement, good food and life aboard his palatial yacht—the rewards of sixty years of hard work since he had landed in the United States as an immigrant boy, without money or skill. President Roosevelt asked Knudsen to put on the uniform of a lieutenant general and teach the War Department how to make war goods. Knudsen accepted.

In New York one of the most respected members of the judiciary was Robert Porter Patterson, winner of combat honors as an infantry captain in the first World War. Patterson was a Justice of the United States Court of Appeals, ranking next to the Supreme Court. He had gone on the bench as a United States District Judge, unanimously recommended by the New York Bar, by appointment from President Hoover. Again the bar had unanimously recommended him when a vacancy occurred in the Court of Appeals and Roosevelt had promoted Patterson to this bench.

One day Roosevelt asked the White House switchboard to find Justice Patterson. He was located, enjoying a holiday from the bench by training as a private in a volunteer unit at a military camp at Plattsburg, N.Y. It was his turn for "K. P." duty. Patterson was peeling potatoes. Roosevelt asked Patterson to resign from his life job on the bench and come to Washington as Assistant Secretary of War, to take a cut in pay, enter one of the hottest political jobs and supervise the procurement of war material. Patterson moved to Washington.

Harry L. Hopkins had become in a few years the most important man among President Roosevelt's intimates. He had succeeded Louis McHenry Howe. No longer Works Progress

Administrator, and having passed through a short term as Secretary of Commerce, he was, until appointed Lend-Lease Administrator in mid-1941, one of the half-dozen "anonymous assistants" to the President. Self-effacing in public, he had broadened his horizons considerably. Still damned by many critics, he had won many friends among New York conservatives—the "Wall Street crowd"—who, if they did not like the New Deal, at least admired Roosevelt's leadership in the crisis of spreading war.

One of the close friends of Hopkins was James Forrestal, two-fisted son of a ward politician in Beacon, N.Y., who worked his way through Princeton, was a naval aviator in World War I, a newspaper reporter and by 1937 president of the great banking house of Dillon, Read & Co.

One day in 1940 the President was talking to Hopkins about the men he needed around him. Hopkins suggested that Forrestal be called to Washington and given an assignment. The President had not met Forrestal, but another of the "anonymous assistant" jobs was vacant. Roosevelt told Hopkins that Forrestal could have it if he would take it.

Forrestal accepted. He was tried out as liaison agent between the White House and the Navy. Within a short time he was appointed Assistant Secretary of the Navy. Very soon afterward, still in 1940, Patterson and Forrestal were promoted to the newly created jobs of Undersecretary of War and Undersecretary of the Navy.

Robert Abercrombie Lovett was another New York banker who was, by all standards, highly successful. At 45 years of age, he was a partner in Brown Brothers, Harriman & Co., of Wall Street, member of many interesting clubs, and interested in half a dozen prominent public societies. He had been a combat aviator in World War I, and a winner of the Navy Cross. Lovett was proud of the distinction given to him by a daughter who called him by the nickname, "Leftie Louie." Invited to take the post of Assistant Secretary of War at Hopkins' instigation, he moved to Washington.

A third friend in this group was Artemus L. Gates, who had moved in 45 years, via Yale University and flying service in World War I, from Cedar Rapids, Iowa, to New York, where he was best known as president of the New York Trust Company. Gates was offered the job of Assistant Secretary of the Navy for Air. He accepted.

These were political appointments. So also were the new civilian administrative jobs that gathered men such as William L. Batt, the ball-bearing king; Chester Bowles, the retired advertising genius; and Edward Stettinius, the financier, in Washington. Yet they were not political. A new type of public servant had appeared in Washington.

These appointees were not old political stand-bys. Neither were they the high-domed type which had characterized the "Brain Trust" and brought into the now permanent life of Washington Felix Frankfurter of Harvard University and his myriad protégés. Even Stimson and Knox could hardly be classed as "political appointees" because the mere acceptance of the jobs handed to them led to an attempt—which bothered neither of them—to read them out of the Republican Party.

True, Bernard M. Baruch came back to Washington—to sleep in the Carlton Hotel and hold conferences on a bench in Lafayette Park—but, although a Democrat, he never held a formal office. He was more like a father-confessor to politicians and businessmen—the true prototype of the elder statesman.

For 140 years the power in Washington had been divided between, or had alternately swung between, the entrenched political leaders and the entrenched elders who often left public office to become the sages of the younger men who held the offices. This contest for power had been fought over dinner tables, in recent years in the more exclusive clubs, and occasionally in the cloakrooms and lobbies of Congress.

Suddenly both groups realized that they had lost authority in a new situation that would give to the new type of "bosses" more power, more opportunity for achievement and more fame. President Roosevelt had begun by disregarding, or at the least listening only tolerantly to, the elder statesmen in the Democratic Party.

As for the Congress, many critics charged that Roosevelt "usurped" its power and got by unfair means delegation of authority that all but nullified it. A more honest statement would be that the Democratic majority in Congress, first frightened half to death by having to face responsibility in the depression and afterward convinced that it could survive only by pinning itself en masse to the Roosevelt coat-tails, had abdicated voluntarily. By 1940, any leadership held by the Democrats in the Congress was merely that deputized to act for Roosevelt.

A free agent to dispose of power as he saw fit, Roosevelt first imported and then built up the new body politic in Washington. It would last beyond V-J Day.

The character of Washington itself was changed.

Chapter Twenty-Four

COMMAND CITY

WORLD WAR II made Washington two cities. It became the actual ruling center with unassailable power over the entire United States. It became, too, with all the reluctance imaginable, the first city of the world.

No wheel turned in the United States without being in some part controlled from Washington. No gun was fired on the side of the United Nations without support in some form from Washington. No one in Washington or in the United States could quite comprehend at first the whole meaning of the change.

Every other city, which in its turn had become the center of the world, had built itself to a degree on military or political conquest. But not Washington. Its new position was thrust upon it.

No longer could the 10 square miles comfortably house the people required by this greatness, as a quarter million new Americans were summoned to the new job. The leaders singled out by Sir Willmott Lewis as living within a single square mile soon overflowed far into the countryside.

In normal times the removal of the German, Italian, Japanese and later the French Embassies and their staffs would have left a noticeable hole in Washington. Actually, they were never missed. The change was gradual, if any flood ever can be described as "gradual." But the date when the change occurred, a date that made the preliminaries no more than curtain raisers, is definite.

Here are random notes of that date:

General George Catlett Marshall, Chief of Staff of the Army, was standing on a ladder pruning the limbs of one of the apple trees on his beautiful estate near Leesburg, Va., when the word came.

Navy Secretary Knox was in his Washington apartment, one day after giving a front-page interview to reporters stating that our Navy was superior to any in the world. Privately he had told one reporter that a war with Japan would be "like shooting fish in a rain barrel."

Secretary of State Hull was rapidly losing patience in one of the interminable conversations with Japanese Ambassador Nomura and special envoy Kurusu.

President Roosevelt was alone in the White House, probably sorting stamps as he did when he was nervous. He was awaiting a reply to his message of the day before personally appealing to Japan not to spread the Asiatic war by using troops massing in Indo-China for an invasion of Thailand.

The main news section of the *New York Times,* leading national newspaper and news Bible for officialdom, ran to 70 pages, mostly padded with page displays of Christmas-gift merchandise.

Maxim Litvinov, the old Russian statesman known as the friend of the Western democracies and dusted off by the Communists as an acceptable new Ambassador to Washington, had arrived in San Francisco on the preceding day.

In Singapore, the British high command invited the foreign correspondents to look over the newest battleship of the Royal Navy, the "invulnerable" *Prince of Wales.*

Washington was unseasonably warm, comfortable out of doors without a topcoat. The writer recalls having gone to a picnic. The food was never eaten. . . .

On this day, December 7, 1941, Pearl Harbor was bombed. The face of Washington was changed for all time.

The Capital City was fortified for the first time since 1861. In 1917 there had been security preparations and guards posted against saboteurs. But in 1942, with warfare moved into the air, the uncertainty of the power and development of the enemy's forces—and with the United States far more helpless than the public was permitted to know—Washington prepared to defend itself.

The tops of the higher buildings downtown bristled with anti-aircraft guns—at first a few were real and many more were dummies—arranged in a perimeter to do all possible to discourage bombing attacks on the White House, the Capitol and Executive Buildings. False terraces hastily thrown up on the White House lawn concealed batteries, which, if once fired, would have broken every pane of glass and dish in the building.

Heavy chains went up on the White House gates. Delicate devices were installed to warn of the entry of any person into the grounds. East Executive and West Executive Avenues, the tiny streets separating the White House from the Treasury and the State Department, were closed (and immediately appropriated as private parking spaces by high-ranking officials). A steam shovel tore into the eastern end of the White House grounds to make an air-raid shelter for the President and foundations for a super-strong headquarters wing to house the President's personal military staff.

Washington shared with other seaboard cities all the rehearsals for warfare that fortunately never came to the United States. In doing so, it proved it was a community like any other city. For a little while jealousies of official position, the division of cliques within levels of position, and the iron-bound caste system seemed to evaporate.

A city already crowded with a population of a little more

than 750,000 became a war headquarters with 950,000 persons jammed into it and other scores of thousands of new arrivals spilling over its boundaries.

The little Swiss Legation, occupied by a Minister and a diplomatic secretary before hostilities, swelled into a working force of eighty persons as Switzerland became custodian for most of the countries with which the United States was at war, and in turn watched over American interests in the enemy countries.

The British Embassy first filled in the space between its two Tudor wings facing Massachusetts Avenue with a small office annex. Next it built a large temporary building at the rear for offices. Finally its missions, with their thousands of employees, moved into great sections of other space—notably the top floor of the Willard Hotel, and the entire apartment building in which Andrew Mellon had once been a tenant.

Every one of the British Dominions, led by Canada, leased new buildings to house military and civil staffs. There was hardly a country that did not increase its representation. The Russians began spreading through the whole northwest residential section. They preferred to lease large houses and install in each a corps that worked and lived in the house. Even in expansion there must be no contaminating contact with Americans or other foreigners.

The Pentagon Building, so large a city remote from "downtown" that the government installed restaurants and shops to serve most of the needs of its 40,000 occupants, rose in a brick pile among a maze of modern roads and parking lots across the Potomac River. Temporary office buildings and barracks for many thousands of soldiers, sailors and marines—together with others for the newly recruited WACS, WAVES and SPARS—began to dot the Virginia countryside and the formerly open parkways of the city.

A picked battalion of Military Police, clad in white leggings, belts and gloves, was assigned to guard the White House. These soldiers walked 100-foot "beats" on its perimeter. They were quartered in a barracks building hastily constructed, complete with garages and laundry, behind the State Department. This barracks was in the shadow of the "Peace Monument" erected shortly after World War I.

Along the western side of the Mall, the Navy erected quarters for WAVES, who relieved enlisted male personnel in office work and hung their laundry up to dry a stone's throw from the Washington Monument.

For the most part, the rule was that office work must first be served, and living quarters considered second. One of the largest apartment houses in the Capital, on Dupont Circle, was taken over bodily as the headquarters for the Civil Defense Command. Office buildings and many downtown apartment houses were purchased or leased, under the threat of condemnation, to house the headquarters machinery of war.

The heart of all this activity was a marble building on Constitution Avenue specially constructed as the permanent headquarters of the Public Health Service. A relatively small structure, shining white, with bronze doors and trimmings, and fountains playing on its lawn, this building was a monument to the determination of the government to serve the peaceful cause of health. A quick survey by military authorities determined that it would be ideal for a far different purpose.

The Public Health Building stands just across Constitution Avenue from the old "temporary" headquarters of the War and Navy Departments. In these, during the first years of war, Chief of Staff Marshall and Admiral Ernest J. King, Chief of Naval Operations, had their offices. Only a two-minute automobile drive distant was the White House, where elderly but vigorous Admiral William D. Leahy worked in the President's office as Roosevelt's personal Chief of Staff for all war operations. These gentlemen became the American members of the Combined Chiefs of Staff—the ultimate operational boss of the entire United Nations war, except Russia.

From London came quiet, almost ascetic Sir John Dill, former Chief of the Imperial Staff, and Fleet Admiral Sir James Somerville, bluff and sociable old sea dog. With great staffs in their train, these two highest ranking British officers joined the three top American planners in the Public Health Building. Admiral Leahy was the final arbiter of their disagreements. In this board of five rested the entire command of the British and American forces in the Pacific and the Atlantic.

President Roosevelt and Prime Minister Winston Churchill held ultimate control over strategy. Whatever they decided must be carried out by the Combined Board. General Douglas MacArthur was given supreme command in the Southwest Pacific and Admiral Chester Nimitz in the Central Pacific, but only within the limits of directives sent from the Public Health Building. The invasions of Africa and Europe were launched by General Dwight D. Eisenhower, but only with the approval of this authority. Supplies went through the Mediterranean or to Murmansk for the Russians, again only with the approval of these five men.

No small group ever carried so much authority. They made Washington the greatest military headquarters of all time. In the long planning period these five met daily, with their advisers and observers sometimes present. A small kitchen was established in the main office suite, so that there need be no interruptions for lunch. One spy with access to the files and maps in this building conceivably could have changed the course of the war.

If there was one primary reason for the existence of Washington in this period it was to carry the task of supporting the military decisions made in the small marble building. The machinery called into being may have been too ponderous, it may have been too wasteful, and sometimes the people in it were frivolous. But even in its weaknesses the machinery made Washington over into its new role.

The British Government recognized the realities. London—

long described in successive editions of the *Encyclopaedia Britannica* as "the greatest city in the world"—sent to Washington all the little pieces of itself necessary to establish complete liaison supporting the Joint Chief of Staff. Its Ambassador in Washington now was Lord Halifax, who had stepped down from the post of Minister of Foreign Affairs to take over direction of this British Government in miniature.

Into the Embassy moved miniature duplicates of each of the major arms of British civil government. It was not necessary, as in 1917-18, for each new decision to be hashed out by cable and correspondence. Now the British had in the Embassy a whole list of ministers and chiefs of missions, each empowered to act in five minutes on important collaborative decisions.

It may have been that the subjection of London to the blitz made it more desirable that headquarters for the world-wide war be established in Washington. But whatever the reason, the world—the important part of it that was staking everything on the preservation of democratic life—moved into Washington.

For a while, Washington had no peer among the world's cities. It was the center of the "One World" dreamed for the future by many thinking people. As yet, there was no clear picture of just what responsibility this would entail.

Beneath the canopy of high official action Washington yet remained a city of people. These people stood in queues at restaurants, drank more liquor than they had in more quiet surroundings, searched frantically for places to live, and worked longer and harder for the most part than they ever had dreamed they would. Modern war did not stop at cocktail time. Washington, therefore, went for the first time on night shifts.

Washington was an American town, with the same rationing of gasoline and food, the same shortages, probably less black market because it was controlled as a "show piece," and the same energetic drive to "Win the War." In only one notable respect was it measurably different from its counterparts in other portions of the country. Washington did not produce things for war; it was the office headquarters. Its war job collectively was a desk job; it was the white-collar headquarters, as naturally would be the case in a Capital whose only first-class industries before the war consisted of a flour mill and a mattress factory.

There were many ways of viewing Washington; but whatever the vantage point, one new and rather startling fact emerged. It became a city, as well as a capital. For the first time in its life, Washington developed interests that brought together the "natives" and the "non-residents."

In black-out practices in the suburbs, at warden posts, Congressional clerks stood watch with the corner grocer and retired service officers. They were doing something for the preservation of their homes—and finally all agreed that Washington was home to each of them. The women of Washington got to know each other in a different light. The caste system, stronger in the Capital than anywhere else in the United States, diminished. It did not evaporate, but it lessened; and it has remained lessened as a result of deep and genuine friendships made and the respect created in that period.

In most established communities, where people have known each other well for long periods of time, the Red Cross and other organizational work represented a continuation of association started through clubs or simply broad friendships. Washington had no such background of association except in a field so limited as to mean nothing in mass work.

Because of its geography, not because of politics, the war gave more than average point to this type of war work.

If the reader will visualize the map of the United States and think of Washington as a city rather than as the Capital, he will see that Washington sits astride the Potomac River about 100 miles from the Atlantic Ocean. There are no cities or crossings over the river below Washington. The tidewater country of Virginia extends inland almost to Richmond on the south, and

Chesapeake Bay makes a deep indentation into Maryland as far as Baltimore.

The direct north-south route of the East must run through Washington. For that reason, Washington became one of the primary routes for troop movements early in the war. Many of its connecting highways were widened and strengthened. Its military airfields were enlarged to the greatest possible extent. The city streets, long after the fighting was over, still were marked with some of the cabalistic signs put up to direct military caravans in their passage through the city.

With the principal training grounds for soldiers in the South, and the greatest ports of embarkation north of Washington, it became a prime transit point—by motor caravan, by train and, in the close-run days of the war, by air.

In addition, the services maintain at Washington two of the largest and most important hospitals—the Army's Walter Reed General Hospital in the city itself and the Navy's skyscraper hospital, completed shortly before the war and located at Bethesda. In peacetime these were great treating and research centers. With their trained staffs, available as supervisors and instructors, both the Army and the Navy enlarged facilities to accommodate as many wounded men as possible in Washington, after the long-range casualties began to come back from the battlefields. A primary place for training amputees to readjust themselves to using artificial limbs was established near Washington.

At the start of the war there were literally hundreds of organizations, many of them prompted more by publicity than by a feeling of service, which sprang into existence. Often they were born at luncheons in fashionable restaurants or over cocktails and teacups in the more elaborate homes. Soon, however, these shook down into working organizations in which social life had no part.

The Red Cross needed and gathered together thousands of women among whom it was more normal for the volunteers to work daily rather than on the peacetime basis of a few hours per month. These did many chores. Some were nurses' aides in the hospitals. The canteen corps workers cooked, washed dishes and scrubbed, and manned coffee and doughnut stands at the most secret air installations on a 24-hour basis daily, to speed men flying overseas or greet those returning.

In one hectic period during the Battle of the Bulge a whole division of soldiers flew through Washington. Each man got coffee and a smile from "Red Cross canteeners" who were beginning to forget the meaning of sleep.

Alongside the Red Cross ranked the American Women's Voluntary Services, whose principal work was providing drivers for cars for official requirements, or simply to make more convenient the lot of the wounded men hospitalized in Washington by the thousands.

Mrs. Martin Vogel, widow of the banker who as Assistant Secretary of the Treasury directed sale of the Liberty Loan bonds in 1917-18, established the Hospitality Corps, through which many of Washington's nicest homes, ranging from the largest to the smallest, were thrown open to entertain lonely service men.

In other words, Washington had an incentive to prove that it was a nice town. It learned, to the surprise of many of its own inhabitants, that it was.

That is the other side of a picture that received almost no prominence in the face of the more exciting descriptions of life in Washington which were featured by the newspapers and the magazines. It also is true that some Washingtonians set records in displays of extravagance, in party-throwing and in spending money. It was the focal point of all the people with something to sell, all the agents with something to "fix" and a horde of aimless and wealthy persons with nothing to do, who settled in Washington to watch the show. For a little while they gave to

Washington a thin veneer similar to the "café society" of New York, but the veneer was very thin.

The hotels all but broke under the strain placed upon them. For 20 years the old "New" Willard, the Mayflower, Washington and Raleigh Hotels had been able to handle comfortably visitors to Washington who wished expensive downtown accommodations. Those with a taste for semi-suburban surroundings were easily accommodated by the Wardman Park and the Shoreham, great sprawling apartment hotels on upper Connecticut Avenue.

Under the pressure of war travel—the legitimate and the other type, but with no way of segregating businessmen from pleasure seekers or members of foreign missions from the mass of well-heeled refugees—Washington found in the middle of the war that it was inadequate for travelers.

One result was the construction at Washington of the only new, large hotel built in the United States after Pearl Harbor and before the end of the war. This was the new Statler. Then, ironically, it had to be constructed twice, despite the shortage of steel and other building materials. When almost completed, it was swept by a disastrous fire that destroyed the walls and twisted the girders.

In the meantime, entertaining rose to the highest pitch. Card leaving and the little formalities that had distinguished Washington were forgotten. These customs were packed away with the tail coats and white ties of the men. Now, people simply invited others to dinner or to cocktails by telephone—perhaps sent along reminder cards later so that their guests would not forget in the confusion of running around. Some men refused to dress for dinner at all, but they ate. The food was as elaborate as ever. The ladies' dinner dresses showed little change; if anything they displayed more of the ladies.

Hospitality forced on the White House the first change in its customs or arrangements since Theodore Roosevelt had redone the mansion. With war as an excuse, the President dared to state, and the Congress finally found excuse to confirm, the fact that the White House was inadequate for the demands made upon it.

It had been bad enough when the King and Queen of England had visited Washington in 1939. At that time, by the most skilled improvising, the White House staff had managed to squeeze into its guest rooms Their Majesties and eight of their personal staff. This could be done once in a great while, but the arrangements were comparable to those in a private home where half the furniture has to be moved to the sun porch and beds brought up from the basement to accommodate an aunt and her family for a week end.

Now, in wartime, the "relations" were flocking to Washington. Heads of states, a royal dignity once in a while, such as Princess Juliana of Holland or King George of Greece, and Prime Ministers in a constant procession.

Presidents of the United States have always been faced by this problem of hospitality, because American custom is to give to a foreign political leader the position his own people consider him to have. Thus, despite fixed American ideas on the subject, royalty is tops. At the same time, a Prime Minister is the elected head of his country's government, and therefore the same thing as a President in the United States. So he, too, is tops.

When royalty or P.M.'s visit Washington the only way to pay them proper courtesy is to invite them to the White House for at least one night. They cannot be sent off to even the finest hotel suite until after hospitality has been served. So heads were put together and a White House annex was "invented."

Across Pennsylvania Avenue from the White House stood the fine old Blair House, which got its name when Jackson's close friend bought it as a residence and made it into headquarters for the group of men known as Jackson's "Kitchen Cabinet." It was still occupied by the Blair family, but they were willing to move. The government purchased the house, gave the front a fresh coat of paint, and for the first time in more than 140 years the White House had a guest house.

Blair House came into the White House picture complete with furniture—of which a few pieces are beautiful—fine old silver, china and linen. Its library remained a tiny memorial to Andrew Jackson. Upstairs are almost a dozen bedrooms and baths. When the house is unoccupied, occasional formal luncheons are given there by the Secretary of State. President Truman slept in Blair House for a while after he succeeded to office. He could not move immediately into the White House until the Roosevelts had removed their personal effects, and the Secret Service would not permit him to continue living in the apartment house that had been his home.

The Secret Service will not permit a President, regardless of his wishes, to sleep in a room with strangers above or below him, or with quarters immediately beyond the walls of his own suite.

Then, for good measure, the government bought another house, next door to Blair House and about as large. It is not an old or famous place, but is called Blair-Lee House. Blair House is for visitors of the top rank; Blair-Lee House greets the members of officialdom of the second rank—cabinet members, chiefs of ordinary missions and the like.

Here again, the pattern of Washington was one of improvisation.

Chapter Twenty-Five

BIG SMALL TOWN

THE NOTES OF A TRUMPET blown on the top of the Washington Monument can be heard clearly 1000 feet away. War veterans will say that is a gross understatement in the light of their war experience with buglers blowing reveille. The fact is noted here, however, because the experiment was performed in Washington, in the spring of 1946, to advertise the opening of the fifteenth season of Washington's only home-town cultural activity —the National Symphony orchestra.

For almost a century and a half a contest has progressed, with no end in sight, over the question whether Washington is culturally an individual community or whether the country through Congress should be responsible for the more esthetic side of life in the Capital. Here again is an example of the curious blending—and conflict—of local and national interests which distinguishes every phase of life in the District of Columbia.

Virtually every other country has, in normal times, some form of nationally supported art expression. The British have long supported symphonic music as a national institution; Italy, opera; Russia, ballet; and most other countries a state theatre or opera. This support has taken the form of direct subsidies, or the provision of buildings and facilities in the capital of the country. These range from the Albert Hall in London to beautifully ornamented theatres in Latin-American capitals so small that few persons know their names.

The score in Washington is different; it is completely minus. The Capital of the United States is supported luxuriously by Congress in its museums and repositories. But the rule of thumb seems to be that such support can be given only to inanimate things, or dead ones. There is no question raised about the needs of the Library of Congress, and little debate was required in the middle of the depression period to obtain an appropriation of $100,000 to purchase a single folio, an original edition of the Gutenberg Bible. The Smithsonian, and its annex, the National Museum, abound in natural history exhibits including a fine specimen of the dinosaur.

Nevertheless, the theatre, music and ballet have encountered a determined opposition based in part on the fear of Congress to seem to be appropriating money for a city other than those in their home districts. Possibly, too, there is a hangover of Puritanism which labels anything connected with the theatre as not quite nice, if not a little sinful. This had led to shadings and subterfuges that at times have been comic, at other times simply ludicrous.

The Daughters of the American Revolution hold a position of privilege in Washington such as no other group does. This organization, a generation ago, built a great auditorium known as Constitution Hall. This was made tax free by law, on condition that it be made available for cultural events. By this backhanded method the Congress avoided spending any money in its capacity as the government of Washington and tried to silence demands that some of the taxes collected in Washington be devoted to this purpose.

The operation proceeded at a fairly even pace for 20 years. Constitution Hall prospered as the scene for lectures sponsored by the National Geographic Society, concerts by visiting artists and orchestras, and the place for meetings of large national and civic groups.

Then, one day, there sprang into national prominence a highly talented singer named Miss Marian Anderson. Miss An-

derson achieved a national reputation. A committee, on which
Mrs. Franklin D. Roosevelt was prominent, decided that she
should sing in Washington. But Miss Anderson happened to be
a Negro. The D.A.R. declined to permit the use of Constitution
Hall for a concert by a Negro.

Since that time the D.A.R. has reversed its stand, but the
argument has grown in favor of the provision of a building in
which representative American artists can give performances
without needing at least the tacit consent of a private group.
And yet, in Washington, when one tries to follow the injunction, "Go and hire a hall," the only one large enough to accommodate a crowd is Constitution Hall.

A certain tradition is served in Washington by the survival of
the National Theatre, which has changed its shell from time to
time. Air conditioning was installed in the summer of 1946.
Through this theatre were strained all of the plays that Washington saw after 1940, with the rare exception of an occasional
special performance that could hardly be classed as commercial.

The National, as it stands today, was one of the older theatres
when Washington had several prospering. The others died in
the depression. Poli's, which once stood opposite the Willard
and Washington Hotels, was torn down to make a parkway in
front of the Commerce Building. The old Belasco, on the east
side of Lafayette Park a few doors from the Dolly Madison
house, has been owned by the government for years. Sometime
it, as well as the Madison home, will be razed and replaced by a
new government structure. The Belasco had a rebirth in World
War II as the headquarters in Washington of the American
Theatre Wing.

Keith's Theatre, once the stopping place for musical extrava-
ganzas, with a vaulted basement promenade as large as the theatre itself, has become a motion-picture theatre. Its only reminder of past glories is a plaque marking the box once reserved
for Woodrow Wilson. Ford's Theatre, farther downtown, is too

old to be usable as a modern playhouse, but it probably will survive most other buildings as a shrine and museum—President Lincoln was assassinated there by John Wilkes Booth. There was a theatre named Knickerbocker in the uptown region, by prewar reckoning, at Eighteenth Street and Columbia Road. This one ended its career in the 1920's when an unusual blizzard put such a strain on the roof that the theatre collapsed and killed several hundred persons. When the building was reconstructed it was turned into a movie showhouse.

There are no concert halls in Washington. When opera came to Washington before World War II, on rare occasions, the Metropolitan might play for a few nights in a large movie house, specially adapted for the occasion, or one of the smaller touring companies might arrange to have the old Belasco dusted out for a week.

Some Washingtonians believe that by the increase in the size of the Capital and the influx of many people of wider interests there is in sight support for more theatre and more cultural activities. They point to the National Symphony Orchestra as evidence of this belief. And yet the symphony is not national; rather it is an example of the pertinacity of a small group of local people who pledged long before the war that Washington should take its place as a true cultural center of the United States, not simply as a political meeting ground.

In 1931 a little group of determined Washingtonians set about founding the symphony orchestra. George A. Garrett, Mrs. C. C. Glover, Jr., Mrs. Walter Bruce Howe and Frank R. Jelleff, owner of one of Washington's more prominent stores, were leaders in the movement. Mrs. E. R. Finkenstaedt and Mrs. Robert Woods Bliss, together with Edward Burling, Jr., and Mrs. Edwin M. Watson, also pooled their time and money to start the music program going. Mrs. Watson was widowed when genial Major General "Pa" Watson, who served as military aide to President Roosevelt for almost a dozen years, died of a heart attack brought on by exhaustion after the Casablanca Conference.

Dr. Hans Kindler became conductor of the National Symphony at a time when it was all idea and very little orchestra. With no money to meet pay rolls, and no facilities other than Constitution Hall, Dr. Kindler recruited musicians who were more interested in music than in pay. Professional musicians, who supported themselves, were joined in the orchestra's early ranks by architects, telegraph operators and clerks who came and brought their own instruments.

From the start, there was a faint hope that the Congress would partially "adopt" the orchestra by giving some support to it. Congress refused to budge. The symphony sponsors thereupon set out to make money. In 1936 the orchestra began a series of popular summer concerts, using for a stage a barge, anchored in the river beneath the Memorial Bridge leading to Arlington. The audience sat on a hillside.

The National Symphony Orchestra, which is "national" only in name, became a top-ranking organization. By 1946 its musicians were paid on a full-time basis, and its reputation was international. Dr. Kindler regularly was commuting to Latin America to conduct a series of concerts in the summer. The season of 1945-46, embracing 24 winter weeks and six summer weeks, was closed with a deficit of $512.38, after the symphony spent approximately $350,000.

The great indoor amusement of Washington is conversation. Collectively the city is a reader of newspapers, periodicals and books. If culture consists of being informed on current events, Washington is the seat of culture. More than one hostess must read the latest edition of the newspaper, or flick on the radio news broadcast while dressing, in order to hold her own with a dinner party of guests, among whom a State Department official and a Senator undoubtedly will discuss the day's events at Paris or Lake Success.

But whatever the conversation, the culture or lack of culture, the wealth or modest circumstances of the Washingtonian involved, he is not likely to be found conducting his discussions in a public place. At lunch, perhaps, but at dinner—never.

The second World War brought to Washington its first boom in night spots in its history. Even in prohibition days, when there flowered in New York and other cities the speak-easies that later blossomed into the most exclusive restaurants, Washington drank as well as ate at home.

The most notable figures among Washington bootleggers were not the operators of plush speak-easies, but the reliable and considerate gentry who delivered good alcohol to homes, and did it promptly. There was no Tex Guinan for Washington in the speak-easy days; interest centered chiefly in the fortunes of The Man in the Green Hat, a figure equally familiar in the corridors of the Senate and House Office Buildings or delivering his jugs along Massachusetts Avenue.

By 1943, with war visitors—spending visitors—there seemed to be the beginning of a Washington Café Society. The cocktail bars became bigger, more colorful, and were crowded to suffocation. Night spots opened in swarms in the area between Fourteenth and Seventeenth Streets from G to K—the region where, within the memory of many people not very old, the most conservative Washingtonians had their homes.

Operators did not hesitate to spend $100,000 decorating a night spot; the waiters counted on tips that averaged as much as $25 a night.

Within a year after V-J Day the owners were wearing long faces and the waiters were thanking customers politely for quarter tips. The restaurant business had made another mistake; it had mistaken visitors for Washingtonians. The war contractors had lost their expense accounts and a new conservatism had come over the people who could afford champagne, but simply would not order it.

It remained difficult to get a hotel room in Washington, but the spending spree apparently was ending quickly after the war. The people who did dine out drank cocktails and ordered decent food, which was not cheap, but "café society" was not for Washington.

Two world wars emphasized the fact that Washington as a city was somewhat different from every other city in the United States. It was Paris with a Middle Western outlook, in living as well as in its dominant thinking.

And nowhere was this more noticeable than in the little compromises which in the aggregate made up its daily life. Take the matter of drinking, for example. Allied Liquor Industries, Inc., was quoted by a national magazine as reporting that in 1944 Washington consumed 16 quarts of liquor for every man, woman and child living there, compared with a national average of five quarts. Due allowance should be made for the fact that the most populous counties of Virginia and Maryland are adjacent to Washington; that in these counties retail sales of liquor were closely rationed, and that the Virginians and Marylanders bought most of their supplies from Washington liquor stores.

Even so, Washington obviously was a hard-drinking town. The point was made that if "outsiders" bought three of the 16 quarts a year that made up the average, Washington still consumed as much liquor per capita as Nevada, with its wide-open cities of Reno and Las Vegas.

Yet, in this city since repeal of prohibition, every bar was closed at midnight on Saturday and remained closed until Monday. There was a 2 A.M. curfew every other night; no all-night "hot spots" could exist under those limitations. There were many cities in which it was commonplace to see café parties breaking up at dawn; but not Washington. The only people on the Capital's streets in the early morning hours were those heading for early jobs.

Also, the laws were enforced. Occasionally a speak-easy

thrived for a while, but only until the police caught up with it. There were from time to time individually dishonest policemen on the Washington police force, but no corruption in the "fixing" sense of the word for many years.

Some of the approaches to morality were amusing. One was the local law, in effect after the repeal of prohibition, that forbade a patron to stand on his feet while he drank in a public place. Bars in Washington cocktail lounges were ornamental affairs where waiters went to get drinks for the customers. A patron at a lunch counter could drink beer while seated at the counter, but not while standing. If he ordered whisky or gin he had to sit at a table.

The Capitol Building itself had for many years some of the best bars in the country, and some of the stoutest drinkers. One story still told concerns two Southern Senators who met at the bar in the Senate cloakroom one afternoon to supervise the broaching of a new cask of bourbon whisky. No new cask could be broached properly without the presence of these two experts.

The first Senator sipped his glass reflectively, and remarked, "I think, suh, I detect the faintest trace of a metal taste in this heah whisky." The second sipped his, and responded, "I beg youh pardon, suh, but it is leather—leather, suh, that mars the taste."

The argument became more heated and almost ended in a duel. It turned into a Senate controversy during the month required to empty the cask of liquor. Almost every Senator—although no others had tasted anything wrong at all—was on hand when the cask finally was emptied, and the bartender smashed it with a bung starter.

Among the broken staves, after careful search, he found a tiny tack, of the kind used by upholsterers, with a metal stem and a head made of leather.

The Capitol and government buildings "went dry" finally in 1903. Repeal of prohibition did not see bars reopened in them.

A few independent legislators, such as the late Senator Key Pittman, of Nevada, put bars in their offices. There are very few of these; by the same token, there are few Senators and Representatives who turn down an invitation to a cocktail party.

Chapter Twenty-Six

WORLD CENTER

FOR THE FIRST TIME in Washington's history the annual dinner given by the President to the Diplomatic Corps had to be broken in 1946 into two parts. The White House dining-room table, extendable to a capacity of about 100, simply could not accommodate all the ambassadors and ministers, with their wives, accredited to Washington.

This was one small measure of the new Washington. Peace did not shrink it. Reluctant, unambitious in world affairs, the quiet, homely city on the Potomac was the nerve center of the world.

The world organization of the United Nations symbolically had started in the old mansion named Dumbarton Oaks. It made little difference, however, that UN had long since moved to New York, or that conferences on peace treaties were held in Europe. The main force that had won the war was the force of the United States. The substance that would do most toward rebuilding a devastated world was in the United States.

And all that was American was represented by Washington. Many of the old faces were gone, and men who were young and vigorous when the first great change occurred in 1933 were old. Personal feuds and political schisms had taken other familiar faces from the scene. But Washington long since had demonstrated that it was more than a man, much bigger than any group that temporarily held control.

In looking backward one saw a paradox in the realization that this Washington, which had jettisoned the League of Nations in 1920, had come to accept as commonplace the model for the United Nations that long antedated the League, an international organization that really worked.

Tourists for a generation had made it a point to visit the Pan American Union. Here stood one of the most beautiful modern buildings in the world, a marble structure conforming to northern architecture but making its bow to tropical lands by enclosing a patio graced by an Aztec fountain. Visitors stopped and gazed at the tropical plants blossoming in this patio, even in midwinter, and they laughed when raucous-voiced macaws protested if they talked too loudly.

These visitors walked through the halls of the Union, past maps and exhibits from all the countries south of the United States, and on into a garden around a lily pond which has been studied by landscape architects from around the world. To native Washingtonians the Pan American was best known as the setting for concerts, in the garden in summer and in the great hall in winter, where one or another of the service bands would accompany artists from Latin America.

These were, however, the superficialities. More important, the Union stood for mutual understanding between the American Nations that had endured since 1890, unaffected on the whole by misunderstandings that sometimes were great, or even by wars between some of the members. For 26 years, until he was killed in an automobile accident, its Director General was scholarly, modest Dr. Leo S. Rowe.

On the morning of each New Year's Day, it had long been the custom for the Secretary of State to entertain at breakfast the chiefs of missions from the Latin-American countries. Such things often were far more important in diplomacy than formal talks among striped-trousered delegations.

The Pan American Union's record never had been perfect as a preserver of understanding between its members. In its lifetime it had seen the United States denounced as the "Colossus of the North," and wars between several of the southerly members. The fact was, however, that it had survived. There was no parallel for the Pan American Union in the world. Its basic strength was the understanding that the Western Hemisphere was made up of peoples and cultures who had the right to respect in their own spheres, and who simply had to get along together.

James G. Blaine, former Secretary of State, fathered the Union at a period when relations among the American Republics might be compared to the fears and jealousies that marked the postwar world of 1946. He called the First Pan American Conference in Washington in 1889-90. This conference set up the International Bureau of American Republics.

There were no great arguments over veto powers, such as marked the birth of the United Nations, but there were jealousies and mistrust. The bureau provided a place where representatives of the Latin-American countries could talk informally. It worked.

By the time a fourth Pan American Conference was held at Buenos Aires in 1910, it had been agreed to christen the 20-year-old child of cooperation the Pan American Union. Andrew Carnegie contributed $850,000 toward the cost of constructing in Washington a home for this league of nations of the Western Hemisphere. The members subscribed $250,000 more to complete the cost of the grounds and buildings. It became permanent.

The Union organized many Pan American Conferences, out of which came greater understanding—agreements not shaken by any of the broader international arguments.

Not much has been printed about the works of the Union in recent years, since these have been overshadowed by greater events. Nevertheless, the 20 other countries which make up the Union consider it sufficiently important to designate their resident representatives at the Union as ambassadors, ranking on a par with their chiefs of missions sent to Washington to deal directly with the Government of the United States.

The absolute equality of all nations within the Pan American Union set an example which at the war's end was rapidly being applied by the United States to all diplomats in Washington. The first step had been to make all chiefs of missions exchanged between this country and the other American countries ambassadors. Thus, little Honduras, with only an ambassador and a military attaché—a total of two officers in its establishment —ranked alongside Great Britain and France. In fact, after Lord Inverchapel arrived in 1946 as British Ambassador, thus becoming for a while the most junior among the ambassadors, he sat far down any dinner table, including the White House one, below Señor Don Julian R. Caceres, the Ambassador of Honduras.

Diplomatic precedence long ago was established purely on the basis of seniority. All ambassadors outranked all ministers, but within the two halves ambassadors had their special places and the ministers their own. The dean of the diplomatic corps was the senior ambassador. Britain had several deans of the diplomatic corps because it customarily left its ambassadors long in Washington.

In the fall of 1946, the line-up of the first 10 ambassadors, in the order of precedence, was Brazil, Spain, Uruguay, the Netherlands, Norway, Greece, Honduras, Nicaragua, Costa Rica and Portugal. Only deaths or transfers could change this order, and inevitably the juniors moved toward the "head of the class" as the seniors retired. Lord Inverchapel would have to wait his turn, as would Ambassador Bonnet of France and all the others.

Being dean of the diplomatic corps meant little except in prestige, and the requirement that the dean have a good digestion. At least once each year the dean had to entertain, and be entertained by, every other member of the corps. And at the White House diplomatic reception, which was separate from the diplomatic dinners, he was the first one greeted by the President.

The changing face of the world probably found more echoes in the diplomatic corps in Washington than anywhere else. The role of Washington as G. H. Q. of the war, and as a major policy center in the peace, accomplished two outstanding things in this field—it put diplomats to work, and it changed all standard ideas about the type of lives they lead. The social requirements of the jobs still persisted, but to an ever-increasing degree these became chores that had to be fitted into working schedules, not the be-all and the end-all of diplomacy.

The late openings and early closings of embassies gave way to the keeping of regular office hours. Staffs multiplied, and the persons on them found that routine work cut sharply into the older and more leisurely lunch and cocktail periods.

On March 8, 1939, when Carlos Martins took up the work of Ambassador of Brazil, his embassy was a cultural center in a large mansion on Massachusetts Avenue, in which an occasional routine report on military, agricultural or financial affairs constituted about the only responsibilities. In 1946, when Mr. Martins was dean of the corps, he presided over an establishment comparable with the headquarters of a great international corporation. A major general of the Brazilian Army, Valentim Benicio de Silva, and a vice-admiral of the Brazilian Navy, Octavio Figueiredo de Medeiros, working on only two phases of his embassy duties, headed large staffs of their own.

The routine of the embassy required the full-time supervision of a minister-counselor, Octavio do Nascimento Brito. There were 23 other officers of diplomatic rank, and these did not include assistants and secretaries and the members of special missions. A large house adjacent to the Brazilian Embassy was exclusively an office building. Argentina and Mexico had staffs almost as large.

Or consider Switzerland, which for 50 years found a single minister and a secretary sufficient to handle its representation in Washington. Minister Charles Bruggmann in 1946 had a staff, with no prospect of shrinkage for a long time, if ever, that included a counselor, several secretaries and attachés for military, naval, and commercial reports.

World interest centered in Washington.

Time was, not far in the past, when the wife of a diplomat was judged exclusively by her entertainments and her clothes, with perhaps some complimentary comment if she was intelligent. But she must not be too intelligent, or too outspoken. That was not ladylike. Above all things, she must never conduct herself in a "public manner."

Such rules were discussed in Washington after World War II only with laughter, if they were discussed at all. The wives of diplomats had won emancipation; they intended to hold it. The second World War gave them an opportunity and excuse to work, and this privilege they would not surrender lightly.

Most of the publicity of war days was given to the "name" ladies who christened ships or presided at this or that benefit function. There was little room for describing the more prosaic bandage rolling, a thing still best done by hand in the atomic age, which occupied, day after day, scores of women working in a large abandoned mansion on Massachusetts Avenue.

Madame Hurban, wife of the Minister of Czechoslovakia, and American born, occasionally kept obligatory engagements, going directly from menial work for the Red Cross and wearing the cotton uniform of her job. "Dish-pan hands," that displaced softly manicured ones, became a mark of pride.

Madame Bonnet, whose husband became the first French Ambassador in Washington after the liberation of France, had not been a diplomatic wife for many years, although she had been a noted hostess when her husband represented his country in Washington before the war. When she returned to resume

her duties as "ambassadress," it was with an established reputation as a milliner, developed during the war when she designed
hats to make a living.

Even before Munich, when the Nazis were penetrating various European countries, one diplomat after another had found
himself torn between changing coats and holding his job or
standing up for principles, regardless of the cost. The cost for
some meant the sacrifice of everything they had.

Madame Boncesco's husband was a Rumanian diplomat.
Wealthy, with every selfish reason to hold onto what they possessed, the Boncescos were popular and distinguished in the
Capital. Madame Boncesco wore a monocle, which gave an
added touch of glamor. Everything the Boncescos possessed was
sacrificed when the minister decided that the changing politics
of Rumania were not his politics. Thereafter, Madame Boncesco became a clerk in a Washington store, and became an even
more popular figure in Washington.

When Hitler perpetrated the *Anschluss* with Austria, Minister
Prochnik was offered every inducement to stay at his post.
He and all the other Austrian diplomats were assured that,
simply by conforming to their new government, their private
estates would be preserved, their pensions assured—life would
be very pleasant. All that Prochnik needed to do was to go to
an office in the German Embassy and obey orders.

For a while, the American Government ruled that the Austrian Legation was in its trusteeship, since Austria no longer
existed. It invited Prochnik to continue to live there with the
rank of Minister of Austria until such time as diplomatic details
resolved themselves. He did not.

Prochnik, a scholar and a prime example of what was termed
a diplomat of the old school, went to work as a university in-
structor. Thereafter he supported himself, while his fortune
went into the Nazi maw. When the Prochniks' daughter, Pa-
tricia, grew up in Washington, she entered society, and then
used an exceptionally good voice to sing in public for pay.

In the more active diplomatic ranks whatever was done by Maria Martins was subjected to the closest scrutiny, because Maria Martins was the wife of the Brazilian gentleman who was made by time the Dean of the Diplomatic Corps. Madame Martins possessed a rare talent for sculpture, which received polite attention long before her husband reached his high distinction.

Ten years ago it was considered all right for a diplomat's wife to have a hobby, and in wartime it was commendable for sculptures to be exhibited at galleries for the benefit of charities and drives. With the end of the war, Madame Martins enlarged her field, exhibited in Paris as well as in New York—and sold her work.

The war freed more than the peoples of the liberated countries; it emancipated the diplomatic women of Washington.

Of course, protocol still persisted. It worried hostesses in the seating of every dinner party with such questions as whether a major general outranked a counselor of embassy, and whether a luncheon could be made to do the work of a dinner. The cost-of-living problem which faced every American housewife reflected itself in the official establishments. Incomes and allowances generally clung to standards that did not keep up with increases in the cost of food and assistance.

It had, too, its amusing manifestations.

Every embassy in Washington tries to display those things for which its country is most noted. The finest wines of France always have been served at the French Embassy. The Chinese Embassy is a museum of China's ancient arts in porcelain and bronze. And so on down the line.

Holland takes its greatest pride in a living exhibit, tulips grown from the choicest bulbs cultivated in the fields along the Zuyder Zee. Fresh shipments of the new bulbs are sent to Washington each year. These are planted in the embassy gardens.

Tulip bulbs, however, do not wear out in one year. They remain fruitful for several years, the only change in their blooms being a slightly diminishing size year by year. It is said that a tulip fancier can tell the rank of a Dutch diplomat by the size of his tulip blooms: the largest belong to the ambassador; the second-year bulbs are in the garden of the counselor—and so on through the list of secretaries and attachés.

Chapter Twenty-Seven

FACES IN THE MIRROR

BETWEEN THE WASHINGTON MONUMENT and the Lincoln Memorial is a long, artificial lake. In the summer small boys sail model boats on its face. In the winters, if Washington has a spell of freezing weather, its surface is thronged by skaters. The lake is called the Reflecting Pool.

Nothing could have been more symbolic of Washington in the gray and thought-provoking days following World War II. The Capital was the mirror of a country. And Washington was the looking glass where all the world studied the mood of a country which promised so much if only it could live up to the bright, strong resolutions of the war days.

Washington, therefore, had come to a point in the long, up-surging history of the United States where its social ascendancy was less important than its political implications. The details of the city had become incidental. It was established. As a capital it was permanent. What mattered now was where it stood, and how it stood its ground, and where next it would move in the cosmos of world affairs—a world living under the shadow of reciprocal suspicions and the dread of the atom bomb.

Yet, as if to prove that there is nothing new in politics, except in degree, Washington again walked late in 1946 along the same road it had traveled in earlier critical periods. To the world, after the elections in November of that year, it was the seat of a divided government, with Harry S. Truman, a Democratic President, constitutionally ensconced in the White House until January 1949, and with the Republican party in firm control of both Senate and House in the new Congress which would convene in January of 1947.

In the personal field of political changes some importance was attached to the switch whereby Senator Arthur H. Vandenberg, of Michigan, a Republican, became chairman of the powerful Senate Committee on Foreign Relations, displacing Senator Tom Connally, of Texas, who became Democratic minority leader of that committee. Actually, the switch was not important in the field of international affairs.

More important was the contrast with previous periods of divided government. These seemed always to come upon the United States when crises required the greatest amount of intelligent, coordinated operations in Washington.

Here was 1917 all over again, or, to take an earlier precedent, the two-year period beginning with the elections of 1894.

President Cleveland began his second term in office in 1893, and in that year there occurred what was known as a "black panic," as all the disturbed forces of Reconstruction, post-Civil War inflation, and indeterminate policies came to a head. In 1894, the country elected a Congress which in both houses was as overwhelmingly Republican as the one elected in 1946. The result was two years of stalemate.

In 1918, with the first World War in its last stages and the peace treaties yet to be considered, President Wilson specifically asked the country to elect a Democratic Congress. He failed in this effort, with the result that his broad program—supported earlier by many leading Republicans—was dead before it had a chance to live.

In 1930, also, President Hoover faced two more years in the White House, a Republican President, with a Democratic Congress sitting in the Capitol.

The precedents were ominous, and prediction was impossible as Washington moved into the postwar world of the late 1940's. But in the mirror of Washington some few things and persons stood out which gave a more hopeful outlook than history might indicate.

There was, at least, the beginning of a new cooperation. That cooperation in Washington was personified by three men—elderly men—to whom the government had given the task of resolving the peace. Possibly none of them would survive the long task ahead, but they were the pacemakers in the work, and they did exemplify one great lesson which Washington had taught its leaders.

The President, under his constitutional powers, makes peace treaties and alliances, and these, to be binding, must be approved by two-thirds of the members of the Senate seated in solemn executive session. But the Senate acts only as a court of review on treaties. It approves or disapproves. Twenty-six years earlier, in 1920, a President, Woodrow Wilson, attempted personally to write a peace treaty involving world collaboration. In 1946 President Truman eschewed the task, and delegated his power to these three men. Two of them were the leaders of Senate opinion on foreign affairs. The third was a former Senator, full of honors, whose titles had included that of Associate Justice of the Supreme Court of the United States.

In planning the role of the United States in world affairs these men were Washington.

On May 2, 1879, an Irish girl gave birth in Charleston, S.C., to a boy who was christened James Francis Byrnes, in honor of his father, who died while he was still very young. The boy's mother took in sewing, and he ran errands to make a little money. While he was in his middle teens, Jimmie Byrnes learned stenography. By the time he was 21, he qualified as a court reporter. Through this door he won admission to the bar. Editor of a small newspaper for a time, a dogged politician, short in stature, and equipped with an Irishman's full quota of humor, Jimmie Byrnes got into Congress at the age of 30.

He left Congress in 1925, after 14 years of service in the House, and until 1931 practiced law and made a little money in Spartanburg, S.C., which he had made his home. He had a cousin, his boyhood chum with whom he had shared a home, named Frank Hogan. This cousin moved to Washington early, set up his own law practice, and before he died became a millionaire and an internationally famous lawyer.

But politics and public affairs pulled harder at James Francis Byrnes than just making money. In 1931 he ran for a seat in the Senate and won it. The job cost him a lot of money in lost earnings. ("There's not much a man can want," Byrnes once remarked to the writer, "beyond a decent home, two tailor-made suits a year, and a reasonable quantity of good bourbon whisky.")

People liked Jimmie Byrnes all the way along the line. Franklin D. Roosevelt liked him. Joseph P. Kennedy, James A. Farley and Cordell Hull liked him.

When Roosevelt decided to name Senator Byrnes to the Supreme Court in 1941, to strengthen the prestige of the court after severe damage by some inferior appointments, the Senate unanimously confirmed the appointment. This was a life job ($20,000 a year, security and no political chores), but a war hit the country, and on October 3, 1942, Roosevelt asked Jimmie to give up all that and take the hot-spot seat of Director of the Office of Economic Stabilization. So Jimmie Byrnes gave it all up and went to work in the war. In time he had a lot of other titles, which generally added up to the job of being Assistant President of the United States.

If Byrnes had any special political ambition it was to be Vice-President of the United States. His Senatorial friends, among them Harry S. Truman, thought he would make a good running mate for Roosevelt in 1944. Truman went out to Chicago to the Democratic National Convention to nominate his friend, if Roosevelt approved. But Roosevelt did not approve.

Fate eventually made Truman President, and his toughest problem was that of international relations. Also he faced the decision of picking a successor if he should die, because now there was no Vice-President and the man who was Secretary of State would be the next man in line. Truman had a tough job to do in firing Edward R. Stettinius, Jr., who had been chosen by Roosevelt to succeed the ill and aging Cordell Hull, but he did it. On July 3, 1945, he delegated to Jimmie Byrnes all his powers of decision in foreign affairs, when Byrnes took the oath of office as Secretary of State.

So Byrnes became the architect of whatever plan was to be followed by Washington in its future role. His face dominated the mirror; it was almost as large as the face of Truman—possibly larger.

Two other faces flanked the face of Byrnes. They were as different in background and type as though they belonged to foreigners from different countries, but they were alike in that both were as American as apple pie.

When Jimmie Byrnes was playing and working in the streets on the poorer side of old, established Charleston, a youngster named Tom Connally was playing around a farm in McLennan County, Tex., soaking up the lore of a state whose elders still recalled when it was an independent country. But Tom did not follow the ordinary pattern of growing up and becoming a ranch hand or a dirt farmer. He went to Baylor University and got his university degree and stayed on to win a law degree. He enlisted in the Second Regiment Texas Volunteer Infantry in the Spanish-American War, and afterward went back home and dug into politics.

Tom Connally was a big man and an impressive orator in a country that bred sonorous phrasemakers. He wore his hair long, and he wore stiff shirts fastened with gold studs. He could talk the left hind leg off a mule, but what he said made sense.

When Tom Connally got into a tight political debate he would tell a story to make a point or to straddle one—or to change the subject. His favorite one, told with variations for a generation, concerned a shiftless man who showed up at the county relief agency to ask for help in supporting a numerous family, including a twelfth child just born.

The agent took him to task for creating responsibilities he could not handle. Texans think a man ought not to bite off more than he can chew. The man swore it would never happen again; said that if it did he would go and hang himself on the nearest cottonwood tree. Within a year he showed up again, needing help for a family including the inevitable new baby.

"I thought you were going to hang yourself if your wife had another baby," the agent said.

"Well, now, I did say that," the man explained. "And I remembered my promise. And when the baby was a-comin' I did go out and I took a piece of rope, and I went out to the old cottonwood tree and I pulled a wagon under a limb to stand on. And I threw the rope over the limb and took a hitch around my neck, and I started to step off, but just then a voice said to me, 'Sam, you may be hangin' an innocent man.' "

A man who can tell stories like that never gets into bitter arguments. Tom Connally talked his way into the House of Representatives in 1916, took leave of absence to serve in World War I, and in 1928 was elected to the Senate. When Senator Key Pittman, of Nevada, died, he succeeded to the Chairmanship of the Senate Committee on Foreign Affairs.

President Roosevelt, seeking to avoid the Wilsonian pitfalls, asked Senator Connally to become Congressional adviser to the United States delegation at the Inter-American Conference at Mexico in 1945. Then the President made him a delegate to the San Francisco Conference in the same year, to help organize the United Nations. President Truman, a fond admirer of his old colleague, made Tom Connally one of the two advisers to Secretary Byrnes at the peace conference meetings.

Grand Rapids, Mich., is known in every part of the United States as the place where furniture is made. It does produce other things, though, and back in 1884 it produced a youngster who was out selling newspapers about the time that Jimmie Byrnes was perfecting his technique as a stenographer. Arthur Vandenberg was a serious youngster, who wound up studying law at the University of Michigan.

The law did not satisfy him, however; he felt a creative urge. He felt it so strongly that he spent more time studying the life of Alexander Hamilton, and he learned so much about Hamilton that he wrote a series of books about him. Ordinarily such a student would wind up in banking, because Hamilton was a master of finance. But Arthur Vandenberg wanted to write. It was not long before he was editor and publisher of the Grand Rapids *Herald*. That got him into politics up to his ears—good, solid Republican politics. In fact, he finally became chairman of the Michigan Republican State Convention.

The next logical step happened in 1928 when Vandenberg was appointed to the Senate to fill a vacancy, then won election to his seat, and was re-elected twice thereafter. Among his committee assignments was the Senate Foreign Relations group. Vandenberg got along with Connally on a purely friendly basis; there was no Democratic-Republican opposition hocus-pocus about their service there. It was here that Vandenberg attained his full stature.

First Roosevelt and then Truman asked Vandenberg to sit alongside Jimmie Byrnes in making the peace treaties. Vandenberg dropped any trace of politics he may have retained and accepted without qualification.

Thus these three—Byrnes, Connally and Vandenberg—became to the world at large the face of Washington in the reflection of international affairs. Nothing like that ever had happened before in all the wars and peacemaking of the United States.

Closer to the mirror, on the streets of Washington, the picture was not quite so clear. It was blurred by the rapid changing of faces, the confusion of people, and the pull and counter-pull of politics in transition. Even Secretary Byrnes resigned after a while to be succeeded by General Marshall. Only the giant trees in Lafayette Park, the lighted lantern hanging from the north portico of the White House, the illuminated dome of the Capitol at night—only such symbols reminded Washington that there is a continuity greater than the individuals passing in procession through office. The pace of the procession had quickened.

If politics and political figures alone had been the face of the Capital the picture would have been one of disillusionment. There was the White House, symbol of everything for which Washington stood, seeming rather small in the shadow of its former great days.

Around it hammered the forces of change, demands for new policies to meet another postwar period, while Paul Porter, as Price Administrator, sought to liquidate in orderly fashion the government controls fastened on production in the period of wartime shortages. John Roy Steelman, the former professor, wrinkled a puckish brow as chief of the Office of War Mobilization and Reconversion, while attempting to stem floods of strikes on the one hand and insistently growing demands by industry that the government "reconvert" by getting out of the reconversion business.

The Democratic Party, of which Truman was chief, encountered a new schism—the charge had long been made that Truman was too "conservative" for the left wing of a party rebuilt by F. D. Roosevelt—when Henry A. Wallace, as Secretary of Commerce in 1946, attempted to rewrite American foreign policy in a speech demanding more consideration for the demands of the Soviets at the peacemaking tables.

Wallace left the Cabinet—after making a speech which had been read in advance and publicly approved by Truman—and the President reiterated his support of Secretary Byrnes. And Averill Harriman, Roosevelt's very early recruit from the ranks of business and finance to the New Deal, resigned his latest diplomatic post as Ambassador to the Court of St. James's to take on the Secretaryship of Commerce. Harriman had been Ambassador to Russia. The Soviet newspapers began to campaign for election of Wallace to the Presidency.

The members of the Congress took to the hustings, 1946 being a by-election year.

And in the White House the President talked to and occasionally swam in the White House swimming pool (it was built in 1933 as a gift to F. D. Roosevelt from the school children of New York) with the new men who were important in Washington. There had been changes—so many in high places that when Wallace resigned, only 17 months after Roosevelt died at Warm Springs, James Forrestal became the only man among 10 Cabinet members who had served under Roosevelt.

But the Cabinet members—as had happened in Jackson's day and in F. D. Roosevelt's time—were not the most important men in Washington, if importance was measured by closeness to the person—particularly to the ear—of the President.

Here were more new faces, new names and new characters. Some people called them a "gang"; *Time* magazine dubbed them "The Regular Guys."

The biggest splash in the White House swimming pool was made when round and jolly George Allen plopped in to frolic with the President. To him Truman gave a picture with the autograph, "My very best to a regular guy, my friend George Allen."

George Allen was a Mississippi boy who grew up under the political wing of a famous character in Congress, "Private John Allen." He was born to fix things. A former hotel man, he succeeded Lawrence Wood ("Chip") Robert as "court jester" for Roosevelt and became entrenched in Washington early in the New Deal days when he was appointed to one of the Commissionerships of the District of Columbia. He studied the effects of the depression by dressing as a hobo and bumming his way across the country. Allen was a born press agent.

A very bright political figure, Allen demonstrated such talents for getting things done that after a few years he enjoyed the income of a wealthy man from directorships of various corporations interested in maintaining Washington contacts. Aviation, steel and insurance companies all appreciated his talents. He worked hard, became the highly successful prototype of a profession that thrives in every state capital but reaches its fullest flower in Washington. There lies the heaven of the lobbyists.

Some politicians consider such an achievement the end of ambition. But George Allen liked politics. By 1944, he had formed a strong attachment for Harry Truman. He was in Chicago at the convention, as confidant of Roosevelt, with an eye out for Truman's prospects. His man got the Vice-Presidential nomination and George Allen smoothed the path in Truman's campaign.

When Truman succeeded to the White House, a telephone call brought Allen back from a vacation and in one night he helped write the three speeches Truman felt it necessary to deliver the next day.

Eventually Truman rewarded Allen by making him one of the five directors of the Reconstruction Finance Corporation, letting him keep some of his better directorships—worth about $50,000 a year. The appointment was only a formality. Allen was the latest in the series of the President's "closest friends."

Another pool habitué was Harry Vaughan, onetime salesman from St. Louis and companion of Harry Truman in the Army in World War I. Now it was Major General Vaughan, in his capacity as Truman's military aide. No White House stag party, either in the mansion or aboard the new Presidential yacht *Williamsburg*, was complete without Harry Vaughan.

And there was Clark Clifford, 39-year-old lawyer from St.

Louis and already noted as an attorney who could make any jury cry. Clifford entered the Navy early in the war with a commission as lieutenant (jg). Soon after Truman became President, Clifford was in the White House, wearing a captain's stripes, as Presidential naval aide. But Clifford was not a court jester. He resigned his commission as soon as Truman could get around to naming Clifford as his special counsel, a post Judge Samuel Rosenman held for many years under F. D. Roosevelt.

Steelman, too, walked in and out of the President's office at will, overshadowing to the point of extinction the massive Department of Labor, where presided the former Senator, Lewis Schwellenbach.

This picture of White House faces, intimate ones, closed with that of John W. Snyder, another St. Louis man. A banker, Snyder had been RFC loan administrator in St. Louis until he disagreed with Jesse H. Jones, of Texas, long the head of the RFC. He was again a private banker when Truman, becoming President, telephoned him from Washington to "come up here right away." Snyder found himself soon thereafter Secretary of the Treasury.

Fanning out from this central group the faces in the mirror of Washington were a jumble of new and old, some active and some inactive—of thousands of officials and clerks liquidating the war while other thousands planned for the future.

Dean Acheson, wealthy and scholarly Undersecretary of State, acted for months as Secretary in place of the absent peacemaker Byrnes, while Sumner Welles, for long the holder of Acheson's office, wrote admonishingly in books and newspaper articles in his library at Oxon Hill. The aged Cordell Hull wrote into his memoirs the full history of his unequaled tenure of office as Secretary of State. And Alice Roosevelt Longworth penned her own reminiscences of more than 40 years in the center of the Washington scene.

On Vermont Avenue, in a granite building whose square block area and fourteen stories could hold only the central core of a tremendous staff, the Veterans Administration attempted to carry out the program for the rehabilitation of some 15,000,000 veterans of World War II. The boss there was General Omar N. Bradley, second in command to Eisenhower in the European theater, and now Veterans Administrator.

Out on the hustings scores of veterans of World War II were campaigning for election to public office, the first wave of a movement that in a few years might see only veterans running the affairs of state.

It was rather difficult to sense the whole picture in walking through the streets of Washington. What the stroller saw was a city with streets less crowded and an atmosphere less hectic than that of New York or Chicago. But it was a busy city, and one so crowded that apparently years would be required to make it comfortable.

It would not grow smaller in size; Washington never had. It faced, in fact, the need to spend an estimated $250,000,000 to bring its streets, its facilities, up to the demands of this new population. The country had crowded in upon it, had made it a metropolis.

The faces in the mirror would change from year to year, even from day to day. The problems would change and the immediate points of interest. Yet something new had been added that could not be changed in the foreseeable future by any amount of wishing for a return of the "good old days."

Washington was no longer just a city, no longer simply the Capital of the United States of America. It was the world capital, the composite face of many countries with common problems, common hopes and common responsibilities. How it would measure up could not be determined by Washington alone. That was a challenge to the country as a whole.

Washington, in the end, would continue to be, as it had been for almost a century and a half, important only as the mirror in which were reflected the people of the United States.

INDEX

INDEX

Jackson, Andrew, 31, 48, 54, 60, 65, 67,
72-74, 76-78, 80, 85, 91, 92, 101, 103,
105, 107, 118, 123, 160, 171, 176, 177,
217, 274, 275, 305; monument to, 101
Jackson, Andrew, Mrs. ("Aunt Ra-
chel"), 72-73, 77
Jacksonia, 171
Japan, 189, 198, 205, 240, 264
Japanese cherry trees, 200, 231
Japanese Embassy, 205, 240, 243-244,
263; Legation, 135
Jefferson, Thomas, 11, 13, 14, 16-18, 19,
21, 22-23, 24, 30, 32, 34, 35-36, 37, 41-
42, 44, 46, 57, 64, 69, 77, 87, 95, 99,
110, 126, 136, 178, 213
Jefferson, Thomas, Mrs., 42
Jelleff, Frank R., 280
Jennings, Paul, 86
Johnson, Andrew, 108, 109, 110, 118
Johnson, Hiram, Senator, 237
Johnson, Samuel, 13
Johnston, Harriet Lane, 162
Johnston, Josiah S., Mrs., 69
Jones, Charles, 15
Jones, Jesse H., 307
Judiciary Square, 98
Juliana, Princess, 274
Jusserand, Jules, 148
Jusserand, Mme., 161

Kalorama, 37, 205, 243
Kantzov, de, Johan Albert, Baron, 56
Keith's Theatre, 179, 279
Kennedy, Joseph P., 300
Key, Philip Barton, 15
Kindler, Hans, Dr., 281
King, Ernest J., Admiral, 267
King, Horatio, 117
King and Queen, British, visit of, 236-
239, 274
Kirkwood Hotel, 100
"Kitchen Cabinet," 274
Knickerbocker Theatre, 280
Knox, Frank, 258-259, 261, 264
Knudsen, William S., 259
Krock, Arthur, 223, 227-228
Krudener, Baron, 74
Kurusu, 264

Labor Department, 220, 248, 307

Laboulaye, de, André, 244
Laboulaye, Madame, 244
Lady of the Manor, 69
Lafayette, General, 65, 101
Lafayette Park, 108, 155, 157, 158, 171,
172, 261, 279, 304
Lafayette Square, 85, 101, 110, 115, 116,
134, 148, 203
La Guardia, Fiorello H., 203-204
Lamont, Thomas P., 152
Lancaster Charity School, 91
Lane, Harriet, 97, 162
Lansing, Robert, 177, 188
Latin America, 146, 240, 252, 277, 281,
288-290
Latrobe, Benjamin, 30, 37, 56, 77
Law, Thomas, 19-20, 55
Law, Thomas, Mrs., 25-26
Lawrence, Amos, 86
Lawrence, David, 229
League of Nations, 197-198, 288
League to Enforce Peace, 189-190, 198
Leahy, William D., Admiral, 267, 268
Lee (Family), 24, 32; "Light Horse
Harry," 32; Mary Fitzhugh, 32; Rob-
ert E., 31, 32-33, 104-105
Leiter, Mrs., 162
Lend-Lease, 228, 236, 238, 260
L'Enfant, Pierre Charles, Major, 30, 57,
135
"Levee Day," 22, 43, 58
Lewis, Willmott, Sir, 203, 263
Liberia, 60
Library of Congress, 69, 87, 199, 248,
278
Lincoln, Abraham, 104, 109, 118, 145,
150, 178, 188, 190, 193, 218, 280
Lincoln, Mary Todd, 105
Lincoln Memorial, 297
Lindsay, Lady, 237
Lindsay, Ronald, Sir, 236-239, 244
Lippmann, Walter, 228-229
"Little Cabinet," 179
Litvinov, Maxim, 264
Livingston, Robert, 13
Livingston, Robert R., 78
Livingston, Robert R., Mrs., 78
Lloyd, Mr. (member of Congress), 38
Lobbe, François, 92
Lodge, Henry Cabot, Senator, 179, 197

314

INDEX

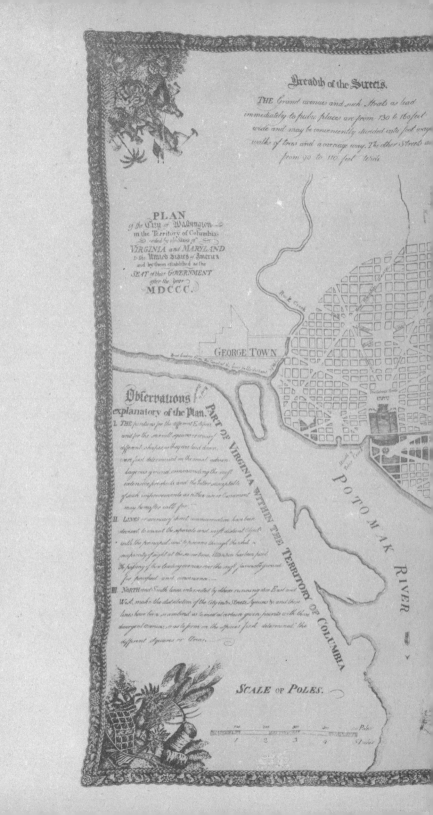

Breadth of the Streets.

THE Grand avenue and such Streets as lead
immediately to public places are from 130 to 160 feet
wide and may be conveniently divided into foot ways
walks of trees and a carriage way. The other Streets are
from 90 to 110 feet Wide

PLAN
of the City of Washington
in the Territory of Columbia
ceded by the States of
VIRGINIA and MARYLAND
to the United States of America
and by them established as the
SEAT of their GOVERNMENT
after the Year
MDCCC.

Rock Creek

GEORGE TOWN

Observations
explanatory of the Plan.

I. THE positions for the different Edifices
and for the several squares or areas of
different shapes as they are laid down,
were first determined on the most advan-
tageous ground commanding the most
extensive prospects and the better susceptible
of such improvements as either use or ornament
may hereafter call for.

II. LINES or avenues of direct communication have been
devised to connect the separate and most distant objects
with the principal, and to preserve through the whole
reciprocity of sight at the same time. Attention has been paid
to the passing of those leading avenues over the most favourable ground
for prospect and convenience.

III. NORTH and South lines, intersected by others running due East and
West, make the distribution of the City into Streets, Squares &c and those
lines have been so combined as to meet at certain given points with those
divergent avenues, so as to form on the spaces first determined, the
different squares or Areas.

PART OF VIRGINIA WITHIN THE TERRITORY OF COLUMBIA

POTOMAK RIVER

SCALE OF POLES.